T. S. ELIOT'S
DRAMATIC THEORY AND PRACTICE

From *Sweeney Agonistes* to

The Elder Statesman

T. S. ELIOT'S DRAMATIC THEORY AND PRACTICE

FROM *SWEENEY AGONISTES* TO *THE ELDER STATESMAN*

BY CAROL H. SMITH

PRINCETON, NEW JERSEY

PRINCETON UNIVERSITY PRESS

1963

Publication of this book has been aided by
the Ford Foundation program to support publication,
through university presses,
of works in the humanities and social sciences

Printed in the United States of America by
Princeton University Press, Princeton, New Jersey

FOR CHARLES

PREFACE

Few topics in modern letters have aroused more animated debate than the vicissitudes of T. S. Eliot's poetic career. In the nineteen-twenties, the poet's conversion to Anglo-Catholicism was regarded as a "defection" by the generation which had hailed the poet of *The Waste Land* as its spokesman. Eliot's second "defection" was of a different order. In mid-career, after readers and critics had adjusted themselves to the idea of T. S. Eliot as a poet of religious experience, the inscrutable Mr. Eliot began to present to West End audiences a series of plays which seemed incompatible with his earlier achievements. While *The Rock* and *Murder in the Cathedral* could properly be considered the work of a religious poet, the plays which followed hardly seemed to be written by the same hand. Eliot's use of modern drawing-room settings and a verse which could scarcely be distinguished from prose caused discomfort both to advocates of poetic drama and to defenders of the realistic theater. The plays seemed on the surface to be within the boundaries of realism, but there were clear evidences of cryptic religious symbolism and even supernatural intrusions into the dramatic action. *The Family Reunion, The Cocktail Party,* and *The Confidential Clerk* mystified and confused audiences, but they fascinated them, as well. How were these plays to be judged when the poet's goals seemed unclear and his dramatic method inconsistent? Eliot's own revelation, in "Poetry and Drama," that he had behind his modern situations classical models from Greek drama and that he felt it necessary to develop a less lyric poetic form for drama in verse, helped very little to explain the principles behind his plays. The result of this dilemma has been a confused, if intrigued, public and innumerable specialized critical studies dealing with Eliot's sources, his dramatic verse, and his developing stage-craft.

In contrast, the purpose of this study is to formulate Eliot's theory of drama in the light of his total religious and poetic development. Eliot is first and last a religious poet, but he is also an experimenter. The evolution of his personal philosophy can be traced in his movement from despair at the disorder of the natural world to his acceptance of a supernatural order which gives meaning and unity to the world's apparent chaos. This movement is clearly evident in his critical writings and his nondramatic poetry. Moreover, there is a clear connection between Eliot's religious perspective and his views on art and drama. His endorsement of classicism, for example, was an effort to require of art a form which could order experience, just as a religious interpretation of existence could order the world of nature. In fact, art's function became for Eliot the microcosmic reflection of divine order.

Eliot found in drama, because of its ritual origins and its capacity to present a completely ordered dramatic world, the perfect vehicle for the expression of his religious insight. The dramatic theme of all of his plays, therefore, has been the plight of the individual who perceives the order of God but who, forced to exist in the natural world, must somehow come to terms with both realms. In order to express this theme, Eliot developed a multi-level drama intended to lead the audience from the ordinary perception of reality to an awareness of a reality transcendent to but immanent in the natural world. Eliot was, therefore, attempting to develop a new kind of theater to fit the special requirements of his dramatic goals.

This study, because it is an analysis of one important element in T. S. Eliot's complex development and attempts to show the importance of the plays in the poet's total achievement, does not deal extensively with Eliot's influence on other writers, nor with the relationship of his work to other movements in the modern theater. Moreover, it is not primarily concerned with an evaluation of Eliot's works by current theatrical standards. It attempts, instead, to determine the principles of the kind of drama and the kind of theater which are behind the conception of all of Eliot's plays, for only after the goals of his drama are understood can a final evaluation of T. S. Eliot's literary achievement be made.

I would like to express my appreciation to Professors Herbert C. Barrows, Jr., Arthur J. Carr, Marvin Felheim, and Jack E. Bender of the University of Michigan for the helpful counsel they have given me in the preparation of this study. Finally, I would like to thank my husband, Charles Philip Smith, for his generous assistance and valuable advice.

C.H.S.

Princeton, New Jersey
August 1962

CONTENTS

PREFACE vii

I. THE PURSUIT OF ORDER 3

II. *SWEENEY AGONISTES* 32

III. *THE ROCK* AND *MURDER IN THE CATHEDRAL* 76

IV. *THE FAMILY REUNION* 112

V. *THE COCKTAIL PARTY* 147

VI. *THE CONFIDENTIAL CLERK* 184

VII. *THE ELDER STATESMAN* 214

BIBLIOGRAPHY 241

INDEX 247

T. S. ELIOT'S
DRAMATIC THEORY AND PRACTICE

From *Sweeney Agonistes* to
The Elder Statesman

CHAPTER I

THE PURSUIT OF ORDER

THE growing number of plays which T. S. Eliot has presented to the public and has carefully seen through production has made it impossible to ignore the importance of the fact that he has chosen to devote the major part of his creative energies in his later years to the theater. Attempts to explain this phenomenon have focused attention on the "dramatic elements" in his nondramatic poetry on the assumption that if he was first a "dramatic" poet, it might be expected that he would later become a poetic dramatist. The origin of this view was probably Edmund Wilson's early statement in *Axel's Castle* (1931) of the dramatic elements in Eliot's poetry. Wilson enumerated as examples of "the dramatic character of his [Eliot's] imagination" the creation of characters such as Prufrock and Sweeney and "the unexpected dramatic contrasts" in Eliot's early poems.[1] Since that time the poet's use of the dramatic monologue in the early poetry, his critical interest in Elizabethan and Jacobean dramatists, and his continuing concern with the issues of verse drama have all been thoroughly investigated.

However fruitful such an approach might be in dealing with Eliot's early poetry, it tends to oversimplify the issues central to his dramatic writing. The problem lies in the

[1] Edmund Wilson, *Axel's Castle: A Study in the Imaginative Literature of 1870–1930* (New York: Charles Scribner's Sons, 1931), pp. 112–13.

fact that it is possible to define the term "dramatic" in such a way as to include almost any kind of poetry. F. O. Matthiessen in *The Achievement of T. S. Eliot,* for example, concludes his discussion of what he calls "the essentially dramatic nature of all his [Eliot's] poetry" with the statement that "the dramatic element in poetry lies in its power to communicate a sense of real life, a sense of *the immediate present."* This element, he says, "demands from the poet a unified sensibility, a capacity of feeling that can closely interweave emotion and thought," and "a mature realization of the existence of both good and evil, an understanding that life takes on dramatic significance only when perceived as a struggle between these forces." [2] By such a definition few great poets would fail to qualify as dramatic. The definition, however, does not help us to distinguish between a play and a poem; instead it simply blurs the distinctions. It does not explain Eliot's decision to write for the theater nor the ideological and artistic ideals which determined that decision.

The inadequacy of the present explanations of Eliot's dramatic career make clear the need for a more searching examination of the relationship between Eliot's poetic goals and his drama and between both of these and his prose writings, for his metamorphosis into a playwright can be explained, I am convinced, only by an understanding of the development and interrelationship of his ideas concerning religion and art. The interdependence of these

[2] F. O. Matthiessen, *The Achievement of T. S. Eliot: An Essay on the Nature of Poetry* (3rd ed. rev.; New York: Oxford University Press, 1958), pp. 67–68.

[4]

elements of Eliot's thought and his creative activity is one of the working assumptions of this study. It is the purpose of this chapter to establish the general outline of his ideological development as a frame of reference within which to place both his plays and his ideas about drama. Each play will then be examined in detail in succeeding chapters.

Although a detailed account of Eliot's development is not possible in the short space of an introductory chapter, it is possible to sketch, by following the general line of his critical writings, his intellectual progress from the early essays collected in the 1920 edition of *The Sacred Wood* to the present. Such an outline can demonstrate, perhaps more effectively than any other means, the struggle toward unity which has been the distinguishing characteristic of his development. Eliot is a poet to whom conscious unity has great importance. This is not to say that contradictions do not exist in his critical writings; many of his critics have been at great pains to point out his inconsistencies. It is also true, of course, that Eliot has changed many of his views during his career; the vicissitudes of his moral and intellectual journey have been better publicized and more eagerly followed than those of perhaps any other literary figure of our time. The point which I wish to maintain, however, is that Eliot appears to have had a compelling need to make some personal order out of the chaos which he found around him as a young man. To a "disciple" of Irving Babbitt at Harvard, a listener to the lectures of Henri Bergson in Paris, a devoted student of F. H. Bradley, and an imitator of the Symbolist fashions of French poetry, the world must have appeared a very relativistic and disorderly place indeed.[3]

From the beginning of his career as a critic, Eliot's view of the necessity of order was apparent. As early as 1919 in "Tradition and the Individual Talent" [4] Eliot enunciated his view of tradition which was to make his name either famous or infamous, depending on one's literary predispositions. The passage deserves to be quoted:

"What happens when a new work of art is created is something that happens simultaneously to all the works of art which preceded it. The existing monuments form an ideal order among themselves, which is modified by the introduction of the new (the really new) work of art among them. The existing order is complete before the new work arrives; for order to persist after the supervention of novelty, the *whole* existing order must be, if ever so slightly, altered; and so the relations, proportions, values of each work of art toward the whole are readjusted; and this is conformity between the old and the new. Whoever has approved this idea of order, of the form of European, of English literature will not find it preposterous that the past should be altered by the present as much as the present is directed by the past." [5]

[3] That Eliot could have taken in the Bergsonian *durée* and Bradley's elaborations and have come out with, not a romanticism of intuition, but a classicism of order is one of the more remarkable of modern literary phenomena. See Anne Ward, "Speculations on Eliot's Time-World: An Analysis of *The Family Reunion* in Relation to Hulme and Bergson," *American Literature*, xxi (March 1949), 18–34.

[4] T. S. Eliot, *Selected Essays* (New York: Harcourt, Brace and Company, 1950), pp. 3–11.

[5] *Ibid.*, p. 5.

Critics arguing for historical perspective on works of art were, of course, nothing new. The remarkable thing here was that Eliot put the matter on the basis of an "ideal" order; he demanded that tradition be recognized as something which has an existence which is incontrovertible and cannot be ignored, an existence which is somehow "given." This alone must have been a shocking idea in most literary circles in 1919, but he went even further by insisting that an ideal order of art not only exists but that the artist, rather than defining that order for himself, or in true romantic fashion imposing his own, is himself defined by that order. The individual mind is less important than the mind of "tradition" and thus the poet should strive not to express his own individual personality but to provide a medium which can best express the impressions, experiences and emotions which are common to all mankind, not those which are unique to him. The poet, in Eliot's own words:

"must be aware that the mind of Europe—the mind of his own country—a mind which he learns in time to be much more important than his own private mind— is a mind which changes, and that this change is a development which abandons nothing *en route*. . . . What happens is a continual surrender of himself as he is at the moment to something which is more valuable. The progress of an artist is a continual self-sacrifice, a continual extinction of personality." [6]

In "The Function of Criticism" (1923)[7] Eliot broad-

[6] *Ibid.*, pp. 6–7.
[7] *Ibid.*, pp. 12–22.

ened the principles which he formulated in "Tradition and the Individual Talent." He quoted his own passage regarding the ideal order of tradition and announced that whereas in the earlier essay he was dealing with the "problem of order" as it affected the artist, he now saw the function of criticism to be "essentially a problem of order too." "If such views are held about art, it follows that *a fortiori* whoever holds them must hold similar views about criticism." Since the end of criticism is "the elucidation of works of art and the correction of taste" the critic should seek standards of judgment which can be commonly agreed upon and applied, just as the artist should subjugate individuality and personal whim to the external criteria of a tradition. Eliot asserts that he envisions criticism ideally to be a "cooperative activity with the further possibility of arriving at something outside of ourselves, which may provisionally be called truth."

But Eliot was not content to stop with an assertion of the possibility of arriving at truth, something, it should be noted, which is outside the individual; he carried the fight to the enemy's quarter. It was Middleton Murry's views that Eliot chose to attack. Murry himself had attacked classicism by saying: "Catholicism stands for the principle of unquestioned spiritual authority outside the individual; that is also the principle of Classicism in literature." Eliot, putting himself on the side of classicism, readily agreed with the similarity his adversary saw. It was to Murry's next statement that Eliot took exception. Murry had said: "The English writer, the English divine, the English statesman, inherit no rules from their forebears; they inherit only this: a sense that in the last resort

[8]

they must depend upon the inner voice." Eliot, calling himself an "Inner Deaf Mute," responded to this statement with a diatribe worthy of the English tradition of Parliamentary debate:

> "For to those who obey the inner voice (perhaps 'obey' is not the word) nothing that I can say about criticism will have the slightest value. For they will not be interested in the attempt to find any common principles for the pursuit of criticism. Why have principles, when one has the inner voice? If I like a thing, that is all I want; and if enough of us, shouting all together, like it, that should be all that *you* (who don't like it) ought to want. . . . And we can like it for any reason we choose. We are not, in fact, concerned with literary *perfection* at all—the search for perfection is a sign of pettiness, for it shows that the writer has admitted the existence of an unquestioned spiritual authority outside himself, to which he has attempted to *conform*. We are not in fact interested in art. We will not worship Baal. 'The principle of classical leadership is that obeisance is made to the office or to the tradition, never to the man.' And we want, not principles, but men.
>
> "Thus speaks the Inner Voice. It is a voice to which, for convenience, we may give a name: and the name I suggest is Whiggery." [8]

The importance of this issue for the present discussion is to suggest how far Eliot had allowed himself to be carried from matters of specifically critical concern. His assertion of the existence of an ideal order of art (and the

[8] *Ibid.*, pp. 17–18.

artist's subservience to that order) led him to the statement that absolute literary standards exist for the judgment of art, indeed that there is even the possibility of
reaching "truth" and that such standards, if absolute, are
outside and above the individual. His comments suggest
that he views the ramifications of these attitudes on art
and criticism as going beyond matters of belles-lettres.
They imply a basic attitude toward human nature. Those
who recognize an order outside themselves accept the fact
of man's limitations and vanities. Those who are convinced they possess an inner voice will not admit that the
voice they hear "breathes the eternal message of vanity,
fear, and lust." Eliot notes that several Catholic hand-
books were written on the exercise of self-examination
"but the Catholic practitioners were, I believe, . . . not
palpitating Narcissi; the Catholic did not believe that
God and himself were identical." As these comments
demonstrate, even this early in his career, Eliot had no
illusions about the nature of man when he is unaware of
a spiritual reality.

There is a direct connection between Eliot's view that
man's nature dictates his need for an ordered universe
and his early views on drama as they emerge in the period
(1919–1927) before his conversion to Christian orthodoxy. His first full statement of his objections to realism
in drama appeared in "Four Elizabethan Dramatists"
(1924)[9]:

"The great vice of English drama from Kyd to Galsworthy has been that its aim of realism was unlimited.
In one play, *Everyman,* and perhaps in that one play

[9] *Ibid.,* pp. 91–99.

[10]

only, we have a drama within the limitations of art;
since Kyd . . . there has been no form to arrest, so to
speak, the flow of spirit at any particular point before
it expands and ends its course in the desert of exact
likeness to the reality which is perceived by the most
commonplace mind. . . . In a play of Aeschylus, we
do not find that certain passages are literature and
other passages drama; every style of utterance in the
play bears a relation to the whole and because of this
relation is dramatic in itself. The imitation of life is
circumscribed, and the approaches to ordinary speech
and withdrawals from ordinary speech are not without
relation and effect upon each other. It is essential that
a work of art should be self-consistent, that an artist
should consciously or unconsciously draw a circle beyond which he does not trespass: on the one hand
actual life is always the material, and on the other hand
an abstraction from actual life is a necessary condition
to the creation of the work of art." [10]

It is apparent from this passage that Eliot's objections
to realistic drama were on the basis of a criterion perfectly consistent with his entire position as outlined above:
he desired in a work of art an ideal relationship of the
parts to the whole which he believed could be achieved
only by abstraction from reality. His dissatisfaction with
the theater of his period was based on the view that all
art, including drama, must be disciplined by adherence
to the "necessary conditions" of its form of creation, just
as man must be disciplined by recognition of his nature
and adherence to restraints administered by guides out-

[10] *Ibid.*, p. 93.

side his own personality. By rejecting the discipline of abstraction, drama condemns itself to "the desert of exact likeness to the reality which is perceived by the most commonplace mind." It thereby forfeits the greatness of universality and timelessness.

That Eliot was interested even in this early period in writing drama which would conform to his own specifications is evidenced by his composition of the two scenes of *Sweeney Agonistes* from 1924 to 1926. The scenes avoid the conventional meters of verse drama of which he disapproved in favor of jazz rhythms,[11] and "abstraction," in Eliot's sense, is certainly one of the distinctive features of the unfinished work. He expresses in this fragmentary piece the theme which, with variations determined by his changing theological position, was to be his throughout virtually all of his dramatic work: the dilemma of the spiritually aware individual forced to exist in a world unaware of spiritual reality. In *Sweeney Agonistes* the emphasis is upon the horror and pain of the spiritual recognition and upon the inability of the newly awakened soul to communicate his experience and awareness to others. *Sweeney Agonistes* is often dismissed as a piece of discarded experimentation, of interest only as it places Eliot in the tradition of the jazz age or as it evidences his morbid state of mind in the nineteen-twenties; it is my belief that, on the contrary, it was a first model for what its author hoped would become a new

[11] The term "rhythm" itself took on important theoretical significance for Eliot and came to be equated with his conception of the ideal relationship of the parts to the whole in a work of art. This aspect of Eliot's dramatic theory is discussed in Chapter Two in connection with *Sweeney Agonistes*.

kind of contemporary drama based on a new set of dramatic ideals. The measure of its importance is the fact that virtually all of Eliot's major dramatic ideas had their first showing in this work: a chorus to convey a response to the hero's dilemma which would correspond to the audience's response, colloquial speech rhythms to enhance the total "rhythm" of the work, conventions from the Greek ritual drama and Greek sources for plot situations, and the development of integrated levels of meaning in his plays.

In Eliot's theme we can see a relationship to his growing religious awareness of the need for an ordered universe in nature and in art. The experience of discovering the world of the spirit and the painfulness of its demands cut through both the intellectual and artistic efforts of the critic-poet of this period and the emotional and spiritual agonies of the convert of the next. The very decision, after 1934, to write more and more exclusively for the theater can also be shown to be, I believe, the product of this same complex of artistic and spiritual principles as they developed throughout Eliot's career. *Sweeney Agonistes* was never completed, for he realized the inadequacy of both dramatic realism and the current types of poetic drama for the expression of his dramatic ideals, and he was aware of the enormity of the task facing anyone who attempted a one-man theater movement along new lines. Other more pressing religious and poetic interests claimed his main attention during the years between 1926 and his return to dramatic writing in 1934.

It was in the preface to *For Lancelot Andrewes* (1928)

that Eliot first announced his acceptance of Anglo-Catholicism. In describing his position he said: "The general point of view may be described as classicist in literature, royalist in politics, and anglo-catholic in religion." [12] This statement is significant, not only because Eliot had become a communicant of the Church of England and had accepted the order imposed by that institution, but because of the way he announced the event. His "conversion" was not only religious, but literary and political as well, as his own statement demonstrates. From the time of the publication of this volume, he speaks as one who knows where he stands ideologically, however defensive he appears at the time of his acceptance of the church and however militant he became in the years that followed. It is a period in which he was consciously broadening his areas of interest.

Whereas before 1928 he spoke as a literary critic or poet whose views sometimes carried implications which he expanded in order to make his position gradually more consistent, after 1928 he speaks as one for whom literary matters provide an entrance to a wider arena. He states in the preface to the second edition (1928) of *The Sacred Wood* that he has passed from the study of the integrity of poetry to the "relation of poetry to the spiritual and social life of its time and of other times." While poetry has in some sense its own life, he says in this preface, it also has a relationship to morals, religion, and politics. Thus he prefers the poetry of Dante to that of Shakespeare "because it seems to me to illustrate a saner atti-

[12] T. S. Eliot, *For Lancelot Andrewes: Essays on Style and Order* (London: Faber and Gwyer, 1928), p. ix.

tude towards the mystery of life." [13] And having enunciated this relationship, he leaves the door open to a criticism which is largely determined by his extra-literary views.

The essays contained in *For Lancelot Andrewes* (bearing the appropriate subtitle "Essays on Style and Order") give a sampling of the views of Eliot the classicist, royalist, and Anglo-Catholic. The critic's evaluations in each area involve value judgments from the other areas. In the essay on Lancelot Andrewes, [14] for example, Eliot is ostensibly dealing with Andrewes as a prose stylist, and he commends Andrewes' style on the basis of its "classic" qualities, its "ordonnance, or arrangement and structure, precision in the use of words, and relevant intensity." But he is fully as interested in Bishop Andrewes as a significant figure in the development of Anglicanism and as an influential force in making "the English Church more worthy of intellectual assent," as he is in Andrewes as a classic prose stylist; just as in the essay on John Bramhall [15] he is interested in the analysis of Bramhall's point of view as an opponent of Hobbes, and Hobbes as an exponent of a materialistic determinism which Eliot sees as analogous in some respects to certain contemporary viewpoints, such as those of I. A. Richards and Bertrand Russell.

In the essay on Machiavelli, [16] Eliot, because he is in essential agreement with Machiavelli's view of human na-

---

[13] T. S. Eliot, *The Sacred Wood: Essays on Poetry and Criticism* (London: Methuen & Co. Ltd., 1928), pp. viii–x.

[14] Eliot, *For Lancelot Andrewes*, pp. 13–32.

[15] *Ibid.*, pp. 33–48.

[16] *Ibid.*, pp. 49–66.

ture, is able to come to the conclusion that Machiavelli was a patriot devoted to his state, a faithful Catholic, and as a Catholic a realist about man's sinful nature:

"The world of human motives which he [Machiavelli] depicts is true—that is to say, it is humanity without the addition of superhuman Grace. It is therefore tolerable only to persons who have also a definite religious belief; to the effort of the last three centuries to supply religious belief by belief in Humanity the creed of Machiavelli is insupportable." [17]

Because of his commitments, Eliot is able to come to a similarly iconoclastic conclusion about Baudelaire in the essay "Baudelaire in Our Time." [18] Baudelaire, because he was a witness to the depravity of man, was neither a true diabolist nor an arch romantic:

"The important fact about Baudelaire is that he was essentially a Christian, born out of his due time, and a classicist, born out of his due time. . . . But Baudelaire was not an aesthetic or a political Christian; his tendency to 'ritual' . . . springs from no attachment to the outward forms of Christianity, but from the instincts of a soul that was *naturaliter* Christian. And being the kind of Christian that he was, born when he was, he had to discover Christianity for himself. In this pursuit he was alone in the solitude which is only known to saints. To him the notion of Original Sin came spontaneously, and the need for prayer. . . . And Baude-

[17] *Ibid.,* p. 63.
[18] *Ibid.,* pp. 86–99.

laire came to attain the greatest, and most difficult, of the Christian virtues, the virtue of humility." [19]

The doctrine of original sin and the virtue of humility were to play an important part in Eliot's drama of the nineteen-thirties, especially in *Murder in the Cathedral* and *The Family Reunion.*

It is in a footnote to the essay on Baudelaire that Eliot's famous strike at what he elsewhere calls "the Life-Forcers" occurs. In referring to the "Ersatz-Religion" of G. B. Shaw and H. G. Wells, he comments that they are "concerned with the spirit, not the letter. And the spirit killeth, but the letter giveth life." This reversal of St. Paul might be taken as Eliot's *leitmotif* during the years immediately after his conversion. What he means by this *bon mot* is at the heart of his frequent attacks on all brands of liberalism and humanism. Perhaps this point of view is most clearly set forth in another essay in *For Lancelot Andrewes,* "The Humanism of Irving Babbitt." [20] It is Eliot's contention that "the humanistic point of view is auxiliary to and dependent upon the religious point of view. For us, religion is of course Christianity; and Christianity implies, I think, the conception of the Church." Because Babbitt's humanism is dependent on Christianity and because only the church can provide the "letter" of religion, humanism as a religion of the "spirit" will sicken and die as it becomes further and further removed from the church. Only a formal religion can provide the necessary moral and ethical framework to sustain itself. Eliot poses this question:

[19] *Ibid.,* pp. 97–99.
[20] *Ibid.,* pp. 126–43.

"Is it, in the end, a view of life that will work by itself, or is it a derivative of religion which will work only for a short time in history, and only for a few highly cultivated persons like Mr. Babbitt—whose ancestral traditions, furthermore, are Christian, and who is, like many people, at the distance of a generation or so from definite Christian belief? Is it, in other words, durable beyond one or two generations?" [21]

Thus in Eliot's literary and religious position during the years immediately after he joined the church the threads which were discernible in the early essays are woven into an integrated position, and their application to literary matters becomes a secondary rather than the primary concern of the critic. His need for order seemed finally and fully satisfied by his religious perspective, and with the relationship of all things thus formalized, he moved on in the nineteen-thirties to encourage others to perceive and embrace the same master plan.

The nineteen-thirties might be called T. S. Eliot's period of militant Christianity. At a time when fascism was making incredible claims and democracy as its major rival was equally boastful if less vocal, it is understandable that the Christian who was irrevocably committed to very different ends and with a set of very different means to achieve those ends, would view with distrust and suspicion both of these ideologies. As a new convert committed to the position of the church on secular matters, Eliot evolved instead his own program and became an active partisan for the Christian point of view. At the end of the decade even his gift of irony seemed to have es-

[21] *Ibid.,* p. 128.

caped him and the tone of his works of "Christian sociology" became almost desperately serious and polemical.

"The 'Pensées' of Pascal" (1931) [22] is a key essay to define the beginning of this period, for it looks both forward and back. It contains an important description of the "Christian thinker" and his motives for the acceptance of faith:

"The Christian thinker—and I mean the man who is trying consciously and conscientiously to explain to himself the sequence which culminates in faith, rather than the public apologist—proceeds by rejection and elimination. He finds the world to be so and so; he finds its character inexplicable by any non-religious theory: among religions he finds Christianity, and Catholic Christianity, to account most satisfactorily for the world and especially for the moral world within; and thus, by what Newman calls 'powerful and concurrent' reasons, he finds himself inexorably committed to the dogma of the Incarnation. To the unbeliever, this method seems disingenuous and perverse: for the unbeliever is, as a rule, not so greatly troubled to explain the world to himself, nor so greatly distressed by its disorder; nor is he generally concerned (in modern terms) to 'preserve values.' . . . The unbeliever starts from the other end, and as likely as not with the question: Is a case of human parthenogenesis credible? and this he would call going straight to the heart of the matter. . . . In the end we must all choose for ourselves between one point of view and another." [23]

[22] Eliot, *Selected Essays,* pp. 355–68.
[23] *Ibid.,* pp. 360–61.

This statement looks back into the origins of belief for Eliot's kind of Christian convert, but it also looks forward by describing the Christian thinker as one who is both greatly distressed by the world's disorder and greatly concerned to "preserve values." The mission of preserving values was to bring Eliot into the contemporary political arena with his own plan for society and with a drama intended to demonstrate in a public art form the superiority of the Christian point of view.

Eliot's developing social concern is most clearly displayed in his prose writings. As a Christian literary man he is especially antagonistic toward the view which he feels is peculiar to, and symptomatic of, the modern world—the view that "poetry is capable of saving us." In the section on "The Modern Mind" in *The Use of Poetry and the Use of Criticism,* Eliot discusses the disturbance of our literary values in consequence of confusing poetry and morals. In this modern attempt to find a substitute for religious faith, he finds I. A. Richards one of the chief offenders. He asserts that Richards is really "engaged in a rear-guard religious action" because he is attempting to "preserve emotions without the beliefs with which their history has been involved." [24]

In contrast to this "wrong" relationship between poetry and morals—poetry as a salvation—Eliot presents, in "Religion and Literature" (1935)[25] the "right" relationship, a view which, even for those who were convinced by

[24] T. S. Eliot, *The Use of Poetry and the Use of Criticism: Studies in the Relation of Criticism to Poetry in England* (Cambridge, Massachusetts: Harvard University Press, 1933), p. 127.

[25] Eliot, *Selected Essays,* pp. 343–54.

his statements two years before, was difficult for "modern minds" to accept as any more than an outright contradiction of his early literary views:

> "Literary criticism should be completed by criticism from a definite ethical and theological standpoint. In so far as in any age there is common agreement on ethical and theological matters, so far can literary criticism be substantive. In ages like our own, in which there is no such common agreement, it is the more necessary for Christian readers to scrutinize their reading, especially of works of imagination, with explicit ethical and theological standards. The 'greatness' of literature cannot be determined solely by literary standards; though we must remember that whether it is literature or not can be determined only by literary standards." [26]

It is important to note that Eliot is speaking to Christian readers. For them he sees the danger of the present literary atmosphere to lie in the influence the modern "cult of personality" can exert in moral and ethical matters. Since literature acts as an influence on actions, he says, and since most contemporary writers do not accept the moral and ethical code of Christians, and, more important still, do not accept the existence of a supernatural order, the influence they exert represents a positive danger to the Christian. Literature, Eliot feels, should never alter morals; morals for the Christian should be based on a foundation out of the reach of temporal literature. On the other hand, he does not want a literature which is

[26] *Ibid.*, p. 343.

Christian propaganda. "What I want is a literature which should be *un*consciously, rather than deliberately and defiantly Christian." In short, he wishes to affirm to his fellow Christians that "the whole of modern literature is corrupted by what I call Secularism, that it is simply unaware of, simply cannot understand the meaning of, the primacy of the supernatural over the natural life: of something which I assume to be our primary concern." It is because of this state of affairs that the Christian reader must superimpose Christian standards of criticism on purely literary ones.

In *After Strange Gods* (1934), subtitled "A Primer of Modern Heresy," and in *The Idea of a Christian Society* Eliot the social planner, the man with a "program," fully emerges. In *After Strange Gods* he begins to lay the groundwork for the structure for which the digging had been done many years before. His remarks, he says, are the bare outline of a theory of tradition and orthodoxy, both of which are to serve as a background for his view of the dangers of authorship when, with "no external test of the validity of a writer's work, we fail to distinguish between the truth of his view of life and the personality which makes it plausible." [27]

He mentions his view of tradition as he conceived it when he wrote "Tradition and the Individual Talent" in

[27] T. S. Eliot, *After Strange Gods: A Primer of Modern Heresy* (New York: Harcourt, Brace and Company, 1934), p. 21. A footnote to the text lists the theorists he has been reading with approval as: "Mr. Chesterton and his 'distributism,' Mr. Christopher Dawson (*The Making of Europe*), Mr. Demant and Mr. M. B. Reckitt and their colleagues. I have also in mind the views of Mr. Allen Tate and his friends as evinced in *I'll Take My Stand,* and those of several Scottish nationals."

1919 and says that while he does not repudiate what he said then, the problem now seems to him more complex and can no longer be treated as a purely literary matter. Now, in 1934, what he means by tradition "involves all of those habitual actions, habits and customs, from the most significant religious rite to our conventional way of greeting a stranger, which represent the blood kinship of 'the same people living in the same place.' " The center of the society must be the local community:

> "The local community must always be the most permanent, and . . . the concept of the nation is by no means fixed and invariable. It is, so to speak, only one fluctuating circle of loyalties between the centre of the family and the local community, and the periphery of humanity entire. Its strength and its geographical size depend upon the comprehensiveness of a way of life which can harmonise parts with distinct local characters of their own." [28]

Social stability, homogeneity of culture, and unity of religious background are all necessary to foster this "largely unconscious" sense of tradition; therefore "a spirit of excessive tolerance is to be deprecated" for tradition must be complemented by orthodoxy, which calls for the exercise of the conscious intelligence.

As these views indicate, in *After Strange Gods* the author, as a literary critic, moves into the wider domain of the society in which literature is produced and enjoyed. His remarks are a valuable index of his ideas in the mid-thirties on the relationship between art and society.

[28] *Ibid.*, pp. 20–21.

Tradition and orthodoxy must exist together if a morally stable literature is to emerge. Moreover, the definition of tradition is expanded to include the fabric of everyday life and custom, as well as a culture's purely artistic and intellectual heritage.

Eliot's whole intellectual movement toward a social mission for himself as a poet which emerged during the nineteen-thirties is, I believe, the most important single fact in explanation of why he turned to the writing of plays. It has been pointed out that despite his early interest in writing drama, *Sweeney Agonistes* was never completed. In 1933, however, he said in the conclusion to *The Use of Poetry and the Use of Criticism:*

> "The most useful poetry, socially, would be one which could cut across all the present stratifications of public taste—stratifications which are perhaps a sign of social disintegration. The ideal medium for poetry, to my mind, and the most direct means of social 'usefulness' for poetry, is the theatre." [29]

Eliot's return to dramatic composition came the next year, 1934, when he was asked to do the choruses for *The Rock.* As an Anglo-Catholic convert, he was engaged in many good works for the church, of which this pageant-play, a fund-raising effort, was only one. Eliot's first complete play, *Murder in the Cathedral,* appeared the next year (1935). His recent comment that he wrote *Murder in the Cathedral* as anti-Nazi propaganda [30] points up

[29] Eliot, *The Use of Poetry and the Use of Criticism,* p. 146.

[30] Reported to me, in conversation, by Donald Hall after he had conducted an interview with Eliot. The interview later appeared as "The Art of Poetry I: T. S. Eliot," an interview by Donald Hall, *The Paris Review,* No. 21 (Spring–Summer 1959), pp. 47–70.

the often-forgotten motive felt by many in High Church circles during the nineteen-thirties—the desire to save the Christian world from the attacks of rival secular ideologies. *Murder in the Cathedral* presents the conflict with which most of his writing of the nineteen-thirties dealt: the conflict between the secular world and the world of the spirit. The play portrays the condition of sainthood but it does not deal solely with the experiential dimension of Becket's condition. It examines as well the necessity for interaction between the two worlds. It is, in other words, the salvation story of both Becket and the women of Canterbury, and it marks an important positive step in the poet's growing conception of the social dimension and responsibility of religion and of his own future literary direction as a poet of religious experience.

Just as a Christian thinker may begin with the recognition of the necessity of a supernatural order, so a Christian poet, in an era when the preservation of his beliefs is threatened, may be expected to emphasize the issue of "saintliness" and its social ramifications to the modern world. In his essay on Pascal, Eliot had said that the unbeliever "does not consider that if certain emotional states, certain developments of character, and what in the highest sense can be called 'saintliness' are inherently and by inspection known to be good, then the satisfactory explanation of the world must be an explanation which will admit the 'reality' of these values." [31] Eliot's chief dramatic effort in this period was expended in finding methods to convey the "reality" of the Christian explanation of the world and the validity of Christian values for society.

[31] Eliot, *Selected Essays*, pp. 360–61.

Eliot's expanded social view is reflected in the modified dramatic world of his plays of the nineteen-thirties and after. Whereas in *Sweeney Agonistes* the world of ordinary humanity is the villain of the piece in that the mystic path demands that "the love of created beings" must be annihilated before union can be achieved, in the plays written since that work there is a greater concern shown for the salvation of other, less spiritually gifted characters. As the author strengthened his conviction of the social mission of the church in the twentieth century, he came to portray, not the awakened soul versus the unawakened ones, but instead the awakened leading the unawakened to a new perception of the meaning of life. Thus, in *Murder in the Cathedral* Becket acts out his passion alone, but the effect of his martyrdom is felt in the lives of the women of Canterbury. In the same way, Harry, in *The Family Reunion,* must go his own way in the end, but his return home makes a difference in the lives of the members of his family. In both cases, however, divine love takes precedence over human love when a choice must be made. While Eliot gradually modifies the stringency of the path, both Celia in *The Cocktail Party* and Colby in *The Confidential Clerk* must make the difficult choice of giving up human for divine love. Only in Eliot's latest play, *The Elder Statesman,* does human love become the earthly reflection of divine love and thus a positive value.

Another ramification of the playwright's new interest in society appears in the dramatic structure of his plays. In each play the stage becomes a dramatic world duplicating in its surface and hidden levels the natural and supernatural orders, and demonstrating the presence of both in human experience, a dramatic method appropriate to the theme of the individual who must exist in both planes at once. In addition, the hierarchy of the orders of being is duplicated in the hierarchy of awareness of the characters within each dramatic world. The penitent and the divine agents who assist him form the pinnacle of awareness in each play, with the other characters in a descending scale from that point.[32]

While the prose writings of Eliot's latest period, the nineteen-forties and nineteen-fifties, do not present any strikingly new trends in his thinking, they do show him moving toward a wider audience, both in his approach to criticism and in his dramatic method. He has shown in a number of essays, collected in the 1957 volume *On Poetry and Poets,* an inclination to redefine or reevaluate his earlier strictures on particular poets, such as Milton, Goethe, and Kipling. His religious interests have also expanded. As C. L. Barber puts it, Eliot has "increasingly chosen as his ground not religion itself, but what leads towards it, goes with it, comes from it." He has demonstrated a wider tolerance for varying forms of belief and unorthodoxy, and unconsciously religious impulses. Eliot's attitude of greater religious tolerance appears in dramatic dress in the plays written since *The Family Reunion* (1939). In *The Cocktail Party* (1949), *The Confidential Clerk* (1953), and *The Elder Statesman* (1958) he gives a more sympathetic treatment to "the incomplete

[32] Eliot's concern with hierarchy in society is clearly manifested in *The Idea of a Christian Society* (London: Faber and Faber Limited, 1939), the fullest development of his vision of a social world organized on religious principles. His dramatic use of this idea is developed in later chapters.

religious impulses of people in ordinary social life." [33]

This tolerance is reflected in *Notes towards the Definition of Culture* (1948). The book mainly concerns the various ways in which the term "culture" is used and, from Eliot's point of view, misused, in the modern world. He continues to assert that "no culture has appeared or developed except together with a religion," but the conditions which he now sees as necessary to foster culture are less rigid than those he insisted on earlier. He still desires an organic social structure which will foster "the hereditary transmission of culture within a culture" by means of social classes and places great stress on the preservation of local cultures; now, however, a "balance of unity and diversity in religion—that is, universality of doctrine with particularity of cult and devotion" is to be allowed.[34]

Several of the essays in Eliot's latest critical volume, *On Poetry and Poets* (1957), further explore the idea of tradition and related matters in a manner important to the understanding of his later drama. "The Social Function of Poetry" (1945),[35] for example, deals with one of the author's central concerns in his latest work—the relationship between language and culture. In his earlier essays he had pictured the poet as having the special function of preserving values; now the poet's function becomes the

[33] C. L. Barber, "The Power of Development . . . in a Different World," appearing as the final chapter in *The Achievement of T. S. Eliot,* by F. O. Matthiessen, pp. 202–04.

[34] T. S. Eliot, *Notes towards the Definition of Culture* (London: Faber and Faber Limited, 1948), p. 15.

[35] T. S. Eliot, *On Poetry and Poets* (New York: Farrar, Straus and Cudahy, 1957), pp. 3–16.

preservation of the very capacity to feel at all—"not merely to express, but even to feel any but the crudest emotions." The poet takes from his society the spoken language of his people and in return expresses the feelings of his people; thus language and culture influence each other through the poet. But beyond poetry's power to express the universal emotions of a people, it serves the even higher function of communicating "some new experience, or some fresh understanding of the familiar, or the expression of something we have experienced but have no words for, which enlarges our consciousness or refines our sensibility." The realm of unexpressed experience which Eliot himself has chosen for his domain is the awareness of a supernatural order which determines and pervades the natural order.

It seems clear from Eliot's comments that he has chosen poetic drama to accomplish his purpose because it can reach a wider public than other poetic means and, more important, because of the possibilities of creating in drama a total dramatic world in which to demonstrate the divine plan. In "Poetry and Drama" (1951) [36] he explains the basis of his choice. While prose drama is wholly adequate to express "the nameable classifiable emotions and motives of our conscious life when directed towards action," there is another range of experience which it cannot express—"a fringe of indefinite extent, of feeling which we can only detect, so to speak, out of the corner of the eye and can never completely focus; of feeling of which we are only aware in a kind of temporary detachment from action." This range of sensibility can only be

[36] *Ibid.*, pp. 75–95.

conveyed by dramatic poetry at its moments of greatest intensity. Therefore the ideal toward which poetic drama should move is different from that of prose drama:

> "I have before my eyes a kind of mirage of the perfection of verse drama, which would be a design of human action and of words, such as to present at once the two aspects of dramatic and of musical order. . . . To go as far in this direction as it is possible to go, without losing that contact with the ordinary everyday world with which drama must come to terms, seems to me the proper aim of dramatic poetry. For it is ultimately the function of art, in imposing a credible order upon ordinary reality, and thereby eliciting some perception of an order *in* reality, to bring us to a condition of serenity, stillness, and reconciliation; and then leave us, as Virgil left Dante, to proceed toward a region where that guide can avail us no farther." [37]

Eliot's final figure of speech, employing one of his favorite religious images, can leave very little doubt that the "fringe of indefinite extent" visible only out of "the corner of the eye" is a vision of religious perfection as it exists in and out of our experience. The poet-dramatist, Eliot suggests, can, like Virgil, lead us to the brink of that other world by making us aware of its existence. After that the path of salvation must be traveled by each soul alone.

It has been the intention of this introductory chapter to demonstrate that the impetus behind Eliot's career as a playwright has been his pursuit of order in religion and

[37] *Ibid.,* pp. 93–94.

in art. The origin of his attempt to develop a new theater is to be seen in his view that, just as man's nature needs to be guided by discipline and order, so dramatic art needs to be given a form which can draw a circle of abstraction around experience in order to make drama conform to the standard of all art—the ordered relationship of the parts to the whole. Believing that of all literary forms drama has the greatest capacity for recreating a complete and ordered world, Eliot developed a dramatic structure which was intended to lead the audience to a sense of religious awareness by demonstrating the presence of the supernatural order in the natural world. His dramatic theme is also the product of his religious concern to integrate the real and the ideal. In each of his plays he has portrayed the plight of the individual who perceives the order of God but, forced to exist in the natural world, must somehow come to terms with both realms.

In the following chapters the evolution of Eliot's theme and the dramatic methods he has developed to express it will be explored in detail. Though Eliot's theatrical methods have undergone many changes, his original intention to portray the impact of the spiritual principle on the lives of men in a form which would be artistically ordered without losing contact with actual experience has remained the basic dramatic goal of all his plays.

CHAPTER II

SWEENEY AGONISTES

❧ THERE has been an atmosphere of mystified fascination surrounding *Sweeney Agonistes* since its first appearance in the *New Criterion* in 1926 and 1927.[1] Many factors contributed to this attitude. Its publication in the form of "fragments" suggested that a complete dramatic work would be forthcoming, using in new roles characters already familiar to readers of Eliot's poetry, but such a work never appeared. Moreover, the epigraphs from St. John of the Cross and the *Choephoroi* suggested erudite and mystical meanings, and Sweeney's macabre description of a ghastly crime, followed by the "hoo-ha" sequence and the mysterious knocking, left the reader with confused reactions. In the face of such esoteric and ambiguous evidence it is no wonder that interpretations are inconsistent and sometimes bizarre.

While there are points of general agreement among interpreters of the play based on the author's early prose statements on drama, there are disagreements on the meanings of the terms he uses. Critics are agreed, for example, that Eliot desired a drama in verse, that he stood firmly against realism and favored instead an art which used devices of abstraction, and that he had formulated a theory of dramatic levels, of which *Sweeney*

---

[1] See, for example, Grover Smith, Jr., *T. S. Eliot's Poetry and Plays: A Study in Sources and Meaning* (Chicago, Illinois: The University of Chicago Press, 1956), pp. 110–18.

Agonistes was an illustration.[2] There is very little agreement, however, on what the poet meant by such terms as rhythm, "circumscribed imitation of life," and dramatic levels. David E. Jones, in *The Plays of T. S. Eliot,* for example, describes the levels of Eliot's plays as reproducing "the different levels—sensuous, logical, psychological, and spiritual—upon which life is lived";[3] Francis Fergusson, in his discussion of *Murder in the Cathedral* in *The Idea of a Theater,* claims that the levels of the play follow the categories of Pascal as Eliot had enumerated them in his introduction to the *Pensées,* "the order of nature, the order of mind, and the order of charity."[4] In fact, the whole body of criticism on Eliot's drama is characterized by disagreement over the meaning of his terms and the inability to perceive the developing pattern of his theories and their demonstration in his plays.[5] There has

[2] After noting, in *The Use of Poetry and the Use of Criticism* (1933), that he viewed the theater as "the ideal medium for poetry," Eliot said that he had "once designed and drafted a couple of scenes of a verse play" which might illustrate the usefulness of levels in drama (pp. 146–47).

[3] David E. Jones, *The Plays of T. S. Eliot* (London: Routledge & Kegan Paul, 1960), p. 15.

[4] Francis Fergusson, *The Idea of a Theater* (Princeton, New Jersey: Princeton University Press, 1949), p. 217. Unable to apply these categories to any of Eliot's other plays, Fergusson concludes that after *Murder in the Cathedral* the playwright turned to realism, a view not borne out, I believe, by an examination of the later plays.

[5] Critics who stress the development of Eliot as a nondramatic poet tend to neglect his dramatic theory when discussing the plays. Helen Gardner, for example, views *Sweeney Agonistes* as "a rather sterile appendix" to *The Waste Land,* not recognizing its importance as a dramatic experiment (*The Art of T. S. Eliot* [London: The Cresset Press, 1949], p. 132). Even those critics who deal with Eliot as a poetic dramatist tend to stress his development of versification for the stage without fully recognizing the dependence of these verse tech-

also been an insistence on judging the plays by the standards of realism, despite Eliot's continued assertions that artistically effective drama must eschew these standards.[6]

It is essential to any complete understanding of Eliot's plays that his insistence on a new kind of poetic drama be taken seriously, and that his principles for its construction be examined against the background of his ideas on religion and art. Eliot was and is a poet of spiritual experience. That fact determined his theme and suggested to him both the inadequacies of other drama of his time for his special purposes and the possibilities of a new drama which might be developed to fit his demands. To discuss his dramatic endeavors as if they evolved independently of his religious and critical goals is to begin at the wrong end. Whether or not his dramatic theories "work" in the theater and whether or not they succeed in embodying his vision of reality are judgments which must be preceded by a more complete understanding of his goals.

---

niques on other elements of his dramatic theory. Thus Jones asserts that Eliot's purpose in writing *Sweeney Agonistes* was "to come to terms with the speech of the time." He concludes that "the comic exaggeration which characterizes much of the play" should "underline the danger of taking too seriously a symbolism which makes fun of itself" (*The Plays of T. S. Eliot*, pp. 29, 38).

[6] Hugh Kenner asserts that *Sweeney Agonistes* was never finished because of Eliot's two interrelated difficulties with drama: "his reluctance to conceive drama as primarily an orchestrated action, and his bias toward a poetry that exteriorizes but does not explicate the locked world of the self" (*The Invisible Poet: T. S. Eliot* [New York: McDowell, Obolensky, 1959], p. 234). Kenner's real objection, it seems to me, is the inadequacy of the realistic theater to handle the theme Eliot has chosen. The point is, however, that Eliot, regardless of his success, has attempted to evolve a new theater which *could* handle his theme.

Eliot shared with the rest of his literary generation an interest in the possibility of poetic drama in the contemporary world,[7] and indeed it was natural that all questions concerning drama should be of interest to a critic who took for his special province Elizabethan and Jacobean drama. The conclusions he came to in "The Possibility of a Poetic Drama" (1920)[8] were that despite the fact that most poets hanker for the stage and that "a not negligible public appears to want verse plays," the contemporary age was too formless to produce an adequate poetic drama. The potential dramatic talents of the present were being wasted because no one poet could accomplish the whole job: "No man can invent a form, create a taste for it, and perfect it too." Another difficulty was that whereas permanent literature is always "either a presentation of thought, or a presentation of feeling by a statement of events in human actions or objects in the external world," the present age had inherited the nineteenth-century "mentality" which attempted to embody a philosophy rather than to replace the philosophy, and a mixed art was the result—"the mixture of genres in which our age delights."

What Eliot found in poetic dramas which were conscientious attempts to adapt Athenian or Elizabethan structures to the contemporary feeling was this same "undigested 'idea' or philosophy, the idea-emotion." Another kind of "attempt to supply the defect of structure

---

[7] The dramatic endeavors of Yeats and the interest of both Yeats and Pound in the Noh drama are also indicative of the interest in a new direction for poetic drama.

[8] Eliot, *The Sacred Wood*, pp. 60–70.

by an internal structure" appeared in plays which ranged from the comedy of ideas to ordinary social comedy. Both these directions of the modern theater, he maintained, failed by artistic standards. The only standard which could be allowed for drama was "the standard of the work of art, aiming at the same intensity at which poetry and the other forms of art aim." By that standard Eliot found the drama of both Shaw and Maeterlinck wanting. He considered both "popularizations," for

"the moment an idea has been transferred from its pure state in order that it may become comprehensible to the inferior intelligence it has lost contact with art. It can remain pure only by being stated simply in the form of general truth or by being transmuted. . . .

"The essential is to get upon the stage this precise statement of life which is at the same time a point of view, a world—a world which the author's mind has subjected to a complete process of simplification. I do not find that any drama which 'embodies a philosophy' of the author's (like *Faust*) or which illustrates any social theory (like Shaw's) can possibly fulfil the requirements. . . . And the world of Ibsen and the world of Tchehov are not enough simplified, universal." [9]

Eliot concludes his discussion with his own suggestion for arriving at a new kind of poetic drama which might satisfy the standards of art:

"Possibly the majority of attempts to confect a poetic drama have begun at the wrong end. They have aimed

[9] *Ibid.*, pp. 68–69.

at the small public which wants 'poetry.' . . . The Elizabethan drama was aimed at a public which wanted *entertainment* of a crude sort, but would *stand* a good deal of poetry; our problem should be to take a form of entertainment, and subject it to the process which would leave it a form of art. Perhaps the music-hall comedian is the best material. I am aware that this is a dangerous suggestion to make. For every person who is likely to consider it seriously there are a dozen toy-makers who would leap to tickle aesthetic society into one more quiver and giggle of art debauch. Very few treat art seriously." [10]

Eliot's remarks indicate that he considered the chief problem to be one of form. The art work must be "pure" and not a popularization; that was of first importance. But it should be noted that his idea of the way to approach the problem was not like that of Yeats—a drawing-room theater for lovers of poetry—but rather by way of audiences who wanted *"entertainment* of a crude sort but would *stand* a good deal of poetry." What Eliot seemed to desire was a broad popular base for the new art form. How this popular audience was to be reached by a play sufficiently "pure" to qualify as "unmixed art" was a question as yet unsolved.

Eliot had faced the same problem of form in his early poetry. His view of experience predisposed him to particular themes which are now well-known: the anguish of frustrated sensitivity, the paradox of sexual automatism which leads to cultural and spiritual sterility, the modern world's materialistic perversion of faith, the loss of the

[10] *Ibid.*, p. 70.

sense of order and wholeness in life which alone can assure intellectual, spiritual, and cultural fertility. And beneath his concern over impotent sensitivity, sterility, and materialism lay two primordial and recurring emotions—the poet's sense of the isolation of every human creature and the resultant horror of life stripped of all illusions. These themes, however, lent themselves to sentimentality and to the excessive expression of personal emotion and "personality." The problem was to give a form to emotion which would make it impersonal and universal. The solution which Eliot evolved was "the impersonal theory of poetry" by which the poet can "transmute his personal and private agonies into something rich and strange, something universal and impersonal." [11]

This process of transmutation demanded its own poetic techniques, and Eliot himself has made known his indebtedness on this score to the late sixteenth-century dramatists and the seventeenth-century metaphysical poets of the English tradition and to the French symbolists, especially Laforgue. Eliot valued the work of these poets and dramatists both for its honesty in looking into the human soul and for its distinctive verbal quality which enabled what he called "the direct sensuous apprehension of thought." [12] He felt that the function of art was to give form to experience, to make artistic order out of the chaos of emotion, and to synthesize experience into a new whole. He was emphatic, therefore, in stressing that the poet must not use ideas as the philosopher did, but must turn them into emotions. "The poet can deal with philo-

[11] Eliot, *Selected Essays,* p. 117.
[12] *Ibid.,* p. 246.

sophic ideas, not as matter for argument, but as matter for inspection." [13] This same view is at the heart of his objection to the plays of Shaw and Maeterlinck, for both, he felt, emphasized ideas at the expense of the standards of art. Form and content must be inextricably bound together. The artist's manipulation of form in a literary work provided a way of giving order and meaning to raw experience. The significance of experience was determined by what the artist's view of reality showed its meaning to be, and its meaning was communicated in turn by the way the artist chose to order experience.

The importance of order in Eliot's personal philosophy has already been stressed. Its role in the creative process was of equal importance and formed a link between his literary method and his spiritual beliefs. His endorsement of the use of myth as a means of ordering experience in the chaos of the modern world came in his review of James Joyce's *Ulysses.*[14] Joyce's use of the *Odyssey,* he said, had "the importance of a scientific discovery."

"In using the myth, in manipulating a continuous parallel between contemporaneity and antiquity, Mr. Joyce is pursuing a method which others must pursue after him. They will not be imitators, any more than the scientist who uses the discoveries of an Einstein in pursuing his own, independent, further investigations. It is simply a way of controlling, of ordering, of giving a shape and a significance to the immense panorama of futility and anarchy which is contemporary history.

[13] Eliot, *The Sacred Wood,* p. 162.
[14] T. S. Eliot, "Ulysses, Order, and Myth," *Dial,* LXXV (November 1923), 480–83.

It is a method already adumbrated by Mr. Yeats, and of the need for which I believe Mr. Yeats to have been the first contemporary to be conscious. It is a method for which the horoscope is auspicious. Psychology (such as it is, and whether our reaction to it be comic or serious), ethnology, and *The Golden Bough* have concurred to make possible what was impossible even a few years ago. Instead of narrative method, we may now use the mythical method. It is, I seriously believe, a step toward making the modern world possible for art. . . ." [15]

The mythical method offered Eliot some distinct advantages. Believing as he did that the artist should turn ideas into emotions and create actions rather than state generalizations, he was obliged to find a means of interpreting experience which would be oblique rather than direct, implicit in actions rather than appended to them. The myth provided a perfect vehicle for effecting this process. The myth itself did not editorialize; nor did it sentimentalize. It simply told a story. But it had two special advantages. First, probably by virtue of its folk origin and long oral tradition, it give a simple and "realistic" rendition of the human soul. Second, it was part of a larger body of human experience which formed a complete "interpretation" of the universe, the origin of man, and the chronicle of his passions. Moreover, it had a long history of use and re-use by generations of creators and their audiences, so that the new user could suggest a universal meaning and be assured that it would be under-

[15] *Ibid.*, p. 483.

stood by his audience by simply modeling his incidents on the pattern of the actions appearing in myth. He could also achieve either analogy or irony according to the way the imitation was handled, and, indeed, in Eliot's case, both were often intended to operate simultaneously.

This new method was made possible, Eliot felt, by the concurrence of psychology, ethnology, and anthropology. What was the nature of this concurrence and in what way did these disciplines help the contemporary artist make sense out of the "futility and anarchy" of the contemporary world? Eliot's notes to *The Waste Land* indicate his interest in the work of Jessie Weston, who considered herself a follower of J. G. Frazer, author of *The Golden Bough*. Her *From Ritual to Romance* (1920) was an attempt to trace the Grail legends back to their sources, which Miss Weston believed to be ancient vegetation rituals. From the point of view of Frazer and his followers, Christianity as well as other religions could be seen as relatively modern versions of age-old pagan celebrations of the earth's yearly death and rebirth, celebrations which later became symbolically the death and resurrection of a god or, in the case of the Grail legends, the sexual maiming of a king and the accompanying loss of fertility of his dependent kingdom until a cure was found which restored his vitality and thus the land's fruitfulness. The primitive analogies between the fertility of the earth and the fertility of man suggested a unity between human and physical nature at the same time that it provided a connection between the sexual and spiritual fulfillment of man.

For Eliot and other members of his generation this

new and, in the early part of the twentieth century, somewhat daring way of looking at these phenomena had the attraction of putting religion on a basis more acceptable to the intellectual and sophisticated mind steeped in the scientific method and in twentieth-century philosophical traditions. Despite the secular and anti-poetic *Weltanschauung* which science had imposed on the modern world, psychology, ethnology, and anthropology—themselves offspring of that *Weltanschauung*—had introduced the view that religion was not the outworn relic of an older culture to be discarded because no longer useful, but, rather, that it expressed ancient and pervasive universal aspects of human experience. Even though Frazer was part of an evolutionary tradition which saw mankind evolving from these primitive forms to a more "modern" and "enlightened" view in which control of nature supplanted propitiation of nature, the new science of psychology under the direction of Jung and Freud emphasized the universal and archetypal aspects of primitive experience which still existed in modern man.

Both Jung, with his belief in the racial unconscious, and Freud, who found the unconscious compulsions he saw in his patients reflected in Greek myth and primitive ritual, used *The Golden Bough* as a source book from which they derived evidence that man's sexual nature kept these primitive roots of human behavior ever green and well-nourished. In addition, ethnology provided evidence of the omnipresence of primitive experience and ritual in every kind of climate and culture in the present-day world, just as classical anthropology provided evidence for its existence in the past. These new sciences gave the indubitability of facts empirically and impartially arrived at. Thus the universality of the relationship between the sexual experience of man and the phenomena of nature provided a rationale for a symbolism which the modern poet, suspicious of the universals of his immediate predecessors, could again use. To the advocate of tradition and culture, which T. S. Eliot had declared himself to be, such a basis for tradition seemed well suited.

Eliot gives abundant evidence throughout his essays of having noted closely the work of another group of Frazer's followers, the Cambridge School of Classical Anthropology, which took as its special province the anthropological study of the classical epoch, with special emphasis on the origins of Greek drama. The members of this group found the basis of classical drama in ancient ritual, in the primitive celebrations marking the phases in the cycles of the earth's productiveness. The works of Gilbert Murray, Francis M. Cornford, and Jane Ellen Harrison emphasized the specific liturgical forms of the fertility ceremonies which were retained in Greek drama.

Gilbert Murray found in the "fixed forms" of the plots of Greek tragedy the sequence of ritual procedure which he summarized as follows:

"1. An *Agon* or Contest, the Year against its Enemy, Light against Darkness, Summer against Winter.

"2. A *Pathos* of the Year-Daimon, generally a ritual or sacrificial death, in which Adonis or Attis is slain by the tabu animal, the Pharmakos stoned, Osiris,

Dionysus, Pentheus, Orpheus, Hippolytus torn to
pieces. . . .

"3. A *Messenger*. For this Pathos seems seldom or
never to be actually performed under the eyes of the
audience. . . . It is announced by a messenger. 'The
news comes' that Pan the Great, Thammuz, Adonis,
Osiris is dead, and the dead body is often brought in on
a bier. This leads to

"4. A *Threnos* or Lamentation. . . .

"5 and 6. An *Anagnorisis*—discovery or recognition
—of the slain and mutilated Daimon, followed by his
Resurrection or Apotheosis or, in some sense, his
Epiphany in glory. This I shall call by the general
name Theophany." [16]

Francis Cornford, following Murray, found the same
primitive fertility ritual underlying the comedy of Aristophanes. In *The Origin of Attic Comedy* (1914) he examined the relationship at length:

"The outline of our supposed ritual plot is now complete. Starting from Aristotle's authoritative statement,
we sought the nucleus of Comedy in the Phallic ceremonies, illustrated by Aristophanes himself in the rites
performed by Dikaiopolis at his Country Dionysia. We
found there, in barest outline, a ritual procedure in
three parts. (1) The procession of the worshippers of
Phales moves on its way, carrying the emblem of the
God on a pole and the instruments of sacrifice. (2) It

[16] Gilbert Murray, "Excursus on the Ritual Forms Preserved in
Greek Tragedy," appearing as a special chapter in *Themis: A Study
of the Social Origins of Greek Religion* by Jane Ellen Harrison
(Cambridge: Cambridge University Press, 1912), pp. 342–43.

pauses at some fixed place for the sacrifice, accompanied by a prayer to Dionysus. (3) The procession moves on again singing the Phallic Song. This *Komos* hymn reflects the two essential elements: invocation and induction of the good influence or spirit, magical abuse and expulsion of evil. The same two elements we found perpetuated in the comic *Parabasis*. In the *Agon* which regularly precedes the *Parabasis* we now have come to see the equivalent of the sacrifice which precedes the Phallic Song. The *Agon* is the beginning of the sacrifice in its primitive dramatic form—the conflict between the good and evil principles, Summer and Winter, Life and Death. The good spirit is slain, dismembered, cooked and eaten in the communal feast, and yet brought back to life. These acts survive in the standing features of the comic plot between the *Parabasis* and the *Exodos*. Finally comes the sacred Marriage of the risen God, restored to life and youth to be the husband of the Mother Goddess. This marriage is the necessary consummation of the Phallic ritual, which, when it takes a dramatic form, simulates the union of Heaven and Earth for the renewal of all life in Spring." [17]

It was Cornford's view that the old ritual drama provided comedy with the stock masks which later led to the development in this form of more and more subtle classifications of all that was ridiculous in human character while the outlines of the ritual plot were retained; tragedy took over different elements inherent in the old

[17] Francis M. Cornford, *The Origin of Attic Comedy* (London: Edward Arnold, 1914), pp. 103–04.

ritual forms, namely "the abstract conception or movement of its plot, and the philosophy of *Hubris*." [18]

It is easy to understand why, with the impetus given by these studies, Greek drama took on a new significance for Eliot. Not only did the dramatic tradition go back to dim antiquity, thus having an honored heritage as a form, but it had surrounding it in the Greek tradition a body of myth existing at several stages of development—in the more primitive ritualistic stage and in the finished master works of Greek drama. It therefore provided the contemporary artist with an inexhaustible source of mythical material at both stages with which to give form and significance to modern life. Moreover, the existence of the earlier forms in the later plays provided a solution to the vexing problem which Eliot had discussed in "The Possibility of a Poetic Drama"—the question of how an artistically satisfying whole could reach all elements in a

[18] Cornford noted Murray's statement on *Hubris:* "Professor Murray has pointed out the affinity between the recurrent life-story of the Year Spirit, the theme of our supposed ritual, and that deep-rooted doctrine of *Hubris,* of the Insolence that brings vengeance on itself as the wheel of Time and Judgment inexorably turns, in which the Greek found the tragic philosophy of life. He says: 'The life of the Year-Daemon, as it seems to be reflected in Tragedy, is generally a story of Pride and Punishment. Each Year arrives, waxes great, commits the sin of Hubris, and then is slain. The death is deserved; but the slaying is a sin: hence comes the next Year as Avenger, or as the Wronged One re-risen: "They all pay retribution for their injustice one to another according to the ordinance of time." ' Our supposed ritual, accordingly, as a representation of the cycle of seasonal life, of the annual conflict of Summer and Winter, provides the essential structure of the tragic plot, the fundamental conception of the tragic reversal or *peripeteia*" (Cornford, *The Origin of Attic Comedy,* pp. 207–08). This pattern with its emphasis on time and judgment has relevance to Eliot's treatment of Becket's spiritual pride in *Murder in the Cathedral.*

heterogeneous public. An underlying mythical structure might provide a deeper level of meaning while the surface presented an analogue palatable to those in the audience who sought entertainment. Meaning would thus be infused through both levels at once, though the key to the connection might be discovered only by those who saw the relevance of the underlying framework. The remaining problem was how to integrate both levels of meaning into an ordered and rhythmic whole.

In "The Beating of a Drum" (1923),[19] Eliot arrived at a solution to that problem by suggesting that perhaps the way forward was the way back, an idea which should not be unfamiliar to his readers. He decided, on the basis of the scholarship already mentioned, "that the *nature* of the finished product . . . is essentially present in the crude forerunner," and he urged other literary men to study the works dealing with the development of tragedy and comedy out of a common form rather than the work of literary critics. He cited the theory of Cornford and Murray as evidence that "the comic element, or the antecedent of the comic, is perhaps present, together with the tragic, in all savage or primitive art." Comedy and tragedy as separate forms are "late and perhaps impermanent intellectual abstractions" which need to be replaced or renewed. Beneath these impermanent forms lies the one essential of drama—rhythm:

"The essentials of drama were, as we might expect, given by Aristotle: 'poetry, music, and dancing con-

[19] T. S. Eliot, "The Beating of a Drum," *The Nation and the Athenaeum,* xxxiv (October 6, 1923), 11–12.

stitute in Aristotle a group by themselves, their common element being imitation by means of rhythm—rhythm which admits of being applied to words, sounds, and the movements of the body.' . . . It is the rhythm, so utterly absent from modern drama, either verse or prose, and which interpreters of Shakespeare do their best to suppress, which makes Massine and Charlie Chaplin the great actors that they are, and which makes the juggling of Rastelli more cathartic than a performance of 'A Doll's House.' As for the catharsis, we must remember that Aristotle was accustomed to dramatic performances only in rhythmic form; and that therefore he was not called upon to determine how far the catharsis could be effected by the moral or intellectual significance of the play *without* its verse form and proper declamation.

"The drama was originally ritual; and ritual, consisting of a set of repeated movements, is essentially a dance. . . . It is . . . possible to assert that primitive man acted in a certain way and then found a reason for it. An unoccupied person, finding a drum, may be seized with a desire to beat it; but unless he is an imbecile he will be unable to continue beating it, and thereby satisfying a need (rather than a 'desire'), without finding a reason for so doing. The reason may be the long continued drought. The next generation or the next civilization will find a more plausible reason for beating a drum. Shakespeare and Racine—or rather the developments which led up to them—each found his own reason. The reasons may be divided into tragedy and comedy. We still have similar reasons, but we have lost the drum." [20]

Sweeney Agonistes, completed in the first draft a year later, was Eliot's most direct effort to get back the lost drum.[21] From the passage just quoted it is apparent that Eliot was seeking beneath the usual classifications of drama for something basic and elemental on which the contemporary poet could rebuild dramatic art. Beneath tragedy and comedy lay primitive religious rites and beneath these rites lay rhythm and man's innate fascination with it. Eliot's comments about the importance of rhythm throw a good deal of light on some of his other statements on drama which at first seem puzzling and on his objections to realism. His objection to realism in drama was that the right relationship of the parts to the whole did not exist where reality was copied directly in art; stylization and abstraction were necessary to achieve an artistic whole. In the passage above the same idea is expressed in a different way. Here, when Eliot says that Rastelli's juggling is more cathartic than Ibsen's *A Doll's House,* he is extending the usual meaning of rhythm as perceived in a juggler's movements to include the ordered relationship of parts to whole, and he understands Aristotle's conception of rhythm to include all these degrees. He conceived the secret of dramatic art to be the effect of the whole. The fact that Eliot extended this principle

---

[20] *Ibid.,* p. 12.

[21] Eugene O'Neill's *The Emperor Jones* (1920) is an earlier and more successful experiment in the use of drum-beats and primitive dramatic rhythms.

even to the creation of character is evidenced by his defense of Ben Jonson [22] as a dramatist: although Jonson's dramatic world is small, it is perfectly proportioned. Jonson's characters are flat, but they fit their world perfectly. While Shakespeare's characters may "represent a more complex tissue of feelings and desires," they are no more "alive" than are Jonson's. Jonson "projects a new world into a new orbit" by simplifying all the details of that world:

> "The simplification consists largely in reduction of detail, in the seizing of aspects relevant to the relief of an emotional impulse which remains the same for that character, in making the character conform to a particular setting. This stripping is essential to the art, to which is also essential a flat distortion in the drawing; it is an art of caricature, of great caricature, like Marlowe's. It is a great caricature, which is beautiful; and a great humour, which is serious." [23]

In short, the term "dramatic" meant more to Eliot than the presentation of an action; it meant the creation of an ordered whole, a total world in which everything is scaled to size, a rhythmic and proportioned totality forming a complete emotional and ideological whole. Even the conception of character was to be reduced to fit the scale. And while rhythm or the ordered relationship of parts could, of course, be present in other literary forms, drama had the advantage of being able to present a whole world more completely than any other literary form, as well as the equally attractive advantage of hav-

[22] Eliot, *Selected Essays*, pp. 127–39.
[23] *Ibid.*, p. 138.

ing ritualistic roots expressing in its original rhythms man's most elemental needs.

Sweeney Agonistes is Eliot's first exploration of these ideas in dramatic form. He first published "Fragments of a Prologue" in the *New Criterion* of October 1926 and "Fragment of an Agon" in January 1927, both under the general title of *Wanna Go Home, Baby?* [24] It was not until 1932 that the two fragments were issued in book form and the title changed to *Sweeney Agonistes: Fragments of an Aristophanic Melodrama.*

The original title clearly conveys the atmosphere of the contemporary déclassé setting. Eliot's choice of jazz verse rhythms to match the jazz-world surface can be explained by his views on rhythm. He was engaged in a search for new metrical forms for poetry to suit contemporary life. In his introduction to his mother's poetic drama, *Savonarola,* published in 1926, he said:

"The next form of drama will have to be a verse drama but in new verse forms. Perhaps the conditions of modern life (think how large a part is now played in our sensory life by the internal combustion engine!) have altered our perception of rhythms. At any rate, the

[24] The sample fragments and a "scenario" were probably completed two years earlier, for in October 1924 Eliot sent them both to Arnold Bennett with a request for criticism. Bennett had noted in his journal of September 10 that Eliot had visited him and announced that "he had definitely given up that form of writing [as characterized by "Wastelands," as Bennett called it] and was now centred on dramatic writing. He wanted to write a drama of modern life (furnished flat sort of people) in a rhythmic prose 'perhaps with certain things in it accentuated by drum-beats.' And he wanted my advice. We arranged that he should do the scenario and some sample pages of dialogue" (*The Journals of Arnold Bennett,* III, 1921-1928, ed. Newman Flower [London: Cassell and Company, 1933], 52).

recognized forms of speech-verse are not as efficient as they should be; probably a new form will be devised out of colloquial speech." [25]

The verse form of *Sweeney Agonistes* was the author's experiment in the creation of a verse derived from a colloquial speech which had been influenced by "the internal combustion engine." Just how literal his intention was (and how close he conceived the rhythms of primitive and modern music to be) is indicated by his instruction to Hallie Flanagan, who presented the fragments at Vassar in 1933.[26] "Diction should not have too much expression. I had intended the whole play to be accompanied by light drum taps to accentuate the beats (esp. the chorus, which ought to have a noise like a street drill)." [27] At the same time, the stylized speeches, actions, and jazz-patters of the characters are an attempt to create a simplified world which is rhythmic in the broader sense which Eliot had developed in his comments on the dramatic world of Ben Jonson.

It should also be remembered that Eliot had come to the conclusion that the new drama should start with a popular audience which wanted entertainment but would

[25] T. S. Eliot, Introduction to *Savonarola: A Dramatic Poem* by Charlotte Eliot (London: R. Cobden-Sanderson, [1926]), p. xi.

[26] There will be no attempt in this study to give a systematic theatrical history of Eliot's plays; only those details of production which illuminate the playwright's dramatic methods and intentions will be discussed. For an informal discussion of the plays' theatrical history see E. Martin Browne "From *The Rock* to *The Confidential Clerk*," *T. S. Eliot: A Symposium for His Seventieth Birthday*, ed. Neville Braybrooke (New York: Farrar, Straus & Cudahy, 1958), pp. 57–69.

[27] Hallie Flanagan, *Dynamo* (New York: Duell, Sloan and Pearce, 1943), p. 82.

put up with poetry.[28] The vehicle for popular entertainment in England in the nineteen-twenties was the music hall. It was there that jazz could be heard in England, and Eliot found in the song-and-dance teams, the jazz patters, the mock-sad comedians, the boisterous and bawdy hilarity of the vaudeville clowns, and even in the art of the jugglers the rhythm "applied to words, sounds, and the movements of the body" which Aristotle discerned as central to drama.[29] Eliot's essay in memory of Marie Lloyd (1923)[30] indicated how highly he valued this form of popular entertainment and the vaudeville performers it produced.

In addition to a sense of rhythm, he found another merit in the vaudeville art; there still remained a social unity in the relationship between the performer and the audience that had disappeared in other forms of dramatic art. "The working man who went to the music-

[28] Eliot's facetious "Five Points on Dramatic Writing" (A Letter to Ezra Pound), *Townsman*, 1 (July 1938), 10, illustrates this aspect of the author's attitude toward his audience:

"1. You got to keep the audience's attention all the time.

"2. If you lose it you got to get it back QUICK.

"3. Everything about plot and character and all else what Aristotle and others say is secondary to the forgoin.

"4. But IF you can keep the bloody audience's attention engaged, then you can perform any monkey tricks you like when they ain't looking, and it's what you do behind the audience's back so to speak that makes your play IMMORTAL for a while.

"If the audience gets its strip tease it will swallow the poetry.

"5. If you write a play in verse, then the verse ought to be a medium to look THROUGH and not a pretty decoration to look AT."

[29] J. Isaacs tells of first taking Eliot to see the English music-hall comedian Ernie Lotinga, whom Isaacs calls a "direct descendant of the phallic comedy of Greece and Rome" (*An Assessment of Twentieth-Century Literature*, [London: Secker & Warburg, 1951], p. 147).

[30] Eliot, *Selected Essays*, pp. 405–08.

hall and saw Marie Lloyd and joined in the chorus was himself performing part of the act; he was engaged in that collaboration of the audience with the artist which is necessary in all art and most obviously in dramatic art." Eliot viewed the fact that the middle classes had no such representative "idol" as Marie Lloyd as an indication of the moral corruption of their class. Unless a new form of drama could be conceived to rescue the public from "the cheap and rapid-breeding cinema," all communal dramatic art, he felt, would disappear. His description of the evolution of *Sweeney Agonistes,* quoted in part earlier, emphasizes the social purposes behind his experiment and deserves to be quoted in full:

"The most useful poetry, socially, would be one which could cut across all the present stratifications of public taste—stratifications which are perhaps a sign of social disintegration. The ideal medium for poetry, to my mind, and the most direct means of social 'usefulness' for poetry, is the theatre. In a play of Shakespeare you get several levels of significance. For the simplest auditors there is the plot, for the more thoughtful the character and conflict of character, for the more literary the words and phrasing, for the more musically sensitive the rhythm, and for auditors of greater sensitiveness and understanding a meaning which reveals itself gradually. And I do not believe that the classification of audience is so clear-cut as this; but rather that the sensitiveness of every auditor is acted upon by all these elements at once, though in different degrees of consciousness. At none of these levels is the auditor both-

[54]

ered by the presence of that which he does not understand, or by the presence of that in which he is not
interested. I may make my meaning a little clearer by
a simple instance. I once designed, and drafted a couple
of scenes, of a verse play. My intention was to have one
character whose sensibility and intelligence should be
on the plane of the most sensitive and intelligent members of the audience; his speeches should be addressed
to them as much as to the other personages in the play
—or rather, should be addressed to the latter who were
to be material, literal-minded and visionless, with the
consciousness of being overheard by the former. There
was to be an understanding between this protagonist
and a small number of the audience, while the rest of
the audience would share the responses of the other
characters in the play. Perhaps this is all too deliberate,
but one must experiment as one can." [31]

This statement points out the elements which led Eliot
to conceive of his theory of dramatic levels. His conviction
of the "social usefulness" of dramatic poetry made him
seek his models in the music hall which might be transformed into a vehicle as valuable to the modern playwright as the Elizabethan theater was for Shakespeare.
A theater with "something for everybody," refined and
disciplined by the standards of art might involve, unify,
and order a society as no other means in the modern
world had succeeded in doing. The dramatic formula
which he evolved at this early stage of his dramatic career
included planes of meaning to match the planes of under-

---

[31] Eliot, *The Use of Poetry and the Use of Criticism*, pp. 146–47.

standing of the audience. Its other ingredients have already been mentioned. They included, first of all, a structure patterned on the model Eliot believed to be beneath both tragedy and comedy—the ritual drama with its agon, its pathos or sacrificial death, and finally its "discovery or recognition of the slain and mutilated Daimon, followed by his Resurrection or Apotheosis or, in some sense his Epiphany in glory." [32] His theme was to be based on the deeper religious meanings of that pattern, which could be suggested by creating situations based on those in later Greek drama which emphasized ritual themes. Finally, the dramatic surface was to be stylized by creating flat characters and patterned actions which would provide entertainment and action to beguile the audience while at the same time suggesting, by their lack of realism and by the presence of serio-comic references to religious meanings, the symbolic dimension beneath the surface, just as the phallic comedy of Greece had.

This mingling of the comic and the serious in the surface is a distinctive characteristic of Eliot's drama. It is a technique based, I think, on his exploration of the favorite poetic device of the metaphysicals—wit. Eliot had defined wit, in his essay "Andrew Marvell" (1921) [33] as "a tough reasonableness beneath the slight lyric grace."

"It is confused with erudition because it belongs to an educated mind, rich in generations of experiences; and it is confused with cynicism because it implies a constant inspection and criticism of experience. It involves, probably, a recognition, implicit in the expression of

[32] Harrison, *Themis,* p. 343.
[33] Eliot, *Selected Essays,* pp. 251–63.

every experience, of other kinds of experience which are possible. . . ." [34]

He found in wit an "alliance of levity and seriousness" which intensified the seriousness, and this feature of style, present in much of his early poetry, is a characteristic feature of *Sweeney Agonistes.*

The new title given to the fragments in 1932, *Sweeney Agonistes: Fragments of an Aristophanic Melodrama,* is an example of Eliot's use of wit to provide clues to the deeper level of meaning. In the new title a kind of ultra-sophisticated effect (for wit is basically a reliance on sophistication) is sought by coupling "Sweeney," previously Eliot's characterization of the natural man, with "Agonistes," suggesting analogies with Milton's *Samson Agonistes* both with regard to Samson's spiritual dilemma and to the Greek dramatic structure used in Milton's work. Thus the audience is intended to get both a comic-ironic impression of the incongruities of Sweeney in Samson's place, while at the same time it perceives on another level the meaning of such a possibility. Samson's dilemma is that of the exile in an alien world who feels compelled by divine will to pull that world down around his own head in order to destroy its iniquities. Sweeney is another spiritual exile in an alien world, and he too must destroy part of himself in his attack on that world. Eliot was trying to achieve comic and tragic effects simultaneously, though on different levels, in an attempt to create a form which would reach through the levels of comedy and tragedy in order to explore beneath the surface of both

[34] *Ibid.,* p. 252.

and of all human experience. His view on this matter was clearly expressed in the following comment:

"To those who have experienced the full horror of life, tragedy is still inadequate. . . . In the end, horror and laughter may be one—only when horror and laughter have become as horrible and laughable as they can be . . . then only do you perceive the aim of the comic and the tragic dramatists is the same: they are equally serious [for] there is potential comedy in Sophocles and potential tragedy in Aristophanes, and otherwise they would not be such good tragedians or comedians as they are." [35]

Perhaps this passage also makes somewhat clearer what Eliot meant to convey by the subtitle *Fragments of an Aristophanic Melodrama*. His play is Aristophanic in that it combines a comic surface of social satire with the ritualistic celebration of death and rebirth which Cornford found to underlie comedy. Eliot's presentation is thus intended to evoke both horror and laughter in those who could see "the potential tragedy" in Aristophanes. It is melodramatic in the older sense of the term, a play combining music and drama, because it is in the music-hall tradition, but it is also melodramatic in another sense. The elements which characterize melodrama, Eliot had said in "Wilkie Collins and Dickens," [36] were an emphasis on plot and situation, flat characters who suggest

[35] T. S. Eliot, "Shakespearian Criticism: I. From Dryden to Coleridge," *A Companion to Shakespeare Studies*, edited by Harley Granville-Barker and G. B. Harrison (Cambridge: Cambridge University Press, 1934), pp. [287]-99.
[36] Eliot, *Selected Essays*, pp. 409-18.

"humour" characters, an atmosphere in which "the co-
incidences, resemblances and surprises of life" are utilized
for emotional effect, and the postponement of the dénouement—"delaying, longer than one would conceive it
possible to delay, a conclusion which is inevitable and
wholly foreseen." I believe Eliot used the term melodrama in the subtitle of *Sweeney Agonistes* to suggest the
conception of a dramatic world he had enunciated in
the Jonson essay, where characters were flat to fit the
world they moved in. In addition, *Sweeney Agonistes*
includes a postponement of the dénouement in the sense
that the play is a commentary on the postponement of
spiritual awakening in modern man.

The epigraphs which Eliot placed at the beginning of
the fragments also hint at the spiritual theme of the
work:

"Orestes: You don't see them, you don't—but *I* see
them: they are hunting me down, I must move on.—
Choephoroi

"Hence the soul cannot be possessed of the divine
union, until it has divested itself of the love of created
beings.—*St. John of the Cross*" [37]

Their arrangement points out a connection between the
purgation of Orestes and of St. John of the Cross. The
first quotation is Orestes' exit line in the *Choephoroi*
when he first becomes aware of the Furies, who haunt
and pursue him after his murder of his mother and her
lover until he has achieved purgation. The passage from
St. John of the Cross is taken from *The Ascent of Mount*

[37] Eliot, *Complete Poems and Plays*, p. 74.

Carmel, which describes the mystical path to union with God. The passage is part of the instruction to the novice who wishes to pass through the first stage of the mystic path—the dark night of the senses in which purification of all human desires must occur before the next stage can be reached. In both passages purgation is the goal; and in both cases the pursuit before purgation can occur is as terrible as it is necessary. This "witty" juxtaposition of seeming incongruities in order to suggest the hidden meanings became a typical feature of Eliot's drama and added to its esoteric effect.

The treatment of the characters in *Sweeney Agonistes* conforms to Eliot's idea of stylized surface. They are undeniably "flat" and, with the possible exception of Sweeney, are sketched in the broad outlines of intentional caricature. Doris[38] and Dusty (a name suggestive of *The Waste Land* imagery) are lower-class London prostitutes. They are both superstitious and superficial and are differentiated only by Sweeney's more sustained attentions to Doris. The world these characters are proportioned to fit is, on the surface level, the demimonde world of the jazz age where men want a spree with women who are willing to give it to them in return for material rewards

---

[38] Perhaps the same Doris who calmly brought the unfortunate epileptic of "Sweeney Erect" (1919) purely physical remedies:

> But Doris, towelled from the bath,
> Enters padding on broad feet,
> Bringing sal volatile
> And a glass of brandy neat.

(Eliot, *Complete Poems and Plays,* p. 26). Grover Smith, Jr. notes that several of Eliot's unfinished poems dealing with "death's kingdoms" were originally entitled "Doris's Dream Songs" (*T. S. Eliot's Poetry and Plays,* p. 100).

and relief from boredom. The fact that jazz symbolized the superficial elements of a modern society of materialistic automatism at the same time that it suggested the primitive side of man's nature in its throbbing rhythms provided the kind of double-edged dramatic device that Eliot liked best. Both analogy and irony could be developed; both the most superficial and the most elemental aspects of the modern world could be suggested by the audible rhythm and the visible setting. The comic and satiric could thus be portrayed on the surface while the tragic and spiritual existed simultaneously beneath.

"Loot" Sam Wauchope, "Cap" Horsfall, and their former war buddies, Klipstein and Krumpacker,[39] now American business men visiting London and "out on the town," remain types, although much of the dialogue is excellently effective and true to the types intended. Swart and Snow seem to be entertainers brought in to provide jazz song and dance routines so popular at parties in the nineteen-twenties.

Sweeney himself is by far the most important and interesting character. He introduces the dimension of tragic horror into the world of Dusty and Doris and the others. In the character of Sweeney some of the ritual elements which Eliot incorporated into the play from the work of

---

[39] Grover Smith (*T. S. Eliot's Poetry and Plays,* pp. 113–14) suggests that Eliot made use of some of the devices of *The Great Gatsby* in his play, such as the telephone conversation for comic effect, the fragment of a popular song for ironic counterpoint, and the long chronicle of names of Gatsby's guests which Fitzgerald so pointedly provides. Whether or not this is true, there is evidence that Eliot was impressed by this book at the very time when he was probably revising his own treatment of the jazz age. He wrote Fitzgerald in 1925 expressing his admiration for the novel.

Cornford and his Cambridge colleagues become apparent. Eliot's intention, I believe, was to make Sweeney an ironical buffoon-hero in Cornford's sense. The hero of comedy hid his wisdom in feigned stupidity which was a mask for cunning and slyness. He battled with his antagonist in the agon by a debate which he won by his wit and his use of ironic abuse which showed up the false claims of his enemy, but he masked his wit in buffoonery. Sweeney re-enacts the role of the hero for he speaks in the play for the principle of spiritual insight won by a horrible agony—in the ritualistic sense, the agony of the old and impotent god who suffers death and mutilation before the regeneration of resurrection.[40]

[40] It is clear from Eliot's letter to Hallie Flanagan, already quoted in part, that he had Cornford's categories in mind, as well as the stylized Noh drama in which Pound and Yeats had become interested: "The action should be stylized as in the Noh drama—see Ezra Pound's book and Yeats' preface and notes to *The Hawk's Well*. Characters *ought* to wear masks; the ones wearing old masks ought to give the impression of being young persons (as actors) and vice versa. Diction should not have too much expression. I had intended the whole play to be accompanied by light drum taps to accentuate the beats (esp. the chorus, which ought to have a noise like a street drill). The characters should be in a shabby flat, seated at a refectory table, facing the audience; Sweeney in the middle with a chafing dish, scrambling eggs. (See 'you see this egg.') (See also F. M. Cornford: *Origins* [*sic*] *of Attic Comedy,* which is important to read before you do the play.) I am talking about the *second* fragment of course; the other one is not much good. The second should end as follows: There should be 18 knocks like the angelus, and then

Enter an old gentleman. He is in full evening dress with a carna-
tion, but otherwise resembles closely Father Christmas. In one hand
he carries an empty champagne bottle, in the other an alarm clock.
THE OLD GENTLEMAN. Good evening. My name is Time. The time by the exchange clock is now nine-forty-five (or whatever it is). I come from the vacant lot in front of the Grand Union Depot, where there is the heroic equestrian statue of General Diego Cierra of Paraguay. Nobody knows why General Cierra is there. Nobody

"Fragment of a Prologue" corresponds to what Cornford described as the first part of the ritual procedure—"The procession of the worshippers of Phales moves on its way, carrying the emblem of the God on a pole and the instruments of sacrifice." The procession was the introduction of and the preparation for the ritual sacrifice. In Eliot's prologue the worshippers of Phales are, of course, Dusty and Doris and their first four guests. The preparation for the sacrifice takes the form of a series of ominous signs of violence and death, since, as the epigraphs have suggested, the negative violence of death must precede the positive state of union or spiritual rebirth. The god must grow old and be mutilated and slain

------

knows why I am there. Nobody knows anything. I wait for the lost trains that bring in the last souls after midnight. The time by the exchange clock is now 9:46.

SWEENEY. Have you nothing else to say?
OLD GENTLEMAN. Have you nothing to ask me?
SWEENEY. Yes.
OLD GENTLEMAN. Good.
SWEENEY. When will the barnfowl fly before morning?
    When will the owl be operated on for cataracts?
    When will the eagle get out of his barrel-roll?
OLD GENTLEMAN. When the camel is too tired to walk farther
    Then shall the pigeon-pie blossom in the desert
    At the wedding-breakfast of life and death.
SWEENEY. Thank you.
OLD GENTLEMAN. Good night.

(As Old Gentleman leaves, the alarm clock in his hand goes off.)" (Quoted in H. Flanagan, *Dynamo,* pp. 82–83.) Since Eliot never saw fit to include this ending in any of the published versions of the second fragment, and since it seems to be written in a style not quite consistent with the rest of *Sweeney Agonistes,* I have not given it special consideration in the discussion of the second fragment. However, the use of the angelus, signifying the union of divinity with humanity in Christ, and the mention of the wedding-breakfast of life and death provide added evidence that Eliot was using Cornford's categories of ritual as well as the Christian symbol of the Incarnation.

before he is revived or reborn as the new god. The first ominous note underneath the comic surface is struck by Pereira's telephone call [41] and the panic it arouses in the girls.

Before the call Doris and Dusty have been discussing whether or not to invite Pereira, who "pays the rent" but never appears in the fragments, to the party to be held that evening. Doris objects that though he pays the rent

> He's no gentleman, Pereira:
> You can't trust him! [42]

Dusty agrees and adds:

> And *if* you can't trust him—
> Then you never know what he's going to do. [43]

When the telephone rings both girls panic, knowing that Pereira is on the other end of the line. Doris insists that Dusty answer and get rid of him somehow:

> Say what you like: say I'm ill,
> Say I broke my leg on the stairs
> Say we've had a fire. [44]

Dusty tells him that Doris has "a terrible chill," that she "just hates having the doctor," and that since "she's got her feet in mustard and water" she hopes to be all right on Monday. On Monday he can "phone through."

[41] Eliot is very fond of the use of a telephone bell or doorbell or knock as an insistent signal of the entrance of divinity. He uses this device in several later plays including *The Cocktail Party* and *The Confidential Clerk*.

[42] Eliot, *Complete Poems and Plays*, p. 74.

[43] *Ibid.*

[44] *Ibid.*, p. 75.

The symbolic identity of this cryptic character is, I believe, important to the meaning of the whole work. His
name is significant; Pereira is a medicine made from the
bark of a Brazilian tree and used to mitigate or remove
fever. It was named after a famous London professor of
materia medica, Jonathan Pereira (1804–1853). Cornford
discusses the role of the doctor as the ritualistic agent for
the rejuvenation of the dead god.[45] In the play Pereira
"pays the rent" in the sense that spiritual existence ultimately depends on him, but in this world of immediate
pleasures he is avoided as long as possible. He represents
a positive spiritual force who keeps insistently calling and
who must some day be reckoned with, even if not now.
From the point of view of those who refuse to exist in
a world of any other kind of "reality" than one which
they can touch, Pereira is viewed negatively. The pursuing
spiritual force is no "gentleman" both because he is unpredictable and relentless and because he demands the
agony of purgation.

The excuse Dusty makes up for Doris is the only one
Pereira is likely to accept even temporarily: that Doris
feels the spiritual chill, that she does not need the doctor

[45] Eliot's interest in the doctor of ritual drama was indicated by a
passage in "Beating of a Drum": "The Fool in 'Lear' is a *possessed;*
a very cunning and very intuitive person; he has more than a suggestion of the shaman or medicine man. . . . The prototype of the true
Fool, according to my conjecture, is a character in that English version
of the Perseus legend, the Mummers' Play of St. George and the
Dragon. The Doctor who restores St. George to life is, I understand,
usually presented as a comic character. As Mr. Cornford suggests, in
'The Origin of Attic Comedy,' this Doctor may be identical with the
Doctor who is called in to assist Punch after he has been thrown by
his horse" (*The Nation and the Athenaeum,* xxxiv [October 6, 1923],
11).

(the enforced spiritual cure) because she is getting along sufficiently well herself with her own spiritual cure. Pereira appears unconvinced for he insists on calling again on Monday, the day after Sunday. The doctor figure with spiritual associations recurs in several of Eliot's plays, most notably *The Family Reunion, The Cocktail Party,* and *The Elder Statesman.* Eliot's continued interest in the medical imagery of fever cures and spiritual doctors is evident in the Christ-the-surgeon passage in "East Coker," particularly the purgatorial stanza:

> The chill ascends from feet to knees,
> The fever sings in mental wires.
> If to be warmed, then I must freeze
> And quake in frigid purgatorial fires
> Of which the flame is roses, and the smoke is briars.[46]

The second suggestion in the prologue of the painful agon to come is the fortune-telling device, familiar from *The Waste Land.* It functions here in several ways: it serves to characterize the girls, showing by their eagerness to "cut the cards for to-night" that while they avoid the true prophecies which Pereira brings, they put their trust in another kind of debased prophecy; it builds up dramatic suspense by cryptically foreshadowing the events to come; and it universalizes the characters and the ensuing action by providing additional mythical symbols based on fertility symbolism.

The fortune they read in the cards begins with the King of Clubs, which they decide "might be Sweeney" or possibly Pereira. The identification of these two char-

[46] Eliot, *Complete Poems and Plays,* pp. 127–28.

acters indicates that neither is very popular with the girls, who associate both with violence, a fact which fore-shadows their dual role as agents of spiritual and pur-gatorial violence. Next the cards show the party and gifts of apparel or money, followed by " 'news of an absent friend' " who is Pereira, they decide. The fortune becomes more frightening as they turn up, after the Queen of Hearts (Mrs. Porter [47] or themselves for "We're all hearts"), the six (" 'A quarrel. An estrangement. Sepa-ration of friends.' ") and the coffin. Both girls are filled with horror but Doris is sure the coffin card is meant for her because she "dreamt of weddings all last night." The cards thus predict the arrival of Sweeney at the party, his news of an absent friend in his concealed spiritual mes-sage, and the threat of violence and death to a Queen of Hearts (but followed by "weddings"). The coffin and the dream of weddings are symbols drawn from Cornford's discussion of the ritual scenes of death and resurrection.[48]

"Fragment of an Agon" corresponds to the second stage of the ritual sequence as described by Cornford. "The *Agon* is the beginning of the sacrifice in its primitive dramatic form—the conflict between the good and evil principles, Summer and Winter, Life and Death," or in Gilbert Murray's words, "Light against Darkness." In the agon of *Sweeney Agonistes* the opposing forces seem to be the unawakened dwellers in a world without a spir-

---

[47] Mrs. Porter and Sweeney were also associated in *The Waste Land:*
    But at my back from time to time I hear
    The sound of horns and motors, which shall bring
    Sweeney to Mrs. Porter in the spring.
(Eliot, *Complete Poems and Plays,* p. 43.)
[48] Cornford, *The Origin of Attic Comedy,* pp. 70–104.

itual dimension, represented in this scene by Doris, and the forces of spiritual purgation and reawakening, represented by Sweeney, who has been reawakened in the past from a state of unawareness and now functions as a spiritual agent. The opening exchange between Doris and Sweeney has a special ritualistic significance which explains the identification of Pereira with Sweeney. He threatens to carry her off to a cannibal isle where he will be the cannibal. When she answers that she will be the missionary and convert him, he retorts:

> I'll convert *you!*

> Into a stew.
> A nice little, white little, missionary stew.[49]

Cornford notes:

> "The Doctor recalls him [the dead god] to life, or the Cook transmutes him from age to youth. This magical process of regeneration, as we have seen, is only a special variety of death and resurrection. The Cook is a magician, a dealer in enchanted herbs, a medicine-man. As such, he is not, in origin, distinct from the Learned Doctor. These two characters are alternative." [50]

A strong piece of evidence for Eliot's use of this source is the statement in his letter to Hallie Flanagan that Sweeney should be scrambling eggs throughout this scene and his remark, immediately after, that Cornford should be consulted. Cornford also mentions the sacramental

---

[49] Eliot, *Complete Poems and Plays*, p. 80.
[50] Cornford, *The Origin of Attic Comedy*, pp. 188–89.

cooking of victims in milk in many primitive rites, which may account for the "white little stew." [51] The egg represents life at its most elemental, but, as in the Easter egg, it is also a symbol for the Resurrection.

Sweeney is offering Doris a painful regeneration by a sacramental means. He gives her his version of what life without a spiritual rebirth really is:

> You see this egg
> You see this egg
> Well that's life on a crocodile isle.
> There's no telephones
> There's no gramophones
> There's no motor cars
>
> .   .   .   .   .   .
>
> Nothing at all but three things
>
> .   .   .   .   .   .
>
> Birth, and copulation, and death. [52]

But Doris says "I'd be bored" and Sweeney agrees. The world she lives in is a crocodile isle and she is, indeed, bored. Sweeney adds that he once went through a painful birth:

> I've been born, and once is enough.
> You don't remember, but I remember,
> Once is enough. [53]

He remembers his birth into the natural world both in the sense that his awareness of another realm of exper-

[51] Flanagan, *Dynamo*, p. 34. In the Vassar production Sweeney wore a cook's apron.
[52] Eliot, *Complete Poems and Plays*, p. 80.
[53] *Ibid.*, p. 81.

ience has awakened him to the awfulness of physical existence and in the additional sense that the knowledge of the need for the purgation of sins makes the state before spiritual rebirth an agony. Doris does not remember her first birth because she has not realized the duality of life. She refuses to accept the description of worldly existence as Sweeney has given it. When Doris cries out:

> That's not life, that's no life
> Why I'd just as soon be dead,[54]

Sweeney tells her:

> That's what life is. . . .
>
> .   .   .   .
>
> Life is death.
>
> .   .   .   .
>
> I knew a man once did a girl in
> Any man might do a girl in
> Any man has to, needs to, wants to
> Once in a lifetime, do a girl in.
> Well he kept her there in a bath
> With a gallon of lysol in a bath.[55]

Sweeney's tale of murder and the awfulness of the life-in-death existence of the murderer is meant to illustrate the process that the penitent must pursue in order to achieve purgation. The tale is a grotesque version of the epigraph from St. John of the Cross: "Hence the soul cannot be possessed of the divine union, until it has divested itself of the love of created beings." According

[54] *Ibid.*, p. 82.
[55] *Ibid.*, pp. 82–83.

to St. John the distance between the creator and the creature is irrecoverable unless the creature is purged of all
human affections, since they represent dependence on the
senses and make demands which cut man off from his
first duty, complete attention to God's love. Thus the
murder and dissolution in a lysol bath (lysol is a cleansing agent, albeit a violent one) of the girl in Sweeney's
tale represents the violent murder of human desire and
dissolution of the old life of "birth and copulation and
death" in the sacramental purgatorial bath which will
bring rebirth.

Sweeney's tale is another version of Eliot's use of the
Lazarus theme. Sweeney returns from the dead to tell the
story of his own horrible purgation, his divestment of
the love of created beings in the form of sensual allure-
ments and purely human attachments in order to achieve
rebirth and union. As one who has been through the
ordeal and has passed from darkness into light, he re-
enacts the battle with those still in darkness. Doris' terror
is caused by her recognition that she, who represents the
old life of the senses in the battle with spiritual forces, is
due for the same murder as the girl in Sweeney's tale.

Thus Eliot sees in the death-rebirth process of the god,
which is the type of the Passion and Resurrection of
Christ, a wider meaning than the final death of the body
and eternal life of the soul after death. He sees that pattern applied to the mystic's process of killing desire in
order to bring to birth the spirit. He pictures the agon as
the representation of that struggle, since humanity living
in earthly darkness in every age, including the modern,
must be brought to awareness of another life of spiritual

light. In the agon in *Sweeney Agonistes* he reproduces a re-enactment of that struggle.

The final song sung by the "full chorus" is a description of the nightmare-like pursuit of the penitent by the purgatorial forces.[56] As the epigraph from Aeschylus suggests, the hoo-ha's serve the same function as the relentless Furies in their pursuit of Orestes. This is Eliot's version of the "Hound of Heaven" theme. The meaning of the hangman should be clear to all readers of *The Waste Land*. The effectiveness of portraying the hanged god of Jessie Weston and Frazer as the hangman lies in the extension of the murder analogy which was begun in Sweeney's tale. Just as a murderer awaits the hangman who will mete out punishment for his crime, here the supplicant awaits the "hanged man" who will mete out purgatorial justice.

It is significant that the final song is sung by the "full chorus," since in Cornford's discussion of the chorus in Aristophanes he describes the attempts of the opponents in the agon to woo the sympathies of the chorus. The chorus takes one side, then the other, and finally is won over to the side of virtue represented by the hero.[57] In *Sweeney Agonistes* the chorus in the beginning of the agon indicates its endorsement of the copulation theme but in the end it too voices the final purgatorial ode.

If this representation of the spiritual path seems overly grim, it should be remembered that it is the bitter, pain-

---

[56] Eliot seems to have based this final song on the Lord Chancellor's song in Act II of the Gilbert and Sullivan operetta, *Iolanthe* (Henry W. Wells, *New Poets from Old* [New York: Columbia University Press, 1940], pp. 70–76). It is, perhaps, not coincidental that Cornford refers to Gilbert as "the Victorian Aristophanes."

[57] Cornford, *The Origin of Attic Comedy*, pp. 105–31.

ful, and relentless pursuit of the purgation period which is being described. Eliot, especially in the period just before his own union with the church, never pictured the path of penitence as an easy one. He is here thoroughly in the spirit of St. John of the Cross and the other Christian mystics, especially in describing the darkness of the nightmare world. In St. John's terms the candidate for union with Christ-the-Bridegroom must go through two separate stages of purgation—the Dark Night of the Senses and the Dark Night of the Spirit. It is the first that St. John refers to in the passage from Book One of *The Ascent of Mount Carmel* which Eliot uses as an epigraph. But even after the desires of the senses are purged, there still remains the darker and more painful purgation of the spirit to make it fit for communication with God. St. John himself deals with the question of why "the Divine light" should be called "dark":

"But the question arises: Why is the Divine light (which, as we say, illumines and purges the soul from its ignorances) here called by the soul a dark night? To this the answer is that for two reasons this Divine wisdom is not only night and darkness for the soul, but is likewise affliction and torment. The first is because of the height of Divine Wisdom, which transcends the talent of the soul, and in this way is darkness to it; the second, because of its vileness and impurity, in which respect it is painful and afflictive to it, and is also dark." [58]

Sweeney's statement, repeated twice, "That's nothing

[58] E. Allison Peers (ed.), *The Complete Works of Saint John of the Cross,* I (Westminster, Maryland: The Newman Bookshop, 1945), p. 406.

to me and nothing to you," is a way of expressing the theme of isolation which is so important in all Eliot's work in this period. The characters in these fragments demonstrate isolation in several ways. The "unaware" characters of the good-time world are isolated from one another because no real relationships can exist between them while they are engaged in the exploitation of one another. But even more, they are isolated from God because they have refused through pride to recognize that life without God is death. On the other hand, the individual preparing for rebirth is not only cut off from his "unaware" fellow men because of his new awakening, but during the long purgatorial path he is terribly and painfully cut off from God until, as St. John of the Cross says, he is sufficiently purified to see the Divine light as other than a fearful darkness. Thus when Sweeney, after telling his tale, says to Doris:

> I gotta use words when I talk to you
> But if you understand or if you dont
> That's nothing to me and nothing to you
> We all gotta do what we gotta do,[59]

he expresses the experiential fact of the mystic path, that God chooses his own and relentlessly pursues them to awareness and that the experience is ineffable and incommunicable until it is personally experienced.

Sweeney Agonistes is Eliot's first dramatic version of the theme of spiritual pilgrimage, the theme he has returned to again and again in his plays. Even though this play exists only in two fragments, it is complete enough

[59] Eliot, *Complete Poems and Plays*, p. 84.

to provide an illustration of his early dramatic theories. And because Eliot's view of man's spiritual pilgrimage and of the way drama can be used to express this subject has been modified but not fundamentally changed in each of his succeeding dramatic works, *Sweeney Agonistes* and the plan on which it was conceived have special significance for this study.

CHAPTER III

THE ROCK AND MURDER IN THE CATHEDRAL

When T. S. Eliot returned to dramatic writing in 1934, it was as a writer of occasional drama, for both *The Rock* (1934) and *Murder in the Cathedral* (1935) were "made-to-order" works intended for church occasions. This fact helps to explain the obvious differences, especially in the poet's attitude toward communication with his audience, between *Sweeney Agonistes* and the two later plays. The former was constructed on the assumption that the average spectator was incapable of perceiving its meaning, which was therefore hidden beneath a surface of contemporary, music-hall-jazz action. In *The Rock*, on the other hand, the meaning was anything but veiled, and the attack on the values of the modern world was made overt. The music-hall tradition was still present but only its most conventional aspect of loosely connected scenes of pageantry and dialogue was utilized. Eliot himself called *The Rock* a "revue" and E. Martin Browne, who directed the production at Sadler's Wells, has recently elaborated on Eliot's term:

"A pageant was called for, to promote the building of churches in Greater London. . . . After many months in which we found ourselves equally puzzled by the problem of how to create an interesting form while retaining the pageant-elements demanded, we agreed on a scenario based on the structure of the type of revue then current under the aegis of Charles Cochran: the difference being that instead of Young Ladies relying on their physical charms, they (together with their male counterparts) wore half-masks and garments of stiff hessian and relied on the application of their vocal agility to Mr. Eliot's verse." [1]

Unquestionably one of the reasons behind this conception was the necessity for communication with an audience which would, if reached by *The Rock*'s message, respond with generous contributions to the Forty-Five Churches Fund. Even *Murder in the Cathedral,* which has often been called limited in its appeal,[2] is limited only by the degree of religious commitment of its public, not by their inability to understand the message. In the later play Eliot has, in fact, gone to the length of providing special devices, such as the Knights' direct address to the audience, to insure that the play's meaning will be brought home to those who view it.

[1] E. Martin Browne, "From *The Rock* to *The Confidential Clerk,*" *T. S. Eliot: A Symposium for His Seventieth Birthday,* ed. Neville Braybrooke, p. 57.

[2] C. L. Barber comments that Eliot's task in the theater has been "the extraordinarily difficult one of presenting the action of redemption to audiences for the most part unconvinced that such an action exists. . . . The public at large beat a path, it is true, to *Murder in the Cathedral.* But most of them went as sightseers, . . . in a spirit which regarded as historical not only the events, but also the Christian values and standards of the play" ("T. S. Eliot After Strange Gods," *T. S. Eliot: A Selected Critique,* ed. Leonard Unger [New York: Rinehart & Company, Inc., 1948], p. 415). R. P. Blackmur also notes that *Murder in the Cathedral* "deals with an emotion I can hardly expect to share, which very few can ever expect to share, except as a last possibility, and which is certainly not an emotion of general interest at all; it deals with the special emotion of Christian martyrdom" ("T. S. Eliot: From *Ash Wednesday* to *Murder in the Cathedral,*" *T. S. Eliot: A Selected Critique,* ed. Leonard Unger, pp. 258–59).

The playwright's change of attitude on the matter of communication can be accounted for by his commitment to the cause of the church in a period when its enemies were in the ascendancy. His membership in the Church of England not only made him aware of his Christian duty to defend his faith, but it also placed him in a group of active Christian theorists within the church who, though few, were extremely vocal. Until a definitive biography of Eliot is written, the details of this liaison, so important to his future direction, will not be known except incidentally as they have been recorded in personal anecdote. Nevertheless, his many articles in church periodicals, his participation in various church seminars, and his work on *The Rock* are ample evidence of the relationship. In addition, Eliot's editorship of *The Criterion* from October 1922 to January 1939 served to place him in the position of spokesman for other neoclassicists, royalists, and Anglo-Catholics, who saw the magazine as an organ which stood opposed to most of the secular political causes current during the period between the wars.

Fundamentally, Eliot's attitude during this period was that expressed in "Modern Education and the Classics" (1932).[3] There were, he felt, only two finally tenable hypotheses about life, the Catholic and the materialistic, and all views of life rooted in materialism, such as liberalism, socialism, and fascism, robbed life of significance. The dangers Eliot saw in liberalism have already been rehearsed: liberalism dangerously elevated the individual to a position where he saw his private will (his "Inner Voice") as an infallible guide to action. In its search for

[3] Eliot, *Selected Essays*, pp. 452–60.

a sustaining creed, liberalism put "Culture" in the place of religion, and the relativism which resulted undermined the one legitimate foundation for ethics and morality. As Eliot pointed out at the expense of Norman Foerster in "Second Thoughts about Humanism" (1928),[4] those who hunger and thirst after righteousness will find "Five Foot Shelf Culture" thin soup.

Socialism and fascism were equally distasteful to Eliot. Both, he claimed, were heresies. In "Catholicism and International Order" (1933)[5] he took issue with the idea of individual liberty based on purely political and social standards:

"The conception of individual liberty . . . must be based upon the unique importance of every single soul, the knowledge that every man is ultimately responsible for his own salvation or damnation, and the consequent obligation of society to allow every individual the opportunity to develop his full humanity. But unless this humanity is considered always in relation to God, we may expect to find an excessive love of created beings, in other words humanitarianism, leading to a genuine oppression of human beings in what is conceived by other human beings to be their interest."[6]

The coupling of St. John of the Cross's phrase with humanitarianism points out quite clearly the direction of Eliot's thought in the nineteen-thirties. The phrase which in *Sweeney Agonistes* stood for the individual's purgation

[4] *Ibid.,* pp. 429–38.
[5] T. S. Eliot, *Essays Ancient and Modern* (London: Faber and Faber Limited, 1936), pp. 113–35.
[6] *Ibid.,* p. 119.

from the desires and affections of this world has now taken on a more social meaning. In the passage above it relates to the outcome for society if the primacy of God's claim on man is not recognized. The "excessive love of created beings" on the social level becomes humanitarianism, which will lead finally to "a genuine oppression" of human beings by others who in their eagerness to save man's physical life endanger his spiritual life. Man must be free, Eliot insisted, from any secular interference which might impede his pursuit of salvation; moreover, society has a positive obligation to provide an atmosphere where man can freely exercise his responsibility for the development of his full humanity "in relation to God."

All of Eliot's plays deal in one way or another with this Christian conception of human freedom. Typically, the dramatic situation involves the hero's discovery of the "Catholic" view of life as the only tenable one, no matter how painful that recognition may be. By recognizing divine necessity, the central character frees himself from subjection to human desires of the flesh, from the horror of the world's apparent disorder, and ultimately from the human limitations of physical death. By recognizing the existence of free-will, he also gains release from the determinism of the modern scientific world view. And typically, as the hero's discovery is made manifest, those around him demonstrate levels of awareness of the true meaning of freedom. Thus in *Murder in the Cathedral* a large part of the significance of the action-suffering motif rests in the realization that to "act" in the illusion of freedom from God's laws is the strongest kind of bondage to the world of the senses, while to exercise the freedom of the will by "suffering" God's will is to be freed from the torture-wheel of life. Thomas' moment of greatest freedom comes with his acceptance of God's will, while at the same moment the Knights exhibit the bondage of unbridled passion because they are tyrannized by the baser purposes of this world—power, greed, and passion. They become, in the imagery of the play, animals; in giving in to their animalistic instincts they have lost their divine gift of soul. The women of Canterbury, on the other hand, in their humility and docility begin by fearing the freedom which Thomas' return and suffering will mean but finally achieve their portion of liberation from the world's wheel by accepting their share of guilt. Allegiance to God's world means freedom from this world, and allegiance to this world means "freedom" from God's world, but the unregenerate who choose the latter can never find freedom from the final domination of death.

In his concluding "Commentary" [7] for *The Criterion* at the end of the decade, Eliot said of his own development during the period of his editorship that the right political philosophy had come more and more to imply the right theology and the right economics to depend on the right ethics. He felt that "real" democracy should be re-established, one which would avoid the excesses of individualism—errors based on the assumption that a majority of natural and unregenerate men is likely to want the right things—and at the same time avoid the dangers implicit in excessive order and authority—the recurring

[7] T. S. Eliot, "Last Words," *The Criterion*, xviii (January 1939), 269–75.

human desire to escape the burden of life and thought by welcoming any regime which offers to assume the entire responsibility for government. He envisioned a limited democracy based on hereditary rights and responsibilities in a community small enough to be homogeneous and therefore able to sustain a religious tradition from generation to generation.

One source which contributed to Eliot's social thought was Christopher Dawson's book, *The Making of Europe*. Dawson pleaded for a point of view toward European culture which would recognize Western Europe as a common civilization, rather than emphasizing the national history of each country. He traced the development of modern Europe from the twin sources of classical culture and the Germanic tribal system. While the Christian and classical social and religious orders were the formative influences in the making of Europe, the human material out of which modern Europe came was the barbarian and his tribe. The essence of barbaric society, according to Dawson, was the principle of kinship, rather than citizenship or the absolute authority of the state. His evaluation of the tribe was laudatory; although it was a relatively primitive form of social organization, it possessed virtues which many more advanced types of society might envy. It was consistent with a high ideal of personal freedom and self-respect and yet evoked an intense spirit of loyalty and devotion on the part of the individual tribesman toward the community and its chief. Consequently its moral and spiritual development was often far in advance of its material culture.[8]

[8] Christopher Dawson, *The Making of Europe* (London: Sheed & Ward, 1932).

Dawson's conception of the tribal group on which Christianity was superimposed became one of Eliot's most important sources for the social organization of a Christian society. He was not, however, very hopeful about the chances of re-establishing this kind of society in the modern world beset with so many alien ideals. The Christian's responsibility was to do what he could to work toward the establishment of a Christian order, but he must not be overly sanguine about the immediacy of success:

> "The World is trying the experiment of attempting to form a civilized non-Christian mentality. The experiment will fail; but we must be very patient in awaiting its collapse; meanwhile redeeming the time: so that the Faith may be preserved alive through the dark ages before us; to renew and rebuild civilization, and save the World from suicide." [9]

The social ramifications of Eliot's Christian views help to explain the modifications in his dramatic works of the mid-nineteen-thirties. It is possible to demonstrate, I think, that once convinced of the necessity for communicating with a world in need of his message, Eliot readjusted his existing dramatic views, both theoretical and practical. It is important to recognize, however, that the changes were readjustments of his previous views, not entirely new constructions. Many of the same ideas which conditioned the theoretical foundations of *Sweeney Agonistes* are present in recognizable, though subtly altered, form in *Murder in the Cathedral* and to some extent in *The Rock*.

[9] Eliot, "Thoughts After Lambeth," *Selected Essays*, p. 342.

The Rock was presented in the spring of 1934, on behalf of the Forty-Five Churches Fund of the Diocese of London as a plea for church building. The severe limitations put on the author are evident in the fact that he has disclaimed full authorship of all but the choruses and one scene, although the printed version announces that the entire book of words is by T. S. Eliot. He explains in his prefatory note:

> "I cannot consider myself the author of the 'play,' but only of the words which are printed here. The scenario, incorporating some historical scenes suggested by the Rev. R. Webb-Odell, is by Mr. E. Martin Browne, under whose direction I wrote the choruses and dialogues, and submissive to whose expert criticism I rewrote much of them. Of only one scene am I literally the author: for this scene and of course for the sentiments expressed in the choruses I must assume the responsibility." [10]

The Rock is called in the printed version "a pageant play." Its scenes depict the efforts and difficulties of a group of London masons involved in building a church. The difficulties they encounter, intended to suggest the obstacles faced by the church in the modern world, include bad foundations, lack of money, the hostility of agitators, and hostile criticism from secular groups represented by the Blackshirts, the Redshirts, and the Plutocrat. The process of construction is seen at every stage from the setting of the foundation to the finishing of the

[10] T. S. Eliot, *The Rock* (New York: Harcourt, Brace and Company, 1934), p. [5].

church in preparation for dedication. Interspersed among the scenes showing the actions of the modern church-builders are a series of pageant scenes from the past showing related situations in the history of the church, including the conversion of King Sabert by Melletus, Rahere's building of St. Bartholomew's, the rebuilding of Jerusalem, the Danish Invasion, the dedication of Westminster Abbey, outbursts of Puritan iconoclasm, and a conversation between Wren, Pepys, and Evelyn. The episodes are linked together by the chorus, which comments on the scenes both past and present. The hooded figure of the Rock, representing the church as eternal witness, sufferer, and martyr, in contrast to the chorus which represents the church in action, is intended to serve the dramatic function of supporting the chorus by putting its commentary on the events witnessed in the framework of the eternal and ever-continuing struggles of the church.

The stereotyped Cockney characters, the stiff historical pageantry, and the hooded figure of the Rock who turns into St. Peter, make it difficult to recognize *The Rock* as the work of the same dramatist who was to write *Murder in the Cathedral* a year later. There are, however, a number of features which correspond to the later play.

In the light of the presence of the choruses and the inclusion of the figure of the Rock, it is probable that Eliot initially conceived the work to be a new exemplification of his theory of dramatic levels. The prose scenes representing the actions of the modern-day builders were to be the surface of the drama, which was to be given an added dimension of historical and cultural importance by the insertion of relevant incidents from the past, one of Eliot's favorite methods of conveying simultaneous analogy and irony. The stereotyped character conceptions might have seemed in scenario to fit very well with his conception of flat humor characters used to achieve a stylized surface which would not interfere with the symbolic level beneath the action.

The chorus was to serve both as the vehicle of social commentary in the Greek sense and, together with the Rock, as the dramatic instrument for piercing through the level of the surface action to the level of the philosophical and theological implications of the action. Since Eliot was convinced that philosophical ideas must be translated into emotions before being presented in poetry, the task of the chorus was to present the ideological commentary on the action in a poetic form which would make the audience feel, as well as understand, the more profound implications of the events. Whereas in *Sweeney Agonistes* the chorus was used only to set the mood as an accompaniment to Sweeney's tale, which carried the burden of the meaning, in *The Rock* the choruses were intended to convey a large part of the meaning as well. In conception, if not in practice, this new use of the chorus marked a move in the direction of a more integrated relationship between the levels, and at the same time toward more direct communication with the audience. Thus Eliot's idea of rhythm, evident in *Sweeney Agonistes* only in the throbbing jazz beat of the verse, became in *The Rock,* at least in its conception, a dramatic rhythm formed by the alternation of the choruses with the surface action in order to give meaning, emotional intensity, and unity to the revue-like variety of the whole.

An examination of this pageant play also brings to light the first full dramatic expression of several of the important themes which Eliot was to use in his succeeding plays. The figure of the Rock, representing the church as eternal witness, sufferer, and martyr, used in conjunction with the chorus, representing the church in action, introduces the actor-sufferer theme and the idea of the perfection of the will, both important in *Murder in the Cathedral*. The chorus, as actor, is counseled by the Rock, as sufferer,

I say to you: *Make perfect your will.*
I say: take no thought of the harvest,
But only of proper sowing.
    The world turns and the world changes,
But one thing does not change.
In all of my years, one thing does not change.
However you disguise it, this thing does not change:
The perpetual struggle of Good and Evil.
.   .   .   .

The good man is the builder, if he build what is good.[11]

Perfection of the will occurs when men, and here institutions, recognize that the only true freedom of action comes in subservience to God's will. Christian patience and humility are achieved when change and "the perpetual struggle of Good and Evil" are seen from the perspective of God. Action and suffering are integrated and tempered by each other in the dual conception of the church presented here: the church in action must continue the fight against evil in each generation but it must

[11] *Ibid.*, p. 9.

simultaneously recognize with humility that the battle will not be won on earth; the church as witness must recognize the eternal nature of the struggle but must continue building in every generation.[12]

Connected with the Christian conception of action and suffering is the theme of the intersection of time and eternity in the experience of religious awareness. The Rock expresses the idea, which became one of Eliot's favorite dramatic utterances, in this manner:

Remember, all you who are numbered for God,
In every moment of time you live where two worlds cross,
In every moment you live at a point of intersection.
Remember, living in time, you must live also now in Eternity.[13]

The point of intersection is also identified with the divine point which moves the wheel of time, "the still point in the turning world." The wheel image, first used in the opening chorus, has been used since by Eliot in both his dramatic and nondramatic poetry. The still point which turns the moving wheel is both the recognition of God possible at every moment and, in history, the moment of the Incarnation:[14]

[12] The description of the Rock, led by a boy like Sophocles' Tiresias and "treading the winepress alone" like Samson, connects this figure with earlier Eliot versions of the character who witnesses human suffering from the vantage point of superior insight, as Grover Smith, in *T. S. Eliot's Poetry and Plays*, pp. 175–76, points out.

[13] Eliot, *The Rock*, p. 52.

[14] See Grover Smith, *T. S. Eliot's Poetry and Plays*, pp. 176–78, for a discussion of the philosophical foundations of this imagery.

There came, at a predetermined moment, a moment in
time and of time,
A moment not out of time, but in time, in what we call
history; transecting, bisecting the world of time, a
moment in time but not like a moment of time,
A moment in time but time was made through that moment: for without the meaning there is no time, and
that moment of time gave the meaning.[15]

Finally, the theme of the temporal forces at war with
the church is presented in *The Rock* in a way which
anticipates *Murder in the Cathedral*. The chorus, after
asserting that the "Son of man was not crucified once and
for all" and that "if blood of martyrs is to flow on the
steps" the steps must first be built, seeks "the young,
the devoted" to help rebuild the Temple and its steps.
They find, instead of devout young Christians, the militant Redshirts and Blackshirts, both of whom denounce
the church. The Redshirts proclaim, in a parody of *vers
libre,* that the church is the deceiver of the people:

REDSHIRTS (*in unison, with military gestures*).
    Our verse
    is free
    as the wind on the steppes
    as love in the heart of the factory worker
    thousands and thousands of steppes
    millions and millions of workers
                                all working
                                    all loving

    in the cities

[15] Eliot, *The Rock,* p. 50.

on the steppes
production has risen by twenty point six per cent
we can laugh at God!
our workers
    all working
our turbines
    all turning
our sparrows
    all chirping
all denounce you, deceivers of the people! [16]

The Blackshirts in turn announce their doctrine in a marching doggerel:

BLACKSHIRTS (*saluting*). Hail!
    We come as a boon and a blessing to all,
    Though we'd rather appear in the Albert Hall.
    Our methods are new in this land of the free,
    We make the deaf hear and we make the blind see.
    We're law-keeping fellows who make our own laws—
    And we welcome SUBSCRIPTIONS IN AID OF THE CAUSE! [17]

[16] *Ibid.*, p. 43.

[17] *Ibid.*, p. 44. F. O. Matthiessen (*The Achievement of T. S. Eliot*, pp. 162, 175) and D. E. Jones (*The Plays of T. S. Eliot*, p. 42) have both pointed out the similarities between these passages and the early drama of W. H. Auden and Stephen Spender. Matthiessen mentions, in particular, Auden's *Dance of Death* and observes that "without Eliot's revolt against the art for art's sake of the 'nineties, his steady insistence that no part of life should be barred from poetry, and his growing example of how a poet can turn for his material both to religion and to politics, Auden's generation would not have found the ground so clear for their own handling of contemporary affairs. But Auden's political plays, as well as Spender's *The Trial of a Judge,* are much more implicated in immediate events, and owe a great deal to the theatre of Berthold Brecht."

Eliot's suspicion of both ends of the political spectrum is evident in the passages quoted above. He pictures the church in the modern world besieged by the twin "heresies" of communism and fascism, both of which march in step to the tunes of this world in their materialistic interpretations of existence. Eliot was to treat the conflict between secular power and the church with more subtlety and universality in the conflict between the Knights and the Archbishop in *Murder in the Cathedral.*

Murder in the Cathedral was written for the Canterbury Festival of June 1935 and, although Eliot was apparently given complete freedom to submit what he pleased, the limitations of a subject appropriate to the festival's purpose and an audience which was expecting a religious drama were nevertheless present.

One instructive glimpse into Eliot's thinking on the subject of his commission by the Canterbury Festival Committee and the whole matter of "Christian propaganda" is provided by an article written for "Notes on the Way" during the composition of the play. He observes that the artist who employs his abilities in the service of a cause does so at his own risk,

"for one danger is that the cause may not be big enough, or profound and permanent enough, not to become somewhat ridiculous under such treatment; and another danger is that you will not succeed in transmuting it into a personal and peculiar passion. The making of great poetry requires a just and delicate sense of values; distorted or incomplete values may easily turn the sublime into the ridiculous. . . . I question whether any of the social causes agitated in our time is complete enough to provide much food for poetry. . . ." [18]

The implication of this statement seems to be that while none of the social causes of his time were complete enough for the great poet, the artist committed to values of un-questionable completeness and truth would not face this difficulty. For the Christian artist, then, propaganda for his cause ceased to be partial and partisan, and became instead a complete and profound interpretation of life which made art possible. Eliot's comment in the same essay that St. Thomas of Canterbury might have pre-ferred as Introit for his Feast day "Princes, moreover, did sit and did witness falsely against me," indicates that Eliot saw in the events leading to the martyrdom of Thomas Becket a situation involving the conflict between the church and world analogous to the modern struggle of the church against its enemies.

Far from giving up the idea of levels in the play's struc-ture, Eliot made perhaps his most effective use of this conception in *Murder in the Cathedral*. The surface level of the action, dealing with the martyrdom of Becket, is divided into two parts which are connected by the "inter-lude" of the Archbishop's sermon on Christmas morning. In the opening chorus, the women of Canterbury express their desire to maintain the quiet sterility of their humble lives, undisturbed by greatness of any kind, "living and partly living." Their presentiment that the return of the

[18] T. S. Eliot, "Notes on the Way" [I], *Time and Tide*, XVI (Jan-uary 5, 1935), 6–7.

Archbishop after his seven years' absence is near and that his return will bring a spiritual as well as a temporal disturbance in their lives fills them with terror. The women are conscious of fear, and desire only "peace" as they understand it; they "do not wish anything to happen." They are only intuitively aware of the greatness of the event—"Destiny waits in the hand of God, shaping the still unshapen."

The reaction of the three priests to the news of Thomas' return represents the next step on an ascending scale of awareness of the event's meaning. Their reactions begin where the women's leave off; they even begin by repeating some of the women's phrases. Within the group of priests, there is also a hierarchy of understanding. The First Priest, knowing his Archbishop's uncompromising nature, fears Thomas' return—"I fear for the Archbishop, I fear for the Church." The Second Priest affirms his loyalty to the Archbishop and sees in his strength a "rock" of God which will dispel "dismay and doubt." He differs from the women in wishing the return but he does not think beyond the comfort of Thomas' presence. It is the Third Priest who, of the three, most nearly approaches Thomas' saintly understanding of the events to come. He says, in language Thomas himself later uses, "For good or ill, let the wheel turn."

In the hierarchy of understanding presented by the characters in Part I, Thomas, of course, stands at the top, although even he is to reach a greater height by the conclusion of his temptations. When Thomas enters and chides the Second Priest for scolding the women, he expresses in his first speech the message of the drama, a message which, when repeated to him later by one of his tempters, takes on a new meaning even for Thomas:

They know and do not know, that acting is suffering
And suffering is action. Neither does the actor suffer
Nor the patient act. But both are fixed
In an eternal action, an eternal patience
To which all must consent that it may be willed
And which all must suffer that they may will it,
That the pattern may subsist, for the pattern is the action
And the suffering, that the wheel may turn and still
Be forever still.[19]

This passage introduces both the action-suffering theme and the imagery of the wheel and the point.[20]

Thomas also answers each of his four tempters in terms of his opening statement. When the First Tempter offers Thomas a return to the life of sensual pleasures of his youth at court, his reply is:

Only
The fool, fixed in his folly, may think
He can turn the wheel on which he turns.[21]

The Second Tempter offers earthly power with which to improve the temporal world and urges Thomas to seek power for present good and to leave holiness to the here-

---

[19] Eliot, *Complete Poems and Plays*, p. 182.

[20] Louis L. Martz gives an extensive discussion of Eliot's wheel-point imagery in "The Wheel and the Point: Aspects of Imagery and Theme in Eliot's Later Poetry," *T. S. Eliot: A Selected Critique,* ed. Leonard Unger, pp. 444–62.

[21] Eliot, *Complete Poems and Plays*, p. 184.

after. Thomas replies that he serves the higher power of the Pope and a higher order than the world knows:

> Those who put their faith in worldly order
> Not controlled by the order of God,
> In confident ignorance, but arrest disorder,
> Make is fast, breed fatal disease,
> Degrade what they exalt.[22]

The Third Tempter offers Thomas both revenge upon the King and domination for the Pope if he will side with the English barons—"Kings will allow no power but their own," thus "Church and people have good cause against the throne." Thomas replies:

> To make, then break, this thought has come before,
> The desperate exercise of failing power
> Samson in Gaza did no more.
> But if I break, I must break myself alone.[23]

The Archbishop thus reveals the contradiction in his thinking. He thinks that he is rejecting the temptation of willing "action" by removing himself from the act of vengeance or of seeking power, but his statement reveals that by "willing" his own destruction he is committing an act incompatible with making his will compliant with God's. The repetition of "I" and the use of "myself alone" in the last line of Thomas' reply carry home this contradiction. At this point the Fourth Tempter enters and his mocking response to the Archbishop's comment is an excellent piece of dramatic irony: "Well done, Thomas, your will is hard to bend."

[22] *Ibid.*, p. 187.
[23] *Ibid.*, p. 190.

The Fourth Tempter offers first the power of martyrdom—"Saint and Martyr rule from the tomb"—and then
the glory of "dwelling forever in presence of God" as a
saint. He urges Thomas to:

Seek the way of martyrdom, make yourself the lowest
On earth, to be high in heaven.[24]

When the Fourth Tempter repeats to Thomas his own
words to the women, he realizes his error at last, that the
pride of willing martyrdom is "the greatest treason: To
do the right deed for the wrong reason." To "act" in such
a way would be to try to turn the wheel himself, rather
than to allow the "will" of the unmoved mover to rule.
Part I ends with Thomas' address to the audience,[25] a
device later duplicated with an opposite motive by the
Knights at the end of Part II:

But for every evil, every sacrilege,
Crime, wrong, oppression and the axe's edge,
Indifference, exploitation, you, and you,
And you, must all be punished. So must you.
I shall no longer act or suffer, to the sword's end.
Now my good Angel, whom God appoints
To be my guardian, hover over the swords' points.[26]

Thomas is saying, in effect, that having endured his
temptations and having reaffirmed submission to God's

[24] *Ibid.,* p. 192.
[25] Eliot's attempt to involve the audience in the action of the play
by directly addressing them has been noted by R. P. Blackmur ("T.
S. Eliot: From *Ash Wednesday* to *Murder in the Cathedral,*" *T. S.
Eliot: A Selected Critique,* ed. Leonard Unger, p. 260) and D. E.
Jones (*The Plays of T. S. Eliot,* p. 57).
[26] Eliot, *Complete Poems and Plays,* p. 197.

will and the divine pattern, he has moved beyond action and suffering, but that the rest of humanity, those too much a part of this world's desires, must endure the suffering implicit in action *and* the responsibility.

The prose "interlude" which separates the two parts of the play is Thomas' sermon in the Cathedral on Christmas morning. The sermon's text, "Glory to God in the highest, and on earth peace, good will toward men" (Luke 2:14), is packed with implication, following as it does the action of Part I. Part I has shown the kinds of worldly glory Thomas has been offered and the kind he has chosen, the glory of God in the highest. The word "peace," also Thomas' first word in the play, has taken on the new significance of the state of the martyr who is beyond action and suffering, and "good will toward men" now has the double import of the martyr's forgiveness of his murderers, and his beneficent influence with God for those who pray for his intercession. The juxtaposition of "God in the highest, and on earth . . ." also suggests the high-low imagery of the wheel. It is, moreover, appropriate that the saint who goes soon to glory should echo the message of the heavenly host to the shepherds at Bethlehem.

In the sermon itself Thomas points out the special significance of the Christmas Mass; it is both the celebration of the joy of Christ's birth and the sorrow of His death. Thomas differentiates God's peace from peace as the world knows it and draws the analogy between Christ and the martyr. He closes the sermon with his newly won insight into martyrdom—that the martyr is not made by his own design but by God's.

[97]

In the first published editions of the play, Part II opened with the entrance of the three Priests carrying the banners of St. Stephen, St. John the Apostle, and the Holy Innocents, and accompanied by the Introits of St. Stephen and St. John. The device was obviously an attempt to unify the time sequence—each banner representing one day which had passed since Christmas—as well as to show the significance of saints and martyrs in the church year and to foreshadow Thomas' own fate of martyrdom. In later versions the opening was replaced by the choral reaction of the women to the Archbishop's sermon. Their earlier fear of the spring and of a spiritual awakening has changed to an attitude nearer acceptance.

When the Knights enter they display, in their appearance and demeanor, a bestiality which is intended to contrast with the mildness and hospitality of the Priests. Their violence symbolizes the animality of man when he does not comply with God's will, but exercises his own instead. In man's desire for freedom from the moral restraints of a higher order, he condemns himself unwittingly to the tyranny of his passions. When Thomas appears the Knights demand to see him alone. They hurl insults at him, ridiculing his humble origins and accusing him of disloyalty to the King and of acting as he has because of ambition and pride. Thomas' reply is that he has always been a loyal vassal to the King: "Saving my order, I am at his command." His comment emphasizes the point that in clinging to the church over the King he is both saving and being saved by his order, which is God's order. His reply also suggests that the man of God is the only really loyal vassal, for all loyalty and morality must be based on divine order. This meaning is enforced when Thomas accuses the Knights of being disloyal themselves and demands that their accusations be made publicly. The angered Knights begin to attack him but are restrained when the Priests and attendants quickly return. The argument which follows explores the meaning of loyalty and treason. The Knights outline the King's grievances—that Thomas had put the King in disfavor with the Pope, that even after being pardoned by the King and reinstated, Thomas had suspended those who had crowned the young prince and denied the legality of his coronation. Thomas insists that he had only acted on the instructions of the Pope and that only the Pope could absolve the bishops. The Knights announce that they bring the King's command that Thomas be exiled but the Archbishop refuses to leave. The Knights depart in a fury, hurling accusations of treason and treachery. To their threats to return Thomas answers that he is ready for martyrdom.

The reaction of the women to the approaching murder is impassioned and even hysterical. Their acceptance of their share of the guilt, echoing Thomas' earlier statement to the audience that all must partake and suffer for such an act, shows that they have arrived at the stage of Christian responsibility, but their passion also indicates that they cannot yet accept or perceive God's will with quietness:

I have consented, Lord Archbishop, have consented.
Am torn away, subdued, violated,
United to the spiritual flesh of nature,

Mastered by the animal powers of spirit,
Dominated by the lust of self-demolition,
By the final utter uttermost death of spirit,
By the final ecstasy of waste and shame. . . .[27]

Thomas comforts the women with the message that they will afterward see the glory of the act which they now witness in horror.

The Priests urge Thomas to flee or hide but he refuses, insisting that he will meet death gladly if it is God's will, but the now-frantic Priests succeed in dragging him off to vespers. The desire for action by the Priests shows that even they have not understood God's will. In the hierarchy of characters only Thomas, who is at the still center of the wheel of action and suffering, experiences peace.

In the Cathedral the Priests have barred the door, but Thomas demands that "the church shall be open, even to our enemies." When the Priests exclaim that these are not men but maddened beasts who attack him, Thomas admonishes them that they argue as the world argues, not as God does. The doors are opened and the Knights enter, maddened with drink, and taunt Thomas in a jazz chant which resembles Vachel Lindsay's "Daniel Jazz,"[28] one of the few remaining echoes of *Sweeney Agonistes* in this play. While the chorus demands a cleansing of the impure world, Thomas is slain by the Knights, who circle around him with outstretched swords, visually forming for the audience a wheel with Thomas as the still point.

The playwright's concern to communicate his message to the audience is evident in many aspects of the play.

[27] *Ibid.*, p. 208.
[28] Grover Smith, in *T. S. Eliot's Poetry and Plays*, p. 182, has pointed out this similarity.

The full involvement of the chorus in Thomas' martyrdom, for example, is intended to enable the audience to observe their own representative group, "the type of the common man," travel the Christian path. The author hoped that those in the audience unable to identify with Thomas could perhaps identify with the women of Canterbury. While Eliot's esteem for the common man has never been high, in his conception of the chorus in *Murder in the Cathedral* he adopted a view at least more complimentary than that which he held when he wrote *Sweeney Agonistes,* when he felt that the majority of the audience would be incapable of sharing any response except that of the visionless and materialistic characters of that play. At least, the chorus has come to an understanding on their own level which can involve them in salvation.

The final appearance of the Knights just before the end of the play is another attempt to establish contact with the modern audience. The Knights address the audience in the contemporary prose of political debate. Eliot's avowed intent was "to shock the audience out of their complacency" and according to E. Martin Browne's account of the 1935 production that effect was certainly achieved.[29] The Knights defend their actions on several grounds and according to the best modern logic. They insist that they were disinterested, that violence was the only way to secure social justice, and that Thomas' death should ultimately be judged "suicide while of unsound mind." The modernity of the language and argumenta-

[29] E. Martin Browne, "From *The Rock* to *The Confidential Clerk,*" *T. S. Eliot: A Symposium for His Seventieth Birthday,* ed. Neville Braybrooke, p. 61.

tion is presumably to emphasize the kind of judgment on martyrdom which the modern secular world would approve—and to convince the audience of the blasphemy of that view.

The insertion of the prose of modern debate in the normally poetic and religious texture of the play is also intended, I believe, to point up the contrast between the "poetry" of the Catholic view of life, in the sense of its order and "rhythm," and the "prose" quality of the disordered, chaotic, and utilitarian materialism of modern existence. The mixture of dramatic moods produced by this device also constitutes a new use of Eliot's earlier ideas on the value of mixing the comic and the tragic in order to arrive at a more fundamental interpretation of events than either genre can afford. Thus the events in *Murder in the Cathedral* are presented as neither tragic nor comic, but Christian, for Thomas goes to glory although he suffers martyrdom. In Eliot's conception of drama, neither laughter nor tears is the desired response, but rather peace which passeth understanding.

The mixture of poetry and prose is matched by a mixture of poetic styles and meters within the verses of the play. E. Martin Browne has pointed out that an appropriate style was worked out for each kind of scene:

"The most superficial level, that of the quarrels between Becket and the Knights, is rhymed doggerel. . . . More subtle, and sometimes rather crabbed, is a four-stress rhyming verse for the Tempters who dramatise the tortuous progress of Becket's inner struggle. . . . There is an easy, near-blank-verse for dialogue with the Priests and Women. . . . And for the Chorus, a very varied series of forms, from the three-stress lines of the women's domestic talk . . . to the long complexes of pleading or of praise. . . . In addition, Eliot has followed the precedent he established with his final Chorus in *The Rock* which is based on the Gloria of the Mass and used the rhythms of two more Christian hymns [*Dies Irae* and *Te Deum*] as ground-bass of choral order." [30]

Eliot's own account of his verse in *Murder in the Cathedral* is found in "Poetry and Drama" (1951). [31] Since he had to take his audience back to an historical event, he felt that "the vocabulary and style could not be exactly those of modern conversation—as in some modern French plays using the plot and personages of Greek drama." On the other hand, he wished to avoid archaic vocabulary and style because he "wanted to bring home to the audience the contemporary relevance of the situation. The style therefore had to be neutral, committed neither to the present nor to the past." He was aware that it was essential to avoid the Shakespearean echo of blank verse "which, after extensive use for nondramatic poetry, had lost the flexibility which blank verse must have if it is to give the effect of conversation." Because he felt that the rhythm of blank verse had become too remote from the movement of modern speech, he chose as his model the versification of *Everyman*. "An avoidance of too much iambic, some use of alliteration, and

[30] E. Martin Browne, "The Dramatic Verse of T. S. Eliot," *T. S. Eliot: A Symposium,* compiled by Richard March and Tambimuttu (London: Editions Poetry London, 1948), pp. 199–200.

[31] Eliot, *On Poetry and Poets,* pp. 75–95.

occasional unexpected rhyme, helped to distinguish the versification from that of the nineteenth century." He came to feel later that from his point of view *Murder in the Cathedral* was "a dead end" because it did not solve the problem of language for future plays. The versification had only the negative merit of avoiding what had to be avoided; it did not solve the problems of idiom or of metrics for later dramas.

On the surface level which has been described, *Murder in the Cathedral* is a stylized dramatization of the historical situation of the martyrdom of Thomas Becket presented both as a psychological study of the saint and at the same time as a portrayal of the twelfth-century power struggle of church and state made applicable to the modern world.

But, in addition to the surface level, there is another level of meaning beneath the surface which shows the play to be a development of the dramatic theory evolved earlier and exemplified by *Sweeney Agonistes*. Eliot's treatment of the second level of meaning in *Murder in the Cathedral,* however, introduces an important modification of his use of Cornford's ritual scheme in the earlier play. Eliot kept the basic formulations of the ur-drama but he cast the murdered god in the role of Christ and developed the ritual sequence of events to conform to the Christian interpretation of that pattern in the Biblical lore surrounding Christ's Crucifixion and Resurrection.[32]

[32] For a discussion of the ritual qualifications for the hero and their application to Christ's life see Lord Raglan, *The Hero: A Study in Tradition, Myth, and Drama* (New York: Oxford University Press, 1937), pp. 178–208, and Herbert Weisinger, *Tragedy and the Paradox of the Fortunate Fall* (London: Routledge and Kegan Paul, 1953).

The playwright integrates this underlying level of meaning with the surface events by constructing an elaborate dramatic analogy between the martyr and Christ, both of whom are portrayed as divine and sin-laden scapegoats who are mutilated and brought back to renewed life. While the martyr as the type of Christ [33] and the presence of elements from the ritual drama [34] have been noted, I believe that neither the completeness of the analogy nor the connection between the theme and the ritual plot has been fully recognized.

Thomas, himself, makes clear the analogy between the martyr and Christ in his Christmas sermon:

"I wish only that you should ponder and meditate the deep meaning and mystery of our masses of Christmas Day. For whenever Mass is said, we re-enact the Passion and Death of Our Lord; and on this Christmas Day we do this in celebration of His Birth. So that at the same moment we rejoice in His coming for the salvation of men, and offer again to God His Body and Blood in sacrifice, oblation and satisfaction for the sins of the whole world.

.   .   .   .

Not only do we at the feast of Christmas celebrate at once Our Lord's Birth and His Death: but on the next day we celebrate the martyrdom of His first martyr, the blessed Stephen. Is it an accident, do you think, that the day of the first martyr follows immediately

[33] See, for example, Grover Smith, *T. S. Eliot's Poetry and Plays,* p. 186.

[34] Both D. E. Jones (*The Plays of T. S. Eliot,* pp. 53-54) and Francis Fergusson (*The Idea of a Theater,* pp. 211-13) mention the presence of the ritual structure.

the day of the Birth of Christ? By no means. Just as we rejoice and mourn at once, in the Birth and in the Passion of Our Lord; so also, in a smaller figure, we both rejoice and mourn in the death of martyrs. We mourn, for the sins of the world that has martyred them; we rejoice, that another soul is numbered among the Saints in Heaven, for the glory of God and for the salvation of men." [35]

The first part of the play, in which Thomas is visited by the Tempters, may thus be viewed as symbolic of Christ's Temptation and the second part, in which Thomas' martyrdom is enacted, as the Passion, Death, and Resurrection of Christ. The opening chorus establishes the analogy between the women drawn to the Cathedral at the Christmas season because of their presentiment of a tremendous event to be enacted and the birth of Christ, in such lines as: "The New Year waits, destiny waits for the coming," and "Shall the Son of Man be born again in the litter of scorn?" The imagery used by the women to express their fear of the coming of life is similar to that used in the opening of *The Waste Land*.

The Herald's description of the coming of the Archbishop into the city echoes Christ's triumphal entry into Jerusalem, even to the colt mentioned in Matthew and Luke and the strewing of garments and branches in Matthew; at the same time it develops the analogy to the procession of Phales mentioned by Cornford and Murray.

Thomas' four temptations, though not exactly analogous to Christ's in the desert, are close enough to be con-

[35] Eliot, *Complete Poems and Plays*, pp. 198–99.

vincing if one equates the Devil's request that Christ turn the stones into bread with the First Tempter's appeal to Thomas' appetites, the Devil's offer of the kingdoms of the world with the inducements of the Second and Third Tempters, and the Devil's attempt to make Christ throw himself down from the pinnacle in order to prove his divinity with the Fourth Tempter's appeal to Thomas' pride in willing martyrdom. In addition, just as Christ's Sermon on the Mount follows immediately Christ's temptation in Matthew, so the Christmas sermon of Thomas follows *his* temptation.

Part II contains the agon of the drama, the struggle of the sin-laden god-figure, in the person of the Archbishop, with his antagonists. It develops, at the same time, several similarities between the Gospel accounts of Christ's passion and Thomas' martyrdom. The most obvious analogy is between the Crucifixion of Christ and the murder of Thomas by the jealous seekers after power in this world, and the acceptance of death by both Christ and the martyr as a part of God's design for the redemption of mankind. But other similarities also exist: for example, the supper the Priests mention in the beginning of Part II may be meant to represent both the Last Supper and the ritual feast, and the Knights' false accusations against Thomas may be intended to suggest both the trial of Christ and the battle of insults engaged in by the god and his antagonist.

Thomas' triumphant statement, just before his death, on the purification of blood,

I am a priest,
A Christian, saved by the blood of Christ,

Ready to suffer with my blood.
This is the sign of the Church always,
The sign of blood. Blood for blood.
His blood given to buy my life,
My blood given to pay for His death,
My death for His death,[36]

emphasizes the reciprocity between Christ's and the martyr's death. Christ shed his blood for the remission of human sin and the martyr, in return, sheds his blood both in repayment for and in re-enactment of Christ's sacrifice. Blood is a multiple symbol in the play and the women view it differently. To them it is symbolic of their blood-guilt in the shedding of the saint's, and by analogy Christ's, blood:

The land is foul, the water is foul, our beasts and ourselves defiled with blood.
A rain of blood has blinded my eyes. Where is England? where is Kent? where is Canterbury?
O far far far far in the past; and I wander in a land of barren boughs: if I break them, they bleed; I wander in a land of dry stones: if I touch them they bleed.[37]

The theme of blood-guilt is also present in Matthew's version of Pilate's offer to give Christ to the multitude:

"He [Pilate] took water, and washed his hands before the multitude, saying, I am innocent of the blood of this just person: see ye to it. Then answered all the people, and said, His blood be on us, and on our children." [38]

[36] *Ibid.,* p. 213.
[37] *Ibid.,* p. 214.
[38] Matt. 27:24–25.

The rain of blood and other lines in the same chorus, including "Night stay with us, stop sun, hold season, let the day not come, let the spring not come," suggest the darkness and earthquake which occurred at Christ's death. The references in the women's chorus to the stones leading to Dante's river of Blood and to the bleeding boughs of the Suicides in the *Inferno* indicate that though the women do not yet realize it, the blood they interpret only as a sign of their terrible guilt will bring them to a penitential state of grace. Thus the death of the martyr and of Christ includes both good and evil, guilt and glory, just as the killing of the god represents both sin and necessity to primitive worshippers.

The concluding lines of the play emphasize a final correspondence between the Savior and the saint. The women, acknowledging their sin, chant:

> Lord, have mercy upon us.
> Christ, have mercy upon us.
> Lord, have mercy upon us.
> Blessed Thomas, pray for us.[39]

The Resurrection of Christ is paralleled by the entrance of Thomas into the ranks of sainthood, and thus the women can pray to both Christ and Thomas for mercy and intercession.[40]

[39] Eliot, *Complete Poems and Plays*, p. 221.

[40] Another aspect of the ritual scheme as described by Cornford and Murray which appears in the play is the winning over of the chorus by the protagonist. It is duplicated in *Murder in the Cathedral* by the women's gradual acceptance of their place in the martyr's triumph. There may also be a connection between Eliot's use of the turning wheel symbolism and the spiritual doctor who revives the god; Grover Smith traces the wheel-point imagery to Aristotle's

In my opinion *Murder in the Cathedral* is Eliot's most successful integration of his dramatic theories. The levels of the play are intrinsically unified by the skillful interweaving of Thomas' story with the imagery of Christ's Temptation and Passion and with the prototype formula of all religion and drama. The hierarchy of characters within the play who perceive the meaning of Thomas' death on their various levels helps to tighten the unity of the drama and to give it the stylized quality Eliot admires. His chorus, occupying a place midway between the chorus in *Sweeney Agonistes,* which is "material, literal-minded and visionless," and the chorus in *The Rock,* which speaks for the church in action, is by far the most successful of the three. By demonstrating the changing attitude of the chorus in *Murder in the Cathedral* from a fear of spiritual realities and a disavowal of responsibilities to acceptance of and participation in both the sin and glory of martyrdom, Eliot has provided a highly effective vehicle for commentary on the action and participation in it.

Most important of all for the play's effectiveness is the new and less literal conception of rhythm which Eliot used. In *Sweeney Agonistes* the "rhythm' was limited to the syncopation of the jazz meter, whereas in *Murder in the Cathedral* the whole structure becomes rhythmic in the sense that the musical form which Eliot has so often mentioned is achieved. The structural rhythm is achieved by the stylized progression of the action with its under-

---

De Anima and the physician-patient theme to another of Aristotle's treatises, *De Generatione et Corruptione*—both of which are treatments of God as unsuffering "first-mover" (*T. S. Eliot's Poetry and Plays,* p. 188).

girding analogies to Christ's life. Part I, presenting the temptation of Thomas, his lowest ebb, and Part II, presenting his passion, death, and victory, his highest point, provide a kind of circular movement which carries out the wheel imagery. The sermon which divides the two parts is contrasted with the Knights' speeches which are intended to lift the audience from their complacency outside the action to an admission of their own communal guilt, as the chorus has been lifted within the play. The alternation of the events of Thomas' martyrdom with the lyrical reaction of the women is a successful use of the same device which had failed in *The Rock*. For once Eliot's distaste for realism seems to have led to the achievement of the kind of ordered whole and aesthetically satisfying surface which his theory demanded.

The playwright, however, feeling that he had been led away from his goal of creating a drama of contemporary relevance, returned in his next play to the idea behind *Sweeney Agonistes*, the portrayal of the Orestes myth in a modern setting. Despite the surface differences between *Sweeney Agonistes* and *The Family Reunion*, the similarities of method and theme show the latter to be a reworking of the material of the earlier unfinished play. *The Family Reunion* thus marks Eliot's return to a religious drama in which he hoped to show the contemporary world the image of its own spiritual needs by means of a dramatic method already developed and refined in his earlier plays.

CHAPTER IV

THE FAMILY REUNION

In *The Family Reunion* (1939) Eliot abandoned both the "furnished-flat" atmosphere of *Sweeney Agonistes* and the historical setting of *Murder in the Cathedral* in favor of the drawing-room world of polite society and a verse somewhat closer to contemporary speech than that employed in his earlier plays. While these changes seemed to be a move in the direction of a more realistic and theatrically conservative theater, the presence of such startlingly expressionistic devices as "beyond character" choral chants, lyrical duets, soliloquies, and the appearance on stage of the ghostly Furies led to confusion about Eliot's dramatic aims. Was his apparent acceptance of the conventions of the realistic theater an indication that he had given up his objections to the basic assumptions of that theater? And if so, how were the frequent and strange interruptions of an otherwise conventional surface to be accounted for? *The Family Reunion* was not a theatrical success, and the public and the critics alike were disturbed by the fact that the play did not seem to fit existing classifications.[1]

[1] Raymond Williams, for example, saw the transitions from the superficial to the profound as "dislocation" and commented that "this kind of failure is what might be expected of Eliot's attempt to come to apparent terms with the methods of the naturalist theatre" (*Drama from Ibsen to Eliot* [London: Chatto & Windus, 1954], pp. 232–37). Denis Donoghue also objected to the transitions but on the grounds that Eliot had "yielded to the temptation to be 'poetical'" and thus became undramatic (*The Third Voice: Modern British and American*

Different as many of the surface features of the play seemed from either *Sweeney Agonistes* or *Murder in the Cathedral,* Eliot had not altered the basic assumptions, evolved in the nineteen-twenties, about the goals and intentions of his drama. His theme of spiritual election and its effects on the secular world was, as before, the starting point of his dramatic ideal. Nor had he changed his ideas about using a dramatic situation with underlying mythical analogies to his theme.

This conclusion is borne out by the fact that Eliot returned in *The Family Reunion,* his first play after his commissioned drama of the nineteen-thirties, to the Orestes story, the same source which he had used in his first dramatic treatment of the theme of purgation. One of the most striking similarities between *The Family Reunion* and *Sweeney Agonistes* is the re-use of the cry of Orestes in Aeschylus' *Choephoroi* when he finds himself pursued by the Erinys. In *The Family Reunion* Harry repeats the cry in his anguished announcement to his assembled family that he, too, is being pursued by his own hounds of hell:

Can't you see them? *You* don't see them, but I see them,
And they see me.[2]

The "hoo-ha's" in the final chorus of *Sweeney Agonistes*

Verse Drama [Princeton, New Jersey: Princeton University Press, 1959], pp. 94–103). C. L. Barber labeled the play "surrealism" ("T. S. Eliot After Strange Gods," *T. S. Eliot: A Selected Critique,* ed. Leonard Unger, pp. 415–43), while John Crowe Ransom praised it for its characterizations and realistic success ("T. S. Eliot as Dramatist," *Poetry: A Magazine of Verse,* LIV, No. 5 [1939], 264–71).

[2] Eliot, *Complete Poems and Plays,* p. 232.

are converted into the Furies of *The Family Reunion*. Moreover, the theme of the murdered girl dissolved in a lysol bath in Sweeney's tale is repeated in Harry's drowned wife, and the same sense of mystery surrounds the event.

These similarities have been widely recognized; other similarities are more obscure. The ritual cooking of the sin-laden god which appeared in the missionary stew and the "you see this egg" sequences of the earlier piece reappear in the reunion dinner party which Amy has planned, and in the hot bath to be drawn for Harry before dinner by the ministering Downing. On the plane of the surface events of the play, it is ludicrous that Amy should try to cure her son's spiritual sickness with a hot bath, but on the symbolic level Amy is unwittingly acting in accord with the ritual sequence of purgation. The same thing is true of the use Eliot makes of Dr. Warburton. He is called in to diagnose Harry's state in medical terms. However, as a symbolic representative of the cook-doctor who brings the old god back to life as a cleansed new god, Dr. Warburton, in his function as the revealer of some of the true facts of Harry's past, is perfectly in keeping with the demands of the eternal order. The effect of these dramatic devices, once the underlying symbolism is understood, is to underline in Eliot's characteristically "Possum" manner the idea that God moves in mysterious ways, the same thought which was emphasized by a grimmer kind of wit in *Sweeney Agonistes*. As these similarities demonstrate, despite the English country-house setting of *The Family Reunion,* the same mythical method was employed. What, then, accounts for the changes in the dramatic surface of the later play?

Between the time of *Sweeney Agonistes* and *The Family Reunion* Eliot learned more about dramatic writing [3] and, while his basic ideals were unchanged, he had modified his ideas about dramatic rhythm and dramatic poetry. He had learned from *The Rock* and *Murder in the Cathedral* what audiences might be expected to respond to and in his first work written specifically for the commercial theater he attempted to put into effect his conclusion that poetic drama must compete directly with the realistic theater on that theater's own terms. It will be remembered that while Eliot had continued to treat the theme of sainthood and the conflict of worldly and spiritual power in *Murder in the Cathedral,* he came to feel that he had been led away from his intention of creating a drama of contemporary relevance using the language of modern life; both the "neutral" language and the historical situation made the play seem to him a "dead end." [4] He was still determinedly against the pretense of stage realism, and the social and psychological themes of the modern stage, just as he was still opposed to both prose and the conventional meters of dramatic verse. His first full-scale attempt to resolve the dilemmas in which he found himself is to be seen in *The Family Reunion.*

In an effort to compete with the commercial theater and to meet his audience on their own ground while avoiding violations of his views on drama, he decided on a new method of handling dramatic levels—a way which

[3] E. Martin Browne has described Eliot's close attention to the craft of theatrical writing in "From *The Rock* to *The Confidential Clerk,*" *T. S. Eliot: A Symposium for His Seventieth Birthday,* ed. Neville Braybrooke, pp. 57–69.

[4] Eliot, *On Poetry and Poets,* pp. 84–85.

might satisfy both his audience and himself at the same time. In *Murder in the Cathedral* he had been successful in sustaining two distinct levels of meaning, the surface actions leading to the martyrdom of Becket and beneath the surface the analogies with the suffering and glory of Christ. The levels were openly merged and communicated to the Cathedral audience at key points in the dramatic structure, such as in Becket's sermon and in the final chorus. At other points less obvious methods were employed, including poetic suggestions which might disclose symbolic connections to the enlightened imagination, verbal echoes of Scripture, and even visual theatrical representations, notably the wheel of swords with Becket at the center. Universality of meaning was conveyed by the ritual sequences embedded in the surface actions and underlying strata. However, the playwright's attempts to make the situation meaningful to the contemporary world were to some degree artificial, as in the final speeches by the Knights and Thomas' occasional addresses to the audience. In *The Family Reunion* relevance to the everyday experience of the audience was to come first but not so much in deference to the expectations of the audience, as in an effort to show them the errors of their expectations. The curtain was to open on the most conventional of dramatic worlds, the English drawing room, but every device at the dramatist's disposal was to be used as the play progressed to shake the audience's confidence in the validity of that world of surface reality as a total representation of existence. This, I believe, was the rationale behind the many "violations" of the theater of realism which disturbed both audiences and critics of this play.

Thus the normality of the everyday world of the play is continually disrupted. In the surface action, the family (and audience) is gathered in expectation of one kind of reunion, but finds another kind of union portrayed. Characters, such as the aunts and uncles, who begin by speaking the most ordinary prose sentiments, break into choral chants; scenes, such as that between Mary and Harry, which begin in the expectation of romance or "love interest," end in rejection of human love in favor of the love of God. Most startling of all and contrived to shatter confidence in the most sacred of dramatic conventions, the belief in the reality of the make-believe occurring on stage, is the appearance of the Eumenides, a "shock-tactic" comparable to the Knights' address to the modern audience in *Murder in the Cathedral.*

Amid the many disruptions, it was necessary to present a coherent guide to the meaning of the action beneath the surface events. This function was served by the use of the Orestes myth and the religious ritual implicit in it. The total effect was intended to be the presentation of a modern counterpart to the universal experience of religious purgation. The audience was to leave the theater having seen an action in modern existence which duplicated the age-old religious pattern and returned to the theater its original function of expressing God's presence.[5]

Along with the modifications in setting and poetic lan-

[5] Audience reaction would indicate that Eliot was overly optimistic in his confidence that audiences would give up either belief in dramatic conventions or confidence in the reality of the external, visible world. Grover Smith, speculating on the audience's reaction to the play, comments: "The audience, if not just giddy by now, leaves the theater with perhaps a suspicion that it has been intellectually 'had' " (*T. S. Eliot's Poetry and Plays,* p. 208).

guage came a somewhat more positive conception of the purgative way in the treatment of the hero's spiritual dilemma. In *Sweeney Agonistes* only the negative side, the horror and desolation of the spiritual pursuit, was emphasized, together with the barrenness of temporal existence; in *The Family Reunion* there is a recognition that the period of desolation is a preparation for a more positive stage of final union with the divine principle. To be sure, the drama ends before Harry has reached that state of union, but it is made clear that he has passed through his worst suffering, the period during which he felt terror in the presence of his Furies because he did not understand their mission.

Interrelated with this new emphasis is the new role played by such characters as Agatha and Mary and Downing, the "watchers and waiters" in the spiritual education of the central character. The prominence of these characters represents, it seems to me, an important alteration in the playwright's attitude toward human love. The instruction of St. John of the Cross to the penitent to divest himself of the love of created beings before the divine union can take place—an instruction issued significantly at the darkest step of St. John's ten stairs—has been replaced in part by Agatha's instructive and curative love. There is, to be sure, a repudiation of human love as represented by Harry's mother's desire to impose her will on his future, by Mary's offer of love which Harry momentarily hopes might save him, and by Harry's wife's attempt to dominate him by her will. Nevertheless, in the character of Agatha, who leads him to the proper recognition of

[118]

his past and his future through her love for him and thus to the "other side of despair," there exists a merging of human and divine Love. This new direction has been followed in Eliot's later plays by a succession of characters who are part human, part divine, and who function to show the penitent his way.

Eliot's treatment of the unaware characters also has been gradually modified. In *Sweeney Agonistes* the chorus is barely differentiated, and it expresses its relation to Sweeney's tale of symbolic purgation by its stylized choral chants of terrified recognition of the awfulness of his encounter with divinity. In *Murder in the Cathedral* the somewhat more positive side of the entry of the spiritual is apparent in the final acceptance by the women of Canterbury of the agony and the glory which Thomas' martyrdom brings into their humble lives. They are not, however, individualized or developed as dramatic personalities. In *The Family Reunion* the chorus is made up of individual members of Harry's family who, though they remain relatively flat characters, are individualized by their differing reactions to the hero's dilemma and by the characteristic verse patterns each is given to speak.[6] Since

---

[6] D. E. Jones gives a valuable analysis of the verse patterns of the choral characters in *The Plays of T. S. Eliot*, p. 86: "The degree of control that the verse gives over characterization and dramatic tension can be illustrated from the scene in which the uncles and aunts discuss 'the younger generation.' . . . Here, the stiff, pompous, insensitive rhythm which characterizes Charles, especially in his more obtuse mood, gives way to an ampler, more relaxed, but still circumscribed movement as Gerald makes his kindly gesture. Mary's pent-up emotion reveals itself in a very jerky movement (the repetitions in 'information . . . generation' and 'I don't deserve. . . . I don't belong'

in this play Eliot was still trying for the stylized effect of Ben Jonson's flat characters (to be unaware of the spiritual world equals spiritual flatness in Eliot's plays), these characters are left undeveloped intentionally in order that they may fulfill their function in the microcosmic dramatic world.

Eliot's manipulation of his characters and theme in this multilevel drama becomes clear when the levels are examined and compared. The clash of the natural and supernatural worlds is present on both levels of the drama. The dramatic conflict implicit in the surface action of the play is between two conceptions of reality or, to express it in the play's own terms, between the two conceptions of the family reunion. The family reunion planned by Amy, Dowager Lady Monchensey, is ostensibly in celebration of her birthday but is actually an effort to establish her eldest son Harry in her place as master of Wishwood and head of the family. Her chief adversary in this plan is Harry himself; he has successfully thwarted his mother's plans in the past by his marriage to a woman who would have no part of the family and by his year of wandering

---

are the more obvious means of achieving a kind of stumbling bitterness). The awkward silence which covers her exit is broken by Violet's sharp decisiveness. Gerald's reaction does not go deeper than bemusement; the rhythm has only a slight hesitancy. With his stolid complacency, Charles moves firmly in to put Mary's outburst into perspective, as he would think. And, finally, Amy with her characteristically domineering rhythm closes the incident. The tenacious rhythm of her monosyllabic half-line 'but life may still go right' prevents us from interpreting it as mere wish; she clearly intends to do what she can to make it go right. The scene demonstrates that poetic drama can have something of the precision of a musical score. Character and dramatic structure are here integrated in the verse rhythm, through which the tension of the awkward moment is built up and resolved."

[120]

since his wife's "death by water." In contrast to Amy's conception of the reunion of the family in order to solidify the family's worldly domain is the spiritual reunion which is the goal of Harry's trial.

Amy has gathered for the meeting of the clan her three younger sisters, Ivy, Violet, and Agatha, her deceased husband's two brothers, Gerald and Charles, and Mary, Harry's cousin and childhood playmate, whom Amy has long planned to establish as Harry's wife. Harry's two brothers, Arthur and John, are expected for the birthday dinner but never arrive. Amy is established from the beginning of the play as a proud and indomitable woman who will brook no opposition to her will. It is also apparent that the family reunion she has planned is in any but a physical sense a pretense. Amy's sisters and brothers-in-law wish they were elsewhere; Harry's brothers never appear; Mary is resentful and anxious about her part in Amy's plan and wishes to escape. The antagonism between Amy and Agatha is apparent from Agatha's first comment that Harry's return after so long an absence will be painful, not joyous. But above all, Harry's state of mind when he arrives home shows how little Amy's plan takes into consideration his actual condition.

He enters in a state of abnormal excitement, and his declaration that the invisible creatures which have pursued him since his wife's death have appeared to him upon returning home shocks his assembled family. When Amy, in an effort to ignore this alarming disclosure, asserts that he can again enter the existence he knew before he left home because she has allowed nothing to change at Wishwood, Harry hysterically retorts that to assume that he is the same person who left would be a useless pretense. Only Agatha seems to understand him and when he looks to her for support, she tries to convince him that if he refuses the pretense of his mother's make-believe world of no-change, he must assume the responsibility of trying to help the rest of his family understand the *new* Harry. He tries to communicate his state of newly awakened awareness in images reminiscent of Sweeney's nightmare world, but realizing his lack of success he concludes with the abrupt announcement of his murder of his wife:

> One thinks to escape
> By violence, but one is still alone
> In an over-crowded desert, jostled by ghosts.
> It was only reversing the senseless direction
> For a momentary rest on the burning wheel
> That cloudless night in the mid-Atlantic
> When I pushed her over.[7]

The escape by violence from the tyranny of the senses by murdering the object of passion is the same experience described in Sweeney's tale. As Sweeney expresses it:

> Any man has to, needs to, wants to
> Once in a lifetime, do a girl in.[8]

Harry's description of isolation in an "over-crowded desert, jostled by ghosts" is the same as that experienced by Sweeney's murderer who "didn't know if he was alive and the girl was dead" or "if the girl was alive and he was dead." In Sweeney's tale this experience stands for a vio-

[7] Eliot, *Complete Poems and Plays*, p. 235.
[8] *Ibid.*, p. 83.

lent application of the instruction of St. John of the Cross to the penitent to divest himself of the love of created beings. The addition of the burning-wheel imagery in Harry's speech connects the murderer's experience with Eliot's other uses of the wheel-point idea. Just as Thomas sought to remove himself from the moving wheel of experience, Harry seeks rest on his wheel, burning with the passions of the life of the senses as in Buddha's Fire Sermon.

Eliot has long been fascinated by murder and its symbolic possibilities. As early as 1917 he explored the meaning of murder in "Eeldrop and Appleplex":

"In Gopsum Street a man murders his mistress. The important fact is that for the man the act is eternal, and that for the brief space he has to live, he is already dead. He is already in a different world from ours. He has crossed the frontier. The important fact that something is done which can not be undone—a possibility which none of us realize until we face it ourselves." [9]

Eliot's extension of the meaning of murder from the literal level of the murderer's state of mind to part of the process of purgation can be accounted for in part, I think, by his connection of this complex of ideas with the ceremonial meanings of murder in the fertility rituals where the god-figure was actually mutilated or dismembered in order to purify him of the iniquities acquired in his sojourn among men.[10] Once the connection is seen between

[9] T. S. Eliot, "Eeldrop and Appleplex. I," *Little Review*, IV (May 1917), 9.
[10] Gilbert Murray vividly describes the importance of such ceremonies to the primitive consciousness in *The Classical Tradition in*

the primitive rite and its re-enactment in Christ's Passion, Crucifixion, and Resurrection, the possibilities of murder for Christian symbolism become clear. Christ took upon himself the sins of mankind and his purification must be imitated by the saint. Murder by drowning also has a ritual significance since the old god was often purified by drowning or boiling. Eliot's earliest uses of the idea of drowning are to be seen in "The Love Song of J. Alfred Prufrock," "Dans le Restaurant," and *The Waste Land,* where its sexual connotations are developed.

Harry, in *The Family Reunion,* is engaged in this same process of purification even before he understands the meaning of the ordeal he is undergoing, and his spiritual agony is juxtaposed against his family's lack of spiritual insight. The assembled family first reacts to the shock of his announcement of murder with disbelief—"Of course we know what really happened, we read it in the papers" —and then with the characteristically inconsistent acts of calling Warburton, the family doctor (on the assumption that Harry is deranged) and questioning Downing, Harry's chauffeur (on the assumption that Harry might have committed the crime). The resistance of the family to the truth is indicated by the "beyond character" pas-

---

Poetry (Cambridge, Massachusetts: Harvard University Press, 1927), p. 229: "This death and vengeance was really enacted among our remote ancestors in terms of human bloodshed. The sacred king really had 'slain the slayer' and was doomed himself to be slain. The queen might either be taken on by her husband's slayer, or else slain with her husband. It is no pale myth or allegory that has so deeply dyed the first pages of human history. It is man's passionate desire for the food that will save him from starvation, his passionate memory of the streams of blood, willing and unwilling, that have been shed to keep him alive."

sages delivered by a chorus made up of the "unaware" members of the family:

> Why should we be implicated,
> brought in and brought together?
>
> · · · · · · · ·
>
> Why do we all behave as if the door might suddenly
> open, the curtains be drawn,
> The cellar make some dreadful disclosure, the roof dis-
> appear,
> And we should cease to be sure of what is real or un-
> real?
> Hold tight, hold tight, we must insist that the world is
> what we have always taken it to be.[11]

They demonstrate in this passage their resentment and fear at being made to participate in Harry's guilt and at being forced to recognize, if only momentarily, the existence of a dimension of experience which they have steadfastly ignored. The demands of Harry's reunion story disrupt the reality of their world. His reunion is a family reunion, not only in the sense that he is helped to understanding by Agatha and Mary, but also in the more important sense that he is shown by them that he must acknowledge the truth about his parents and become reunited with his past as a means to self-knowledge and ultimate union with God. He is made to realize that part of his burden of sin and guilt is a family heritage.

The main action in Harry's personal drama begins with his realization upon returning home that only there do the Furies visibly appear to him. He returned home because

[11] Eliot, *Complete Poems and Plays*, pp. 242–43.

he had assumed that there he could escape into the re-membered happiness and security of the past. Instead, his pursuers are more real and terrible to him than ever be-fore. His spiritual education is conducted in three stages. From Mary, who shared his childhood, he hopes to find out the truth about the past which lies behind the façade of changelessness which his mother has constructed at Wishwood. He discovers from his cousin that neither of them was happy as children because both were deprived of freedom by the domination of Amy. On the most literal level of the drama Mary's comment refers to Amy's direc-tion of the family and thus to the destruction of the free-dom of those closest to her—her husband, her sisters, and her children. On another level, however, Mary's comment applies to Harry's spiritual liberation from the wheel and represents release from the domination of the willful de-mands of this world and freedom to follow, instead, the demands of the spiritual world by freeing one's self from lower, and thus destructive, kinds of human love.

In response to Mary's confession of her own "ordinary hopelessness," Harry answers that she cannot know what complete hopelessness is, "the sudden extinction of every alternative." But Mary reminds him that even his agon-izing experience may be a deception, that his return home showed some sign of hope that the past could save him. Mary suggests that it might be something inside himself which Harry needs to alter. For the first time, he feels the possibility of the painful renewal of life within him, but he is confused about its meaning. Because Mary has brought him the first glimmering of hope he has felt, Harry thinks for a moment that her love might be the destination of his painful journey, but just as he rapturously declares his newborn hopes, the Eumenides reveal themselves to him more forcefully than ever before. He realizes then that they will allow him no peace to accept the message of "sunlight and singing" which Mary's love seems to offer.

Harry's plea to the Furies to allow him to accept the path of purely human love shows an analysis of his dilemma and its causes which Agatha is later to show him is false:

Why do you show yourselves now for the first time?
When I knew her, I was not the same person.
I was not any person. Nothing that I did
Has to do with me. The accident of a dreaming moment,
Of a dreaming age, when I was someone else
Thinking of something else, puts me among you.
I tell you, it is not me you are looking at,
Not me you are grinning at, not me your confidential looks
Incriminate, but that other person, if person,
You thought I was: let your necrophily
Feed upon that carcase. They will not go.[12]

Harry mistakenly believes that his past self is completely separated from his present self and that by loving Mary he can recapture the innocence of his childhood. He believes that his wife's death was "the accident of a dreaming moment . . . when I was someone else," and he refuses to accept responsibility for the actions of that other self, though he obviously cannot avoid feelings of guilt. The freedom he desires is from guilt and responsibility,

---

[12] *Ibid.*, p. 253.

but the Furies show him that he must accept both before he can be truly free.[13]

Harry's next attempt to learn the truth about the past takes place in his interview with Dr. Warburton. The scene is ingeniously constructed to bind together three separate aspects of the action—the efforts of the family to discover Harry's mental condition by sending Dr. Warburton to talk with him, the efforts of Dr. Warburton to communicate to Harry the seriousness of his mother's condition and thereby inadvertently further Amy's design for her son's future, and Harry's own efforts to discover the truth about his past from the family doctor. In asking Warburton about his father, Harry remembers an all-

---

[13] F. O. Matthiessen, in *The Achievement of T. S. Eliot,* pp. 167–68, quotes a letter which Eliot wrote to E. Martin Browne describing his intention in this scene: "The scene with Mary is meant to bring out, as I am aware it fails to, the conflict inside him between . . . repulsion for Mary as a woman, and the attraction which the *normal* part of him that is left, feels toward her personally *for the first time.* This is the first time since his marriage ('there was no ecstasy') that he has been attracted towards any woman. The attraction glimmers for a moment in his mind, half-consciously as a possible 'way of escape,' and the Furies (for the Furies are *divine* instruments, not simple hell-hounds) come in the nick of time to warn him away from this evasion—though at that moment he misunderstands their function. Now, this attraction towards Mary has stirred him up, but, owing to his mental state, is incapable of developing; therefore he finds refuge in an ambiguous relation—the attraction half of a son and half of a lover, to Agatha, who reciprocates in somewhat the same way. And this gives the cue for the second appearance of the Furies, more patently in their role of divine messengers, to let him know clearly that the only way out is purgation and holiness. They become exactly 'hounds of heaven.' And Agatha understands this clearly, though Harry only understands it yet in flashes. So Harry's career needs to be completed by an *Orestes* or an *Oedipus at Colonnos."* Eliot's mention of *Oedipus at Colonus* as the end of the purgation experience is significant in light of the fact that he was to use this Greek work as his source for *The Elder Statesman.*

important event in his childhood—the kiss his mother gave him when news of his father's death came, a kiss which began her possessive domination of Wishwood and her sons. Harry learns from the doctor that Agatha knows the secrets of the true relationship between his mother and his father and, though he has never before dared to ask, he now determines to learn the truth.

The third step in Harry's enlightenment occurs in his interview with Agatha. He learns that she and his father had discovered their love for one another in "a present moment of pointed light" on "a summer day of unusual heat for this cold country." His father had conceived a plan for murdering Amy three months before Harry's birth, but Agatha had stopped him, feeling that the child was in a sense her son as well as Amy's, since she would have no other. Agatha's story brings Harry the saving insight that his own relationship to his dead wife was a repetition of his father's desire to kill his mother and that his conviction that he pushed his own wife overboard was a dream, not an act which he actually committed.

Harry, for the first time, experiences a moment of complete happiness. By discovering the truth about the past he has freed himself from the hold of "phantoms," the events of the surface of life which he has been forced to accept as real since childhood.[14] He sees for the first time that the Eumenides are to be followed, not fled from, for to those who are permitted to view them they are more real than the illusions which the world imposes.[15] He

---

[14] Grover Smith, in *T. S. Eliot's Poetry and Plays,* p. 208, cites the last two *Quartets,* especially "Dry Salvages," as examples of Eliot's development of these same themes in his nondramatic poetry.

[15] It is interesting to compare Eliot's treatment of the Eumenides

realizes, however, that although acceptance of their reality means the end of one kind of suffering, another and equaly difficult kind will follow—the self-inflicted ordeal of the mystic path. That is the journey which Harry now sees as his future course.

When Harry leaves Wishwood it is at the cost of his mother's life. She realizes that she has lost her battle to keep her son, and she is incapable of understanding that the ways of divine love take precedence over the ways of human love. Harry's decision to accept his calling even at the price of his "murder" of his mother is endorsed by Agatha. Her line:

> Love compels cruelty
> To those who do not understand love [16]

might well stand as the modification of the instruction of St. John of the Cross which *The Family Reunion* expresses. Although human love is now not altogether denied, it is accepted only insofar as it provides a means to achieving reunion with God.

At the close of the play, Harry's reunion has won out over his mother's.[17] Agatha's summary of the play's climax

---

with Jean-Paul Sartre's in *The Flies,* where they are portrayed as swarming, noisome insects representing remorse sent by the vengeance-seeking Gods as a means of holding men in intellectual bondage. This difference in treatment emphasizes the fundamental difference of attitude toward remorse and purgation in the two writers, one espousing Christianity and the other atheistic Existentialism. Sartre sees remorse and religion in general as standing in the way of man's freedom, while in Eliot's view Christian freedom, as described above, means the denial of personal will in order to accept the will of God.

[16] Eliot, *Complete Poems and Plays*, p. 279.

[17] There have been a number of complaints registered against the ending of *The Family Reunion*. Grover Smith, in *T. S. Eliot's Poetry*

is intended to express the symbolic meaning of the events
portrayed:

What we have written is not a story of detection,
Of crime and punishment, but of sin and expiation.
It is possible that you have not known what sin
You shall expiate, or whose, or why. It is certain
That the knowledge of it must precede the expiation.
It is possible that sin may strain and struggle
In its dark instinctive birth, to come to consciousness
And so find expurgation. It is possible
You are the consciousness of your unhappy family,
Its bird sent flying through the purgatorial flame.
Indeed it is possible. You may learn hereafter,
Moving alone through flames of ice, chosen
To resolve the enchantment under which we suffer.[18]

---

and Plays, p. 200, has objected to the absence of specific information
about what will happen to Harry after the curtain falls. (Michael
Redgrave asked Eliot the same question during rehearsal for the
London production and is reported to have received the reply that
Harry and his chauffeur "go off and get jobs in the East End"!
[D. E. Jones, *The Plays of T. S. Eliot,* p. 101.]) F. O. Matthiessen
has raised a more serious objection which reveals the same disposi-
tion to overlook the "allegorical" quality of the events. He objects to
Harry's lack of "humanity" in his treatment of his mother (*The
Achievement of T. S. Eliot,* pp. 170–71). The surfaces of Eliot's plays
are intended, I think, to provide fables which carry the attention of
the audience to the deeper level of interpretation. The plays are "abstract" and "stylized" in the sense Eliot developed in his writings
about drama during the nineteen-twenties and cannot be viewed by
the standards of the realistic theater without distorting their meaning. It is my conjecture that one of the reasons behind Eliot's change
to a comic surface in his next play, *The Cocktail Party,* was the
greater tolerance of audiences for "abstraction" in comedy than in
other dramatic forms.

[18] Eliot, *Complete Poems and Plays,* p. 275.

Agatha's comment makes explicit for the audience Harry's divine mission. She also implies that he is to be a kind of sacrificial scapegoat for his entire family. When she addresses him as "the consciousness of your unhappy family" and suggests that he is "to resolve the enchantment under which we suffer," she connects his personal identity with all saviors who suffer and are purged of the sins of others. Symbolically, the family on whose behalf he suffers is the family of man.

Agatha's statement that the events of the drama are not a "story of detection, Of crime and punishment, but of expiation" points out to the audience that the "thriller" [19] aspect of the play (for example, the sudden visit of the police chief, the family's questioning of Downing, and their other attempts to discover if Harry murdered his wife) is an intentional misrepresentation of events. It is another example of the author's attempt to build up one kind of expectation in the audience only to shatter it with a different and unexpected interpretation of events. In the reference to Dostoevski's *Crime and Punishment* the playwright hints at a precedent for his device, for *Crime and Punishment* also begins as a murder mystery and ends as a tale of spiritual purgation. The fact that the *Oresteia* also follows the same pattern suggests the connection of this theme with ritual and myth.

Eliot's use of his mythical source in *The Family Reunion* was prophetic of his method in later plays. The ritual struggle between the dominion of earth and the

---

[19] Eliot's interest in "thrillers," detective fiction, and crime has been discussed by Grover Smith in *T. S. Eliot's Poetry and Plays*, pp. 116–18, and in "T. S. Eliot and Sherlock Holmes," *Notes and Queries*, cxciii (October 2, 1948), 431–32.

dominion of heaven provided the fundamental conflict of the play, and the events in Aeschylus' version of the myth provided a situation with dramatic possibilities which the playwright explored in modern terms. All of the Greek sources which Eliot has so far used have been chosen because they have seemed to him particularly rich in religious meaning, especially Christian meaning. He converts the Greek plot into Christian terms but keeps these meanings concealed in the events of the contemporary situation; the characters do not preach Christian doctrine as Thomas did in his sermon. It is important to note, however, that the "inevitability" and universality of interpretation which Eliot achieves when he is most successful are the product of a careful process of selection and emphasis. In the case of *The Family Reunion* this process is less effective than it might be because of the discrepancies in the meanings and events of the playwright's mythical levels.[20]

In Eliot's source Orestes commits an act of violence against Clytemnestra and must suffer the agonies of purgation before the sin is judged by Athena to be a necessary act which will end the curse on the house of Atreus. In *The Family Reunion*,[21] the curse on the house of Atreus becomes original sin, and the father being revenged be-

[20] Eliot himself has commented in "Poetry and Drama" that the play's "deepest flaw" was "in a failure of adjustment between the Greek story and the modern situation. I should either have stuck closer to Aeschylus or else taken a great deal more liberty with his myth" (*On Poetry and Poets*, p. 84).

[21] Several studies have examined the analogies between *The Family Reunion* and the *Oresteia*, including Rudolf Stamm, "The Orestes Theme in Three Plays by Eugene O'Neill, T. S. Eliot, and Jean-Paul Sartre," *English Studies* (Amsterdam), xxx, No. 5 (1949), 244–55; Maud Bodkin, *The Quest for Salvation in an Ancient and a Modern Play* (Oxford: Oxford University Press, 1941); and T. R. Henn, *The Harvest of Tragedy* (London: Methuen & Co. Ltd., 1956), pp. 217–32.

comes the heavenly Father. Attempts to push the analogies further, however, encounter difficulties which can
be solved only by understanding the ritual foundations.
A problem is presented, for example, when Agamemnon's
sacrifice of Iphigenia is equated with Harry's father's
contemplated murder of Amy and their unborn child,
for that murder is prevented by Agatha and the child
is spared. Moreover, Harry's pursuit occurs *before* his
mother's "murder" and, though it occurs after what he
believes to be his murder of his wife, Agatha makes clear
that Harry has only imagined this act. Nor have the
scenes involving Mary, Agatha, and Dr. Warburton counterparts in the *Oresteia*. It is only by understanding the
symbolic equation between Harry's wife and mother as
representatives of the domination of the senses and of the
human will that the analogy can be maintained at all, and
that equation depends on interpreting Amy as a representative of a corrupt spiritual principle which must die
in order to renew itself.

The conflict between Harry and his mother which was
described earlier is patterned on the ritual plot with its
agon between the sin-laden and impotent representative
of the old year and the reborn and sin-free god of the new
year.[22] By emphasizing features of the surface action which
correspond to the ritual sequences, Eliot invests the actual
events of the play with the symbolic values implicit in his

[22] One source of Eliot's interest in the ritual elements of the *Oresteia*
may have been Gilbert Murray's comparative study of Hamlet and
Orestes as ritual heroes in *The Classical Tradition in Poetry*, pp.
205–40. Murray demonstrates the presence of the ritual sequence in
the myths surrounding both heroes and describes Orestes as a representative of the new year who must war against the corrupt Earth
Mother figure (Clytemnestra).

model, though often interpreted in terms of his own religious perspective. The portrayal of Amy as an old woman near death is an example of a change in characterization made to emphasize the ritual pattern.

The opening scene of the play provides abundant examples of the correspondences the playwright wished to establish. The time of the action is late March, the time of the spring fertility ceremonies and, in corresponding Christian terms, of Easter. In the first speech of the play Amy complains of her old age and winter confinement and of her fears of approaching death in words which suggest the terminology of the fertility rituals:

O Sun, that was once so warm, O Light that was taken
    for granted
When I was young and strong, and sun and light un-
    sought for
And the night unfeared and the day expected
And clocks could be trusted, tomorrow assured
And time would not stop in the dark!
Put on the lights. But leave the curtains undrawn.
Make up the fire. Will the spring never come? I am cold.[23]

The reference to the season of renewal as a season of death is an idea familiar from Eliot's earliest use of the fertility material of Jessie Weston, and the building of the fire suggests the sacrificial fire used for the cooking of the old god, as well as being the mystical symbol for purgatorial flames.

While Amy represents the old principle which must be destroyed before the new principle can be born, she stands,

[23] Eliot, *Complete Poems and Plays*, p. 225.

in more specifically Christian terms, for the human will or self unwilling to receive divine guidance. Her willfulness and pride are made clear by her determination to impose her plan on those around her. Her refusal to accept change is based, ironically, on her belief in the world of time; if change can be avoided, the clock can be turned back. She will not acknowledge that the only realm of changelessness is the timeless world of eternity. The name of her domain, Wishwood,[24] indicates the illusion of her desires, and the events of the play indicate the impossibility of her plan. Her fears that the clock will stop in the dark emphasize her exclusion from the realm of spiritual consciousness for, in the words of "Burnt Norton," "To be conscious is not to be in time." [25]

Amy's alignment with the "wrong" side and her failure to appreciate the efficacy of any realm beyond the physical is pointed up by the fact that she is invariably proved wrong by events. Her two sons, who she is sure will arrive for her birthday party, never show up, while Harry, whom she considers the most unpredictable, appears. She is similarly sure that he will not wish to talk about the painful events of his past, but he wishes to talk of nothing

[24] Roy Battenhouse, in "Eliot's 'The Family Reunion' as Christian Prophecy," *Christendom,* xx (Summer 1945), 317, comments that "the very name Wishwood is intended by Eliot to stand for universal man's Dream House, located in a wood of wish and memory—turned to by man for refuge but discovered to be only an asylum for ghosts." Tennessee Williams, in *A Streetcar Named Desire,* uses the symbol of the family home for a similar purpose.

[25] Anne Ward discusses the clock symbolism in the play in relation to the time philosophies of Bergson and Hulme ("Speculations on Eliot's Time-World: An Analysis of *The Family Reunion* in Relation to Hulme and Bergson," *American Literature,* xxi [March 1949], 18–34).

else. Throughout the play, virtually every statement she makes proves to be incorrect. At the very climax of the play, the birthday party she has so carefully arranged to complete the family reunion becomes her death-day celebration.

Harry's identification with the spirit of the new year struggling for rebirth, while made less explicit in the imagery of his speeches, is nevertheless clear. It is apparent from his first entrance that he is in the presence of a spiritual reality which places him in continual conflict with the will of his mother and with the elements of self which must be purged from his own nature, both of which qualify him as a representative of the scapegoat. And in at least one scene he uses the imagery of the ritual sacrifice of rejuvenation. In his "beyond character" dialogue with Mary he says:

> Spring is an issue of blood
> A season of sacrifice
> And the wail of the new full tide
> Returning the ghosts of the dead
> Those whom the winter drowned
> Do not the ghosts of the drowned
> Return to the land in the spring? [26]

And she responds in like terms:

> I believe the moment of birth
> Is when we have knowledge of death
> I believe the season of birth
> Is the season of sacrifice

> .   .   .   .

[26] Eliot, *Complete Poems and Plays,* p. 251.

And what of the terrified spirit
Compelled to be reborn
To rise toward the violent sun. . . ?[27]

The ritual battle is thus re-enacted between Amy and Harry as representatives of the human will or self and of the spirit. The old principle is defeated so that the new may be reborn.

Eliot made use of the spiritual assistants in the rejuvenation ordeal as described by Cornford by creating his own counterparts for these helpers. The climax of Harry's departure is built up to with three scenes, in each of which the hero is led one step nearer enlightenment by an assistant of the divine order. It is established in the play that Agatha, Mary, and Downing are conscious agents of divinity. Agatha makes clear in her final instructions to Downing that both she and Mary have "seen" Harry's pursuers, and he responds that he "wondered when his Lordship would get round to seeing them," indicating that he has seen them, too.[28] All three recognize that Harry's Furies are positive, not negative, agents (as Downing puts it, "There's no harm in *them,* I'll take my oath"); they also realize that Harry will not be needing them for long. Their specal status of "knowing" more than the hero knows and yet standing below him in the spiritual hierarchy is conveyed by Agatha's consolation of Mary:

[27] *Ibid.,* pp. 251–52.
[28] Grover Smith calls Downing "Harry's faithful Pylades . . . who in the last scene assumes the role of a guardian Apollo" (*T. S. Eliot's Poetry and Plays,* p. 203).

We must all go, each in his own direction,
You, and I, and Harry. You and I,
My dear, may very likely meet again
In our wanderings in the neutral territory
Between two worlds.[29]

Dr. Warburton, on the other hand, is an "unconscious" spiritual assistant. That is, on the surface level of the drama he acts as if he were another of the unaware members of the cast of Amy's plot; however, both the effect of his actions and the obviously double meanings of his remarks connect him with Harry's salvation drama. He fulfills, I am convinced, the ritual role of the cook-doctor which Cornford described and takes his place as one of a long series of serio-comic, symbolic, cook-doctors in T. S. Eliot's plays, beginning with Pereira in *Sweeney Agonistes* and including Sir Henry Harcourt-Reilly in *The Cocktail Party*, Eggerson in *The Confidential Clerk*, and the doctor who orders Lord Claverton to the sanatorium in *The Elder Statesman*. The cook-doctor sequences of the ritual drama include the representation and imagery of illness, fever cures, and sacrificial boiling or stewing of the old god. This painfully curative process was followed or accompanied by a procession and feast in celebration of the renewal and conversion of the old into the new. Sweeney's sardonic threat to convert Doris into a stew in *Sweeney Agonistes* was Eliot's first dramatic treatment of this idea. In *The Family Reunion* the same pattern is followed. When Harry's malady becomes apparent, the doctor is called in. The order of the curative action is as follows:

[29] Eliot, *Complete Poems and Plays*, p. 285.

Harry's talk with Mary, his "hot bath" before dinner, the procession into dinner, followed by his interview with the doctor which eventuates in his complete enlightenment in the scene with Agatha. The conversation before dinner between Harry and the doctor "who has known him longer than anybody" is ostensibly a Hamlet-Polonius scene,[30] but it conceals some important symbolic meanings conveyed in the imagery of illness and disease. In an apparently "polite" conversation about Harry's childhood illnesses, Ivy comments on the unpleasantness of "coming home to have an illness," and Violet adds that as a child he would never stay in bed because he was convinced that he would never get well.

These remarks are meant, I believe, to reveal the symbolic meaning of the surface events. Harry has returned "home" to become spiritually ill because only there can his cure begin. Until his final awakening he has refused to submit to the cure because no possibility of spiritual health was apparent to him. But he learns from Agatha that what he had viewed as terrible pursuers to be avoided because of the horror, guilt, and contamination they make him experience are in reality positive guides to be followed through the terrors of purgation to "the other side of despair."

The exchange between the doctor and Harry which follows further develops the relationship between two of Eliot's favorite images, disease and murder:

[30] F. O. Matthiessen notes the Hamlet-Polonius quality of the scene (*The Achievement of T. S. Eliot*, p. 169). Gilbert Murray's discussion of the "remnants of the old Fool" in the feigned madness of Hamlet and Orestes may have influenced Eliot's portrayal of his hero (*The Classical Tradition in Poetry*, pp. 209–16).

Warburton:

    We're all of us ill in one way or another:
    We call it health when we find no symptom
    Of illness. Health is a relative term.

   ·   ·   ·   ·   ·   ·   ·   ·   ·

          . . . My first patient, now—
    You wouldn't believe it, ladies—was a murderer,
    Who suffered from an incurable cancer.
    How he fought against it! I never saw a man
    More anxious to live.

Harry: Not at all extraordinary.
    It is really harder to believe in murder
    Than to believe in cancer. Cancer is here:
    The lump, the dull pain, the occasional sickness:
    Murder a reversal of sleep and waking.
    Murder was there. Your ordinary murderer
    Regards himself as an innocent victim.
    To himself he is still what he used to be
    Or what he would be. He cannot realize
    That everything is irrevocable,
    The past unredeemable. But cancer, now,
    That is something real.[31]

A Christian interpretation of these remarks seems plausible in the light of the playwright's theme. Man, the spiritual doctor's "first patient," despite his disease of original sin which determined in a doctrinal sense the Crucifixion or "murder" of Christ, refuses to recognize his condition. He is in this sense the murderer who cannot realize or take responsibility for his act, who, as Harry

---

[31] Eliot, *Complete Poems and Plays*, pp. 255–56.

says, "regards himself as an innocent victim." Man, cursed
with death since the Fall, combats an "incurable cancer"
from the moment of birth.[32] He fights a futile battle to
maintain physical life dominated by his will, not God's,
rather than learning the lesson ensuing death should
teach: that physical life must end but eternal life can be
gained by humility and the acknowledgment of sin. Harry,
though he does not know it at this point in the play, is
going through the nightmare of purgation necessary to
enable him to escape from the usual lot of unaware man to
a state of awareness of spiritual reality. He is suffering the
guilt, not of his wife's drowning, but of man's universal
"family" sin and mutual responsibility for evil.

There are other clues to identify Warburton with the
doctor of the ritual drama. His remark that since Harry
left he has had no patient at Wishwood suggests, as
Dusty's telephone conversation with Pereira in *Sweeney
Agonistes* does, that Amy, like Doris before her, refuses to
have the spiritual cure administered. Physical health has a
negative value in Eliot's symbolism. There is an irony in
Amy's refusal of the doctor's cure because his urgent message to Harry in the next scene is that only Amy's will is
keeping her alive and that she indeed needs the medicine
of salvation which she rejects. Violet's remark that Amy
seems not a day older than ten years before "except that
she can't get about now in winter," suggests the aging and
corrupt old year which must be destroyed at the end of
winter in order to bring forth the new and fruitful year in

---

[32] See D. E. Jones' discussion of original sin in relation to Harry's
guilt (*The Plays of T. S. Eliot*, pp. 115–16).

the spring. The ritual procession and feast are introduced by Amy's request to the doctor to escort her in to dinner, "since we are very much the oldest present" and "as we came first, we will go first, in to dinner." (The procession to dinner is overtly ritualized by Agatha's mystic rune.) The doctor's comment that he hopes next year will bring him the same honor and that it is only when he gets an invitation to dinner that he ever gets to see Amy, hints at the continuance of the annual fertility rites despite Amy's refusal to accept her dependence on the realm of existence which he symbolically represents.

In Harry's interview with the doctor after dinner, Eliot achieves an ingenious kind of dramatic irony which is one of the most original features of his spiritual dramas. On the surface level in this scene of symbolic cross-purposes, Dr. Warburton, who has been called in by the "unaware" members of the family to diagnose Harry's "illness," spends the entire interview trying to impress Harry with the seriousness of Amy's illness and imminent death, symbolically expressing the ritual fate of the impure old god. But Harry, by insisting on ignoring Warburton's mission in his own search to find out the truth about his past, assists the cook-doctor's purposes by moving one step closer to his victory over the old god. While Warburton tries to tell Harry about his mother's illness, Harry is concerned only to find out about his father. Symbolically Harry has been born of the marriage of human will and divine spirit; he is, like all men, a child of earth and heaven. (Agatha's love affair with his father is intended to convey *her* love for the divine.) Harry senses that knowledge about his divine Father is necessary before he can find his way to spiritual insight, and his conversation with Warburton can be viewed in this symbolic light:

Harry:
>   But I want to know more about my father.
>   I hardly remember him, and I know very well
>   That I was kept apart from him, till he went away.
>   We never heard him mentioned, but in some way or
>   another
>   We felt that he was always here.
>   But when we would have grasped for him,
>   there was only a vacuum. . . .
>
> .   .   .   .

Warburton: . . . You know that your mother
>   And your father were never very happy together:
>   They separated by mutual consent
>   And he went to live abroad. You were only a boy
>   When he died. You would not remember.

Harry: But now I do remember. Not Arthur or
>   John,
>   They were too young. But now I remember
>   A summer day of unusual heat. . . .
>
> .   .   .   .

>   *That* was the day he died. Of course.
>   I mean, I suppose, the day on which the news ar-
>   rived.[33]

(It should be remembered that Agatha also discovered *her* love for Harry's father on a "summer day of unusual heat.") Harry, the first born of the union of human will

[33] Eliot, *Complete Poems and Plays*, p. 260.

and divine spirit, dimly remembers his heavenly Father's death before his mother's domination began with her kiss.

It is also significant that the three characters called by Amy to be present at her death are Agatha, Mary, and Dr. Warburton, all representatives of the spiritual world. By their assistance they help usher out the old principle of will and officiate in the rebirth of the new Harry (out of the "Old Harry"). The ceremony celebrating Harry's departure toward spiritual life and Amy's departure toward physical death is conducted by Agatha and Mary as they circle around the "birthday cake with lighted candles." [34] The blowing out of the candles is intended to indicate, I think, that while Amy's birthday has become her death-day it has also been transformed into Harry's birth-wedding day, his day of union with eternity.

The final feature of the ritual plot to be discussed and one which Eliot has used in some manner in every one of his dramatic works so far considered is what Cornford referred to as the "winning over of the chorus." The function of the chorus as a reactor to and reflector of the dramatic action is pointed up in *The Family Reunion* by the use of theatrical imagery by the chorus members, Ivy, Violet, Gerald, and Charles. They continually see themselves as unwillingly playing parts assigned to them by Amy. Their kinship with Amy and with her husband indicates that they are meant to represent the "type of the common man" which might, but usually does not, perceive the spiritual dimension of life. While all of the mem-

[34] F. O. Matthiessen suggests the church ritual of Tenebrae, which commemorates the darkness of Thursday, Friday, and Saturday of Holy Week before the light of Easter Sunday, as the source for this scene (*The Achievement of T. S. Eliot*, p. 170).

bers of the chorus in their "beyond character" speeches feel an uneasiness at the knowledge that "something strange" is happening, only Charles, appropriately a brother of Harry's father, expresses any glimmering of insight on the conscious level of the dialogue:

> It's very odd,
> But I am beginning to feel, just beginning to feel
> That there is something I could understand, if I were
>   told it.
> But I'm not sure that I want to know. I suppose
>   I'm getting old.[35]

In the conflict between the two realms of existence represented by Amy and Harry, the role of the chorus is to show, first by their unwilling acceptance of membership in Amy's cast of characters, then by their gradual confusion at the disruption of the events they expected to occur, and finally by their fear and glimmering awareness, the gradual victory of the eternal over the temporal.

This is Eliot's last use of a formal chorus, for in *The Cocktail Party* he found in the conventions of comedy what he felt to be a less obvious and more effective means of conveying the impact of the spiritual principle on the lives of modern men—the theme which was to remain, despite all changes of dramatic surface, the fundamental concern of all of Eliot's plays.

[35] Eliot, *Complete Poems and Plays*, p. 288.

CHAPTER V

THE COCKTAIL PARTY

The Cocktail Party was presented to the public in 1949 with the phrase "A Comedy" conspicuously appended to the title. The evident seriousness of Eliot's religious message in *Murder in the Cathedral* and *The Family Reunion* and the earnestness of his determination to have that message accepted by the public made his adoption of the mode of comedy seem startling and, to some, perverse.[1] In part, the same motive determined his use of a comic surface in *The Cocktail Party* as that which lay behind his disruption of the expectations of his audience in *The Family Reunion:* the desire to destroy and clear away conventional modes of thought and interpretations of events in order to reveal the hidden meaning and the divine plan behind appearances. The conventions of the comedy of manners led audiences to expect a gay and superficial treatment of the surfaces of life in the orderly world of comedy, where dilemmas are magically resolved in the last act and endings are happy, if sometimes cynically rendered. What Eliot attempted was a reversal of the terms of that world so that what first appeared to be a

[1] Both Raymond Williams (*Drama from Ibsen to Eliot,* p. 237) and E. Martin Browne ("From *The Rock* and *The Confidential Clerk,*" *T. S. Eliot: A Symposium for His Seventieth Birthday,* ed. Neville Braybrooke, p. 64) testify to the sense of expectation which preceded Eliot's first postwar play and the impact it had on audiences. C. L. Barber ("The Power of Development . . . in a Different World," in *The Achievement of T. S. Eliot,* by F. O. Matthiessen, p. 235) mentions the strong objections of many to the British-comedy surface of the play.

playing along the surfaces of life became a probing among the depths. The orderliness of the comic world where all dilemmas are resolved at the end of the play was maintained, but the neatness became a product of divine order and the "happy" ending a product of spiritual guardianship.[2]

The origins of Eliot's decision to use the methods of comedy in *The Cocktail Party* are to be found, I think, in the theatrical failure of *The Family Reunion*. In the earlier play he had attempted the same transformation of one view of reality into another by gradually replacing the audience's expectation of seeing a family "murder mystery" in the style of Agatha Christie with a reinterpretation of the meaning of family crime and punishment. Eliot was, no doubt, prepared for the audience's reluctance to accept a new interpretation of reality, but he had not contended with their reluctance to give up their belief in the dramatic conventions he exploited. Audiences, he found, were all too easily convinced by the initial presentation of events and resisted the dramatist's attempt to shatter the illusion of that initial reality. Their reaction was likely to be either confusion or, even more disastrous for the author's purposes, amusement pro-

[2] The view that the comic surface of *The Cocktail Party* is present to appease or distract a Shaftesbury Avenue audience from the "real" meaning of the play, while very common in the criticism, is, I believe, incorrect. (See, for example, Grover Smith, *T. S. Eliot's Poetry and Plays,* p. 216, and Denis Donoghue, *The Third Voice,* p. 115.) It is true that Eliot wished to use a convention familiar to his audience, but distraction was not his aim. He wished rather to transform one set of events into another set by demonstrating the spiritual meaning behind them. In the service of this purpose, both levels of interpretation are important, for the second is dependent on and necessary to the first.

duced by the discrepancy between the expectation and the actuality.[3] Laughter coming at the wrong time and, more important, directed at the spiritual interpretation of events, rather than at the illusions of the natural world, could destroy the dramatic effect sought. Eliot himself had made use of the incongruity of "wit" in his early plays but in order to provoke thought, not laughter, just as he had used the lysol bath to represent purgatorial cleansing in *Sweeney Agonistes* in order to produce horror, not thrills. Eliot's observation that beneath great comedy there is horror and beneath great tragedy there is laughter[4] is a clear indication of the seriousness of his intention in invoking alternative dramatic moods.

Faced with the failure of *The Family Reunion*, Eliot appears to have concluded that if the surface of his dramas were made comic these difficulties might be resolved and the audience's tendency to laugh at incongruity might be turned into an advantage. Audiences of English comedy had had long training, in tragicomedy, romantic comedy, and even farce, in moving from broad comic effects to the belief in a situation of romance or pathos. No damage would be done to the serious intention of the dramatist by

[3] The continual danger that laughter might result from the Knights' address to the audience in *Murder in the Cathedral* has been described by E. Martin Browne ("From *The Rock* to *The Confidential Clerk*," *T. S. Eliot: A Symposium for His Seventieth Birthday,* ed. Neville Braybrooke, p. 61); Eliot has given his own account of the difficulties involved in presenting to a contemporary audience evidences of the supernatural world in the form of the Furies in *The Family Reunion* (*On Poetry and Poets*, p. 90).

[4] T. S. Eliot, "Shakespearian Criticism: I. From Dryden to Coleridge," *A Companion to Shakespeare Studies,* edited by Harley Granville-Barker and G. B. Harrrison, pp. [287]-99.

leading the audience from the world of comedy to a set of serious meanings implicit in that world. The shock of incongruity would be less jarring because the audience's involvement in a comic situation was less great, and, moreover, incongruity was the *raison d'être* of comedy; thus the audience's attention to the poet's themes and meaning would not be obscured by involvement in the surface events.

One indication of Eliot's developing concern with the comic form during the years between *The Family Reunion* (1939) and *The Cocktail Party* (1949) is to be found in his interest in S. L. Bethell's *Shakespeare & the Popular Dramatic Tradition,*[5] for which Eliot wrote a highly complimentary introduction. His interest in Bethell's book has a special relevance for his conception of levels of meaning and for his own use of comedy. Bethell's thesis is that Shakespeare's dramatic art cannot be understood without recognizing his use of the popular dramatic tradition, the chief characteristic of which is the "audience's ability to respond spontaneously and unconsciously on more than one plane of attention at the same time."[6] In the light of this tradition, Bethell chides nineteenth-century attempts to interpret Shakespeare's settings and characters in terms of naturalism. He compares a performance of Ibsen, where the audience remains passive while the actors create an

[5] S. L. Bethell, *Shakespeare & the Popular Dramatic Tradition* (London: P. S. King and Staples Limited, 1944).

[6] "This is the core of my present thesis: that a popular audience, uncontaminated by abstract and tendentious dramatic theory, will attend to several diverse aspects of a situation, simultaneously yet without confusion" (Bethell, *Shakespeare & the Popular Dramatic Tradition,* p. 28).

illusion of real life on a picture-frame stage, with the Elizabethan, or the modern experimental, theater.[7] In the latter two "there is no illusion of actual life; but the audience are vividly aware of acting in progress, and the communication, through their cooperative goodwill, of a work of dramatic art. If the one type of production is more realistic, the other is essentially more real." Bethell describes the advantage of the nonnaturalistic method over its naturalistic competitor as follows:

"This double consciousness of play-world and real world has the solid advantage of 'distancing' a play, so that the words and deeds of which it consists may be critically weighed in the course of its performance. . . . Naturalism must engage in a constant effort to delude the audience into taking for actuality what they are bound to know, in their moments of critical alertness, to be only a stage performance. To gain a hearing, naturalism destroys the critical awareness necessary for appreciation: it is hardly surprising that a method thus divided against itself has produced little of permanent value."[8]

Bethell observes that especially in Shakespeare's comedies the scenes in which emotion might run too high are

---

[7] Bethell says of *Murder in the Cathedral:* "There is one recent play which may be a 'sport' (as biologists say) or perhaps the forerunner of revival. *Murder in the Cathedral,* with its complex demands upon the audience, is the nearest modern approach to serious art in the popular tradition. Mr. Eliot has significantly written in praise of the old music-hall, and in this play he exploits music-hall devices in the service of the highest dramatic aims" (*Shakespeare & the Popular Dramatic Tradition,* p. 29).

[8] *Ibid.,* p. 33.

sometimes toned down by means of verbal patterning, by reminders to the audience that they are viewing an "improbable fiction" on stage, and by using such devices as a play within a play.[9] "The tendency throughout is to pass lightly over whatever has the potentiality of heightened emotion, in order, presumably, to keep the intellect unclouded and to concentrate serious attention upon certain themes. . . ." There is, in addition, a still more important dramatic purpose served by Shakespeare's exploitation of this tradition. By pointing up the unreality of the play world, "the solidity of the first plane of reality, the plane of our terrestrial life, is seen to be illusory." [10] Poetry, he maintains, is the natural vehicle both for suggesting mean-

---

[9] Bethell also mentions Shakespeare's frequent metaphorical use of plays and players to remind the audience that it is make-believe which is being enacted (*ibid.*, p. 40). It will be remembered that Eliot also used this same imagery in his treatment of the chorus characters in *The Family Reunion*.

[10] Bethell's principal example is *The Tempest*, where Prospero reminds the audience that, as his spirit actors in the Masque of Ceres have vanished, so

> the great globe itself
> Yea, all which it inherit, shall dissolve
> And like this insubstantial pageant faded,
> Leave not a rack behind. We are such stuff
> As dreams are made on, and our little life
> Is rounded with a sleep.
>
> (*Tempest,* iv. i. 153–58)

Bethell concludes that Shakespeare is thus able to assert, through the series of illusory worlds in the play, "the existence of an eternal order behind the relatively trivial and impermanent phenomenal world, as the 'real' world exists in comparative stability behind the shadow world of the theatre" (*Shakespeare & the Popular Dramatic Tradition*, p. 41). C. L. Barber has compared Sir Henry Harcourt-Reilly, in his role of magical physician who directs the dramatic events, with Shakespeare's Prospero ("The Power of Development . . . in a Different World," in *The Achievement of T. S. Eliot,* by F. O. Matthiessen, pp. 235–37).

ings beyond the particular and for "distancing" over-emotional scenes.

In his introduction to Bethell's book, Eliot discusses the relevance of this material to his own endeavors in poetic drama. Just as the tradition which Shakespeare utilized allowed him to explore deeper levels of reality than our everyday world discloses, so the creator of modern verse drama must create a form containing characters who, while they "perform the same actions, and lead the same lives as in the real world," disclose "a deeper reality than that of the plane of most of our conscious living." For the accomplishment of this ideal, poetry is a necessary instrument because poetry can express, as imitations of actual speech cannot, the underlying reality:

"A verse play is not a play done into verse, but a different kind of play: in a way more realistic than 'naturalistic drama,' because, instead of clothing nature in poetry, it should remove the surface of things, expose the underneath, or the inside, of the natural surface appearance. It may allow the characters to behave inconsistently, but only with respect to a deeper consistency. It may use any device to show their real feelings and volitions, instead of just what, in actual life, they would normally profess or be conscious of; it must reveal, underneath the vacillating or infirm character, the indomitable unconscious will; and underneath the resolute purpose of the planning animal, the victim of circumstance and the doomed or sanctified being. So the poet with ambitions of the theatre, must discover the laws, both of another kind of verse and of another kind of drama. The difficulty of the author is also the difficulty of the audience. Both have to be trained. . . ." [11]

In *The Cocktail Party* Eliot employed several of the ideas which Bethell discussed in order to "remove the surface of things" by replacing profane meanings with religious ones. Just as Shakespeare was able to emphasize the illusory nature of "the plane of our terrestrial life" by pointing up the unreality of the play world, so Eliot wished to point up the illusory nature of surface appearances by revealing other meanings in those events and by introducing continual reminders of another world. In *The Cocktail Party,* while there are no Furies visible to the audience, Sir Henry's song "One-Eyed Riley" and the mysterious toasts drunk to the hearth and to the journey remain as interruptions in the comedy-of-manners surface. Moreover, the fundamental rationale for all of the dramatic action is the revelation that Alex, Julia, and Sir Henry are in league as spiritual guardians for the rest of the characters. Thus, by the divinely operated circle of reciprocal cures wrought by Eliot's three guardians, what begins as a comedy of misdirected love affairs and marriage triangles, is transformed into an exposition of the multiple meanings of Christian love and marriage.

Eliot also exploited another major advantage provided by comedy—the ability to "distance" scenes which might otherwise cause too great an emotional involvement on the part of the audience and thus cause the theme or meaning to be overlooked. The marital arguments of Edward and Lavinia and Sir Henry's office interviews with both sets of characters are handled with the methods

[11] T. S. Eliot, Introduction to *Shakespeare & the Popular Dramatic Tradition* by S. L. Bethell, p. [9].

of comedy and deliberately flattened in order to keep the audience awake to the symbolic implications.[12] The most crucial use of this technique occurs in the treatment of Celia's martyrdom, which is surrounded in the third act by the buffoonery of Alex and the manifestation of the beneficial effects of her death on the others.[13] Eliot's use of these aspects of comedy is thoroughly consistent with his early views on the usefulness of verbal rhythms, flattened characters, and stylized actions in producing a rhythmic dramatic surface. The conception of a popular dramatic tradition also appealed, no doubt, to the author's desire to reach a large and varied audience.

By the move to comedy Eliot hoped, I think, to turn an

[12] C. L. Barber comments on Eliot's use of comedy in the "masterful second act" in Sir Henry's consulting room: "By a classic comic mechanism, he [Sir Henry] deftly switches Edward and Lavinia into a head-on collision. . . . They cut down each other's false pretenses: our hilarity as we watch the process is an experience of the weakness of such pretenses, blown away in laughter—after which Edward and Lavinia can start to make a new beginning. Because the process is positive, conveying the comic sense that life is larger than personalities, their encounter and change of heart makes an effective preliminary and foil to Celia's interview. The reversals of expectation in Celia's case are not for the most part laughable, but some of them are. . . . Her interview belongs to comedy, even when we are moved, perhaps to tears, by her expression of her plight, because it presents her situation being opened up by Reilly's redefinition of it—there is a turning of the tables which makes way for fulfillment" ("The Power of Development . . . in a Different World," in *The Achievement of T. S. Eliot,* by F. O. Matthiessen, pp. 237-38).

[13] There has been a varied critical reaction to Eliot's treatment of Celia's martyrdom. W. K. Wimsatt, Jr. asserts that the major flaw in the play's tone comes in the third act when the author, at the climax of the double outcome, matches the comic treatment of Edward and Lavinia with the sensational details of Celia's death ("Eliot's Comedy," *Sewanee Review,* LVIII [Autumn 1950], 667). Denis Donoghue agrees with this judgment and adds that, while Celia's path can be explained in intellectual terms, "the degree of explicitness in Alex's report remains an artistic flaw because the details, however easy to 'explain,'

audience accustomed to the methods of commercial comedy into an audience trained to attend to "more than one
plane of attention at the same time" as Shakespeare had.
Bethell's presentation of the product of the popular dramatic tradition as a stylized multilevel drama which operated by the "cooperative goodwill" of an audience which
realized that they were viewing a work of dramatic art
and thus retained the critical faculty which could lead to
enlightenment lent valuable support to the theory Eliot
was attempting to evolve. *The Cocktail Party* marks the
beginning of the playwright's effort to lead his audience,
by means of the comedy of Shaftesbury Avenue, to an
understanding of life best exemplified by the comedy of
Dante.

Eliot's use of the methods of comedy to transform the
orderliness of the comic world into a symbolic microcosm
representing the order of God was only one part of a more
complex dramatic plan. With the expansion of his social
goals and his eagerness to reach a larger audience had
come a desire to include a wider segment of Christian life
in his drama. In his desire to discover the "laws, both of
another kind of verse and of another kind of drama"
which could "remove the surface of things," Eliot hoped,
I think, to construct a plan for his drama which could im-

---

impress their own quality on the 'feel' of the play. . . . No rhetorical
law demanded the crucifixion near an ant-hill" (*The Third Voice*, p.
129). Raymond Williams disagrees with the view that Eliot's presentation of Celia's path is a dramatic mistake: "It has been frequently said
that Celia's motives are unsubstantiated, that the play does not prepare
us for her decision. It seems to me that this criticism is a rationalisa-
tion, covering an essential antipathy to the nature of her experience.
. . . By making Reilly the guardian of those who follow both ways,
he [Eliot] has achieved, in the most striking possible way, the reali-
sation of a particular pattern of values" (*Drama from Ibsen to Eliot*,
pp. 242–43).

pose a pattern on a more complex dramatic universe than he had yet presented. The principle upon which he settled and which pervades every aspect of *The Cocktail Party* was the conception of a "musical" pattern which could impose unity on diversity. The ideal he had in mind was a rhythmic ordering of experience which could create harmony out of seeming discord and show apparent incongruities to be variations on a single, all-encompassing theme. This contrapuntal ideal can be perceived in every facet of *The Cocktail Party* from the use of a comic surface to portray the underlying seriousness of religious experience to the choice of a verse form which could express both the lyric and mundane. The cocktail-party atmosphere of fashionable London was to be the unexpected starting point of two paths to salvation, and the interdependence of each path on the other was to emphasize a pervading spiritual unity in experience.

Eliot's effort to show unity in diversity is most clearly evident in the intellectual fabric of ideas behind the dramatic events of the play. In the history of Christian mysticism from the time of the writings attributed to Dionysius the Areopagite, there have traditionally been two paths by which the soul could come to God—the Negative Way and the Affirmative Way. Followers of the Negative Way believe that God may be reached by detaching the soul from the love of all things that are not God, or, in the terms Eliot most frequently chose to use, by following the council of St. John of the Cross to divest oneself of the love of created beings. The Way of Affirmation, on the other hand, consists of the recognition that because the Christian God is immanent as well as transcendent, everything in the created world is an imperfect image of

Him. Thus, all created things are to be accepted in love as images of the Divine. The Way of Affirmation, while less rigorous, has its own implicit difficulties, for the price of loving created beings ultimately involves suffering and loss.

In Eliot's plays up to the time of *The Cocktail Party* the predominant emphasis was on the negative aspect of the Christian experience. In *The Cocktail Party,* however, while the Negative Way is present in Celia's path to martyrdom, dramatic attention is divided equally between Celia's marriage to God and the Affirmative Way of Christian marriage represented by the Chamberlaynes.[14]

The case for the Way of Affirmation and its origin in

[14] Eliot's treatment of the two paths in his nondramatic poetry is to be found in *Four Quartets,* especially "Little Gidding" (1942). The following passage could stand as an epigraph to *The Cocktail Party* for it not only emphasizes the different paths taken by Celia and the Chamberlaynes and the state of "unknowing" from which they both start, but it also stresses another frequently overlooked aspect of the play, the use of a mastery of the past to attain Christian freedom from desire, a theme Eliot also used in *Murder in the Cathedral* and *The Family Reunion:*
There are three conditions which often look alike
Yet differ completely, flourish in the same hedgerow:
Attachment to self and to things and to persons, detachment
From self and from things and from persons; and, growing between
    them, indifference
Which resembles the others as death resembles life,
Being between two lives—unflowering, between
The live and the dead nettle. This is the use of memory:
For liberation—not less of love but expanding
Of love beyond desire, and so liberation
From the future as well as the past.
(*Complete Poems and Plays,* p. 142.) Even the structure of the play corresponds to the three conditions mentioned: Act One shows the state of indifference to God's will, Act Two shows the use of memory for liberation through the agency of Sir Henry, and Act Three presents the two conditions of "attachment" and "detachment."

the Doctrine of the Incarnation is perhaps best expressed by Charles Williams, who along with Eliot was an active member of the Anglo-Catholic intellectual movement of the period before and during the Second World War. This movement was profoundly interested in the role of the church in the social scheme of the modern world. The position put forth by this group has been discussed earlier; briefly, it consisted of an intense interest in the various movements of regionalism in the British Isles and in America and sought to establish a social plan built around the unit of indigenous communities held together politically, ethically, and spiritually by their geographic and religious bonds of kinship. It was commonly thought among Anglican intellectuals that, though the traditional emphasis in Western thought has been on the Negative Way, probably because of the influence of monasticism, the Way of Affirmation might prove to serve the function monasticism served in the Middle Ages. John Heath-Stubbs, in an introduction to the work of Charles Williams, expresses the concern churchmen felt during and after the Second World War when the preservation of Christian values became a matter of desperate immediacy:

"Monasticism arose as a result of the condition accompanying the breakdown of the Roman Empire. Men withdrew from the world for the sake of the world, in order to salvage, in safe refuges, something of the values which were everywhere being destroyed. We must be profoundly grateful that it was so. Today, European civilization is faced with a situation analogous to, yet also different from, that which heralded the approach of the Dark Ages. Perhaps once again it will be the task of the Christian Church to preserve for posterity our threatened values. But many believe that this can be done, not by a return to the monastic ideal, but by some organization of an essentially 'lay' kind, of Christian living and working in the world, yet under the law of Grace." [15]

In addition to the social implications of the Doctrine of the Incarnation, Williams described the Affirmative Way as the way of the poet and lover, and he cited Dante as the leading exponent of this path to salvation. In imitation of Dante, Williams extended the Affirmative Way to the doctrine of romantic love. He felt that the image of the beloved was for the lover, at the moment of first falling in love, an image of the divine perfection. Dante, he said in *The Figure of Beatrice* (1943),[16] saw Beatrice as God saw her, in the image of her perfection, that is, as she would have been had there been no Fall of Man and as she may potentially be when she is restored to heaven. But there were dangers in this Way. In *Descent into Hell* (1937) [17] he dealt with one of the most terrible of these dangers— the treatment of the beloved as a mere instrument upon which romantic emotion may be projected. The most difficult thing in the world, said Williams, was to realize that other people exist. The moment of falling in love was only the beginning of the Way, for the experiences of life and death entail a more complex series of affirma-

[15] John Heath-Stubbs, *Charles Williams* (London: Published for the British Council by Longmans, Green [1955]), p. 17.

[16] Charles Williams, *The Figure of Beatrice: A Study in Dante* (London: Faber and Faber Limited, 1943).

[17] Charles Williams, *Descent into Hell* (New York: Pellegrini & Cudahy, 1949).

tions. For Dante this process involved the acceptance of his beloved's marriage to another and her death; today the more usual kind of acceptance is of the responsibilities and disillusionments of marriage. John Heath-Stubbs describes the influence of Dante's conception of love on Williams' development of the Affirmative Way:

"There is, of course, much in common between this view of love, and that set forth by Plato in the *Symposium*. But the aim of the Platonic lover is to pass from the contemplation of phenomenal beauty in the person of the beloved to a purely intellectual and abstract ideal. Charles Williams' thought, however, is Christian, not Platonist. The aim of the Way is not the exaltation of Eros to a transcendent plane, but its transformation into Agape—Christian love within the framework of Christian marriage. Williams is bound by his belief in the Incarnation, which implies an affirmation of the importance of the particular, and of material experience. It may well be, as M. Denis de Rougemont has suggested, that the characteristic western view of Romantic love originated, among the Provençal troubadours, in heretical (Dualist) circles. But Dante brought what had hitherto been a purely secular ideal into harmony with the whole framework of medieval Catholic theology. This harmonization of Dante's Williams aimed to perpetuate, and to reinterpret for the world of today." [18]

It was Charles Williams' exposition of the two Ways which provided, I believe, the theological framework of *The Cocktail Party*. In *The Descent of the Dove* (1939)

[18] Heath-Stubbs, *Charles Williams*, p. 22.

Williams gave the following description of the two methods sanctioned by the ancient church for the achievement of salvation:

> "Both methods, the Affirmative Way and the Negative Way, were to co-exist; one might almost say, to co-inhere, since each was to be the key of the other. . . . The Communion of the Eucharist, at once an image and a Presence, was common and necessary to both. The one Way was to affirm all things orderly until the universe throbbed with vitality; the other to reject all things until there was nothing anywhere but He. The Way of Affirmation was to develop great art and romantic love and marriage and philosophy and social justice; the Way of Rejection was to break out continually in the profound mystical documents of the soul, the records of the great psychological masters of Christendom." [19]

The Cocktail Party reflects Eliot's attempt to cast the Christian idea of the two Ways, as well as Williams' multi-level conception of "falling in love," in the form of drawing-room comedy. Williams' assertion that the Communion of the Eucharist, "at once an image and a Presence," was common and necessary to both Ways may have been behind Eliot's use of the latter-day Communion service in the guise of a cocktail party.[20] The audience is introduced in the first act to a situation typical of the comedy of manners, including the customary extra-marital

[19] Charles Williams, *The Descent of the Dove: A Short History of the Holy Spirit in the Church* (reprinted ed.; New York: Meridian Books, 1956), pp. 57–58.

[20] D. E. Jones comments: "The cocktail party can be the secular counterpart of the Communion Service if given in the right spirit, the titbits and the short drinks the equivalent of the bread and wine. The play is almost a piece of metaphysical wit in its discovery of analogy in unlikely places" (*The Plays of T. S. Eliot*, p. 143).

amours and intra-marital quarrels of a couple in fashionable London society. The characters are also predictable comic types: the faithless husband and wife, their romantic partners, the dowager eager for gossip, the aging playboy, and the understanding friend of the family who acts as confidant.

The curtain opens on a cocktail party in full progress,[21] but while the host is in evidence, it soon becomes apparent through the insistent questioning of Julia and the clumsy avoidances of Edward, that the hostess is not only absent, but that she has left her husband. Edward has been forced to go on with a party he could not cancel in time. The only hint of mystery in the otherwise conventional events is the presence of a mysterious stranger who resists all of Julia's attempts to identify him. When the other guests have left, Edward confesses to the stranger that his wife has left him. Instead of sympathy, the guest gives his congratulations and when Edward becomes angry he receives the ominous reply that

> to approach the stranger
> Is to invite the unexpected, release a new force,
> Or let the genie out of the bottle.

[21] E. Martin Browne has described the conscientious efforts expended to make the first production as conventional as possible: "In the setting for *The Cocktail Party*, Anthony Holland gave a good conventional Shaftesbury Avenue idea of a West-End flat and consulting-room—and nothing more. The actors were dressed by the same firms who would clothe any comedy shown on the London Theatre Guide; cigarettes were by Abdulla and stockings by Kayser Bondor. When the curtain rose on the chatter of the cocktail party no one who had not read the name of the author would suspect that anything out of the ordinary was going to happen on that stage" ("From *The Rock* to *The Confidential Clerk*," *T. S. Eliot: A Symposium for His Seventieth Birthday*, ed. Neville Braybrooke, p. 64).

It is to start a train of events
Beyond your control.[22]

From the moment of this cryptic utterance the comic tone of the play is combined with a suggestion of the magical, of secret cures wrought by secret forces. The guest, by playing the devil's advocate, makes Edward realize that he must get his wife back in order to find out what has happened during their five years of marriage. "I must find out who she is, to find out who I am." Once Edward has made his decision, the mysterious guest announces that his wife will be returned in twenty-four hours.

The exhausted Edward, who wants only to be left alone, is bombarded by the good intentions of his friends who return one after another, in the rapid pace of farce, ostensibly to minister to his needs. In one interview after another the comic implications of the entangled relationships of the play are revealed. Peter confesses his love for Celia and Edward gives him second-hand the same advice which he had himself rejected from the stranger. The comic irony of Peter's confession is revealed when Celia returns and it becomes apparent that she and Edward have been having an affair. (When it later is made clear that Lavinia has been Peter's lover, the romantic circle of reversals is complete.) Celia, when she learns that Edward wants his wife back, realizes that she has loved the man she wanted Edward to be, not the man he really was.

When the twenty-four hours have elapsed and Edward is awaiting his wife's return, the guests of the party of the day before arrive, the unknown guest to remind Edward

22 Eliot, *Complete Poems and Plays,* p. 306.

[164]

of his decision, and Julia, Alex, Celia, and Peter with wires ostensibly from Lavinia summoning them to witness her return. When Lavinia arrives, however, she denies that she sent any wires and the aura of mystery is again renewed. The act ends with Edward and Lavinia again in discord, but forced to face their need to do something about their marriage.

Act Two takes place several weeks later in the consulting room of Sir Henry Harcourt-Reilly, who is revealed to be the unidentified guest at Edward's party. Alex and Julia, now seen to be in league with the doctor, have arranged appointments for Edward and Lavinia, and for Celia. By Sir Henry's magical ministrations Edward and his wife are reconciled in an uneasy union because, he tells them, they are "exceptionally well-suited to each other" since neither is equipped to be of any value to anyone else:

And now you begin to see, I hope,
How much you have in common. The same isolation.
A man who finds himself incapable of loving
And a woman who finds that no man can love her.[23]

Celia, on the other hand, finds in her consultation with the doctor that her real love affair is with God. She is sent to Sir Henry's "sanatorium" for which he found Edward and Lavinia unfit. The act ends with a libation drunk by Sir Henry, Julia, and Alex to the paths chosen by Edward, Lavinia, and Celia—toasts to the hearth and to the journey.

The last act is intended to demonstrate the outcome of the cures wrought by Sir Henry and the other guardians.

[23] *Ibid.,* p. 355.

The action takes place two years later just before another cocktail party given by the Chamberlaynes. This time, however, both Edward and Lavinia are present and at peace with each other. All of the guests of the first party appear except Celia, whose martyrdom while serving the natives of Kinkanja Alex reports. Celia's death acts as a spiritual catalyst to all those present whose lives had been involved with hers. Through Sir Henry's vision of the "triumph" of her death, Edward and Lavinia gain a new insight into the other path which they are not equipped to follow, while Peter has a glimmering perception that he might someday share her path. The play ends with the guardians hurrying off to attend another cocktail party, presumably to effect additional spiritual cures in other social circles.

Beneath the comic treatment of affairs of the heart, the playwright reveals the spiritual condition of the human creature and the possibility of the two Ways to salvation which can be achieved through Christian love. The point of the comic situations of unreciprocated love— Lavinia in love with Peter, Peter in love with Celia, Celia in love with Edward, and Edward in love with himself— is that the human condition without grace involves misguided and mismanaged attempts to "find oneself" through the adoration of the chimerical image of another. The author's point is not that the world is without love nor that the creature is without the capacity to seek love but rather just the reverse. The human creature is conceived with the necessity for love implicit in his being. His dilemma is that without grace, without the recognition of his dependence on God, he continually seeks improper objects for his love. When unregenerate man falls in love, his worship of another person is in reality a love affair with an image of his own needs. He denies the spark of divinity in other creatures and, like Narcissus, sees in the face of another a reflection of himself or, even worse, of the self he imagines he would like to be. From the Christian point of view this kind of love affair can lead only to the mutual disillusionment and destruction of both persons. The proper view of Christian love necessitates both the recognition of the spark of divinity in every other creature and the act of loving as a reflection of love for the creator.

In the several misguided love affairs of the play, the ramifications of improper loving are explored. Edward and Lavinia, as representatives of the Affirmative Way to Christian love, demonstrate in their early conduct the dangers in that path. When Edward feels the need to confess to someone that his wife has left him and chooses the stranger at his party, he hears, instead of flattering sympathy, the ugly truth about his own nature. When he insists that he wants his wife back, even though he had thought he was in love with Celia, Sir Henry points out to him that what he feels is not the loss of another person he loves, but rather the loss of his own personality. His own identity is insecurely based on the image he sees reflected back from his wife, rather than on knowledge of himself. Sir Henry confronts him with this unpleasant fact and describes how the loss of purely human love operates:

> There's a loss of personality;
Or rather, you've lost touch with the person

You thought you were. You no longer feel quite human,
You're suddenly reduced to the status of an object—
A living object, but no longer a person.
It's always happening, because one is an object
As well as a person. But we forget about it
As quickly as we can.[24]

When Edward demands to know where the doctor's un-asked for diagnosis leads, Sir Henry replies, "To finding out What you really are." Only by acknowledging that he is fundamentally defined by his relationship to the creator can the creature discover any stable ground for identity. Man without belief in the existence of the spirit can base his view of himself only on what others think him to be. Particularly in a non-Christian world, where spirit goes unacknowledged, he is likely to be treated merely as an object, a body without a soul, and he will soon find himself left with the suspicion that others are right and that he *is* only an object. The scene is intended to point out that a surer foundation than public opinion is necessary for spiritual selfhood. Only faith in the fatherhood of God can insure identity.

While Edward is incapable of loving, Lavinia is incapable of being loved. When they meet each other in Sir Henry's office, he reveals to both of them that they have been lying to him, to themselves, and to each other. Honesty is the first step in the cure for the "self-deceivers." Just as Edward's abandonment of Celia has forced him to admit that he did not love her, so Lavinia deceived herself in her feelings about her husband's unfaithfulness. Sir

[24] *Ibid.,* p. 307.

Henry points out that it was not the discovery of her husband's deception which prostrated her but rather the recognition that Peter loved Celia instead of her:

When you had to face the fact that his feelings towards her
Were different from any you had aroused in him—
It was a shock. You had wanted to be loved;
You had come to see that no one had ever loved you.
Then you began to fear that no one *could* love you.[25]

Thus, as Sir Henry says, both Edward and Lavinia as lovers of self and self-deceivers have in common "the same isolation" and are therefore admirably suited to each other. He agrees with Edward when he says that all they can do is make the best of a bad job but adds:

When you find, Mr. Chamberlayne,
The best of a bad job is all any of us make of it—
Except of course, the saints—such as those who go
To the sanatorium—you will forget this phrase,
And in forgetting it will alter the condition.[26]

Before Christian marriage can be achieved, Edward and Lavinia must learn the lesson expressed by Sir Henry: "We die to each other daily." Sir Henry tells Edward that he and his wife must meet as strangers and begin anew. By the end of the play they have mastered the past and have become different persons. The eternal nature of salvation is manifested by the perpetual possibility of their choices and the help awaiting in the form of the

25 *Ibid.,* p. 355.
26 *Ibid.,* p. 356.

guardians, once their choice to accept the conditions of the Affirmative Way has been made.

The plight of Celia and, to some degree, Peter, is different. Whereas people like Edward and Lavinia are concerned to find themselves and to make peace with their new identities, Celia and those who go to Sir Henry's "real" sanatorium are concerned to lose themselves in the larger identity of God. When Sir Henry explains to Edward and Lavinia why they are not fitted for his sanatorium, he says:

If I had sent either of you to the sanatorium
In the state in which you came to me—I tell you this:
It would have been a horror beyond your imagining,
For you would have been left with what you brought with
     you:
The shadow of desires of desires. A prey
To the devils who arrive at their plenitude of power
When they have you to themselves.[27]

In other words, the isolation Edward and Lavinia feel is caused by an absence of self-knowledge. They need the balm and comfort of Christian love and fellowship which is to be found in communion and marriage in order to attain the necessary knowledge of themselves. The saint, on the other hand, must endure the attacks by the "devils" because the goal of the Negative Way demands the dissolution of self in order to purify the spirit for union with God. The "real" sanatorium cures the disease of self.

Celia's interview with Sir Henry is the reverse of Edward's and Lavinia's. They insisted on the severity of their

[27] *Ibid.*

illness and, without understanding its true cause, were convinced that someone else was to blame. Celia, on the other hand, is afraid she is wasting the doctor's time. Her two symptoms are "an awareness of solitude" and "a sense of sin." The first has made her perceive the spiritual truth that man without God is separated from real understanding of others or himself:

No . . . it isn't that I *want* to be alone,
But that everyone's alone—or so it seems to me.
They make noises, and think they are talking to each
    other;
They make faces, and think they understand each other.
And I'm sure that they don't.[28]

Her sense of sin is connected with the Christian doctrine of atonement:

It's not the feeling of anything I've ever *done,*
Which I might get away from, or of anything in me
I could get rid of—but of emptiness, of failure
Towards someone, or something, outside of myself;
And I feel I must . . . *atone*—is that the word?[29]

Celia has been brought to this realization by her affair with Edward. She, unlike Edward and Lavinia, is capable of loving (she has loved Edward) and of being loved (she has been loved by Peter) but she realizes that she herself has created the object of her love:

           Can we only love
Something created by own own imagination?

[28] *Ibid.,* p. 360.
[29] *Ibid.,* p. 362.

Are we all in fact unloving and unlovable?
Then one *is* alone, and if one is alone
Then lover and beloved are equally unreal
And the dreamer is no more real than his dreams.[30]

Celia's disillusionment is based not so much on losing
Edward as on her fear that no love relationship can really
exist; she is puzzled, however, by her feelings of guilt at
not having found something which she is convinced must
be an illusion. Sir Henry replies that her condition is
curable, but that she must choose the form of treatment.
To accept the first cure, the Affirmative Way, she must
give up the ecstasy of her vision and be contented with

the morning that separates
And with the evening that brings together
For casual talk before the fire
Two people who know they do not understand each other,
Breeding children whom they do not understand
And who will never understand them.[31]

The second cure, the Negative Way, is a "terrifying journey" and requires courage:

The second is unknown, and so requires faith—
The kind of faith that issues from despair.
The destination cannot be described;
You will know very little until you get there;
You will journey blind. But the way leads towards pos-
session
Of what you have sought for in the wrong place.[32]

[30] *Ibid.*
[31] *Ibid.,* p. 364.
[32] *Ibid.,* pp. 364–65.

When Celia asks which of the two Ways is the better, Sir Henry replies that neither is better and that both are necessary and lonely:

> But those who take the other
> Can forget their loneliness. You will not forget yours.
> Each way means loneliness—and communion.
> Both ways avoid the final desolation
> Of solitude in the phantasmal world
> Of imagination, shuffling memories and desires.[33]

Celia chooses the second path and Sir Henry pronounces the same benediction, the dying Buddha's instruction to his disciples, that he has used for Edward and Lavinia, but he addresses Celia as "my daughter":

> Go in peace, my daughter.
> Work out your salvation with diligence.[34]

Celia has chosen to conduct her love affair with God rather than to be content with the reflection of God's love in the love of creature for creature. The price of looking directly into the face of light is great and blinds the lover to reflected glory.

As the Chamberlaynes' fulfillment of their chosen path is presented in the final act, so Celia's fulfillment of her path is described by Alex. The function of the story of her martyrdom serves a double dramatic purpose. It carries out the structural pattern of the play's spiritual "before" and "after" scheme, showing in Sir Henry's evaluation of the triumph of Celia's death the full meaning of the

33 *Ibid.*, p. 365.
34 *Ibid.*, p. 366.

eventuation of the Negative Way. At the same time it demonstrates in the attitude of the Chamberlaynes toward the event that their path has enabled them to "know that they do not know" what Celia's path involves. Lavinia notes that Sir Henry had an expression of "satisfaction" when he heard about Celia's death. Sir Henry replies by quoting the "magus Zoroaster" passage from Shelley's *Prometheus Unbound,* which describes the two worlds which coexist on either side of the grave and which account for the presence of ghosts or visions.[35] Sir Henry saw such a *Doppelgänger* of Celia when he first met her at the Chamberlaynes' first cocktail party:

I saw the image, standing behind her chair,
Of a Celia Coplestone whose face showed the astonishment
Of the first five minutes after a violent death.[36]

He explains that he did not foresee what sort of death because it was for Celia to choose "the way of life To lead to death." His function was to direct her in the way of preparation which, when accepted, led to her death. (Celia herself emphasized this conception of Christian freedom when, in her parting comment to Sir Henry, she said, "I know it is I who have made the decision.")

Both Edward and Lavinia feel a new sense of Christian responsibility and guilt for Celia's death, but Sir Henry explains to them that it is because they feel her death was

[35] Grover Smith notes that Eliot's source for this passage was Charles Williams' novel *Descent into Hell,* the first chapter of which contains part of the same passage and is entitled "The Magus Zoroaster" (*T. S. Eliot's Poetry and Plays,* p. 226).
[36] Eliot, *Complete Poems and Plays,* p. 384.

a waste that they feel themselves to blame; when they accept the fact that her death was triumphant they will be able to dismiss their sense of guilt about Celia.

The conclusion of the play emphasizes the harmony of diverse paths leading to a common spiritual goal. The quality of awareness which Edward and Lavinia feel comes from their new understanding of Celia's course and of their own. At first they do not want Julia, Sir Henry, and Alex to leave, nor do they want their party to begin, but once the first doorbell sounds Lavinia says, "Oh, I'm glad. It's begun." Eliot is attempting to point out that during the moment of awareness ordinary life seems impossible to endure, but once the moment of awareness recedes it is remembered as an interval of painful intensity and it is with a sense of relief that one again enters the everyday world. Most people experience the spiritual dimension of life only in these occasional moments and their understanding of the Celias must, of necessity, be limited. Nevertheless, each approach to God in some way involves the other; thus Eliot has composed a final scene which demonstrates the reciprocity.

Edward's and Lavinia's understanding of and sympathy for Peter is also an illustration of the circularity of salvation. They extend to him the benefit of their experience and wish to share his burden. Edward's comments contrast with those he made in the first act of the play when he offered Peter Sir Henry's second-hand advice as a means of getting rid of him. Now both Edward and Lavinia share with Peter the knowledge they have each learned. Peter has created an image of Celia which was based on his needs rather than on Celia's true nature.

Lavinia tells him that he must regard his love for her not as worthless, but as a new beginning. The play ends with a whole series of new beginnings, ranging from the beginning of the new cocktail party, finally fulfilling its true function of secular communion, to the beginning of a new series of cures to be carried out at another cocktail party by the departing guardians.

An additional feature of the author's plan for the integration of diversity is evident in his continued use of a mythical stratum of meaning in *The Cocktail Party*. Eliot himself, in "Poetry and Drama" (1951), announced as his Greek source the *Alcestis* of Euripides. He was determined, he said, to use his source "merely as a point of departure, and to conceal the origins so well that nobody would identify them until I pointed them out myself." [37] In this he succeeded, atlhough once the source has been pointed out the similarity of the *Alcestis* to the surface situation of *The Cocktail Party* becomes clear.[38] In the *Alcestis* Heracles arrives as an unknown guest at the house of Admetus and, unaware of the death of Alcestis, Admetus' paragon of a wife, makes himself unpopular with the king's servants by his revelry during the mourning of the household. When Heracles discovers that Alcestis has chosen to die in her husband's place and that Admetus, now realizing his loss, wants her back, Heracles, because of the hospitality extended to him in a time of suffering,

---

[37] Eliot, *On Poetry and Poets*, p. 91.

[38] Two studies which discuss in detail Eliot's use of Euripides are: Robert B. Heilman, *"Alcestis* and *The Cocktail Party,"* *Comparative Literature,* v (Spring 1955), 105–16; and William Arrowsmith, "The Comedy of T. S. Eliot," *English Stage Comedy,* ed. W. K. Wimsatt, Jr. (New York: Columbia University Press, 1955), pp. 148–72.

brings her back from the dead. Eliot has made clear that Sir Henry Harcourt-Reilly is his modern-day counterpart to Heracles:

"Those who were at first disturbed by the eccentric behaviour of my unknown guest, and his apparently intemperate habits and tendency to burst into song, have found some consolation in having their attention called to the behaviour of Heracles in Euripides' play." [39]

In Eliot's play Sir Henry first arranges for Lavinia's disappearance in order that both she and Edward may come to realize that "we die to each other daily" and that every moment is a new beginning.[40] Then, as an unknown guest at Edward's party, Sir Henry hears Edward's confession that his wife has left him, but warns him that to confess to a stranger may start a chain of occurrences which release mysterious (and, it is implied, divine) forces of which he is unaware. Sir Henry, as Heracles, then brings Lavinia back from "the dead" in order to begin the couple's spiritual cure. Lavinia's refusal to discuss where she has been corresponds to Alcestis' inability to speak until the third day after her return from the dead when she has been unsanctified by the appropriate rites. And

---

[39] Eliot, *On Poetry and Poets*, p. 91.

[40] Eliot has recently commented: "*The Cocktail Party* had to do with Alcestis simply because the question arose in my mind, what would be the life of Admetus and Alcestis be, after she'd come back from the dead; I mean if there'd been a break like that, it couldn't go on just as before. Those two people were the center of the thing when I started and the other characters only developed out of it. The character of Celia, who came to be really the most important character in the play, was originally an appendage to a domestic situation" ("The Art of Poetry I: T. S. Eliot," an interview by Donald Hall, *The Paris Review*, No. 21 [Spring-Summer 1959], p. 61).

just as Admetus does not know his wife at first, so Edward does not "know" Lavinia nor she him.

Beneath the surface analogies of the problems of marital love and sacrifice lies the same theme which Eliot has used in his other plays—the theme of renewal and rebirth —for *Alcestis* is a story of literal death and resurrection carried out by divine agency. The use of myth is thus intended, as it was in Eliot's earlier plays, to integrate the various levels of meaning implicit in the theme. Eliot uses the rebirth theme in the case of the Chamberlaynes to emphasize the daily rebirth which constitutes the Affirmative Way of Christian marriage. In the *Alcestis,* while Heracles' decision to rescue Alcestis from the regions of the dead makes up the chief dramatic action, Admetus had also been saved from death earlier by Apollo's arrangement of the ransom of another's life for the life of the king. Both husband and wife are saved from death just as Edward and Lavinia are both saved from spiritual death.

Moreover, Celia's story, the other end of the Christian continuum in *The Cocktail Party,* is also an echo of the *Alcestis* theme. As a representative of the Negative Way of Christian sainthood and martyrdom, Celia also suffers spiritual death and rebirth, but in reversed terms. In her discovery that she had loved an imagined creation of her own making, she suffers the death of her hopes for a life in the world, but in her acceptance of the Negative Way she is reborn in Christ. In her martyrdom she suffers physical death but achieves eternal life, just as she achieves another kind of Christian marriage in the union of the saint with God. Eliot saw both Celia's and Alcestis' ransom of their lives for others as analogous to the sacrifice of Christ. His desire to stress the literalness of the analogy is made clear by the crucifixion Celia endures.

Eliot's casting of his Heracles-figure as a doctor is a clear evidence of the ritual elements which form a framework of relevant clues for the religious meanings of *The Cocktail Party*. Sir Henry Harcourt-Reilly is the doctor of the ritual drama who achieves the return to life or the cure from sickness of the corrupted divine spirit. It is in this role that he brings Lavinia and Celia back to life. As the unknown guest he represents the eternal presence of divinity, and he is equipped to effect a cure of human lovesickness if his patients will only make the proper choices. The emphasis on choice for both the Chamberlaynes and Celia is another manifestation of the idea of Christian freedom. Choice is free for the Christian, but the price of the wrong choice is a state of death-in-life, while the reward of the right choice is ultimate illumination.

Sir Henry's ritual identity is suggested by his continual drink of gin with a drop of water (he is adulterating his spiritual nature with a drop of water, representing time, flux, and humanity). His buffoonery and bawdy revelry [41] are echoes of the traditional actions of the cook-doctor who hides his curative power and canny ability to outwit his opponents in the guise of a fool. As his helpers, both Alex and Julia share the traits of buffoonery. Julia is a

---

[41] According to Grover Smith, most versions of the song he sings, "One-Eyed Riley," are bawdy. Smith also discusses the ritual origins of Sir Henry (*T. S. Eliot's Poetry and Plays*, pp. 217–18).

busybody who knows all and leaves her spectacles and umbrella conveniently handy for her return at the most inopportune moments of intrigue. She is also responsible for Sir Henry's presence at the Chamberlaynes' party.

Alex, in the guise of a globe-trotting playboy, carries out the function of the ritual cook who is instrumental in the purification of the impure old god. The exotic dish he concocts out of the half-dozen eggs in Edward's kitchen suggests one of Eliot's favorite symbols, the egg as a sign of fertility. Even the farcical conversation between Julia and Alex which opens the play is filled with religious and ritual symbolism, such as wedding cake, champagne, and tigers (suggesting Eliot's Christ-the-tiger passage in "Gerontion").

The structural organization of the drama also reflects the ritual sequence. In the first act the corruption of the lovers and the distortion of spiritual love is evident at the first cocktail party and its aftermath. Even the party food is scarce, as Julia points out, suggesting spiritual starvation. Sir Henry's interviews with his patients in the second act are the equivalent of the ritual purgation of the impurities portrayed in the first act. The act ends with the libation drunk by Alex, Julia, and Sir Henry to the two Ways, as in the Greek ceremonial celebration of the purification feast. The third act presents the triumphant union and renewal of the Chamberlaynes and Celia and provides the groundwork for Peter's discovery of his Way. Eliot even presents a triumphal marriage procession, like that at the end of the ritual drama, when all the guests of the first party, except Celia, appear before the beginning of the second. The renewed marriage of the Chamberlaynes and the marriage of Celia with God are thus symbolically celebrated in ritual terms.

One final feature of Eliot's plan for the integration of diversity is evident in his treatment of the problems of poetic form in *The Cocktail Party*. He desired to create as part of his musical pattern a verse form flexible enough to allow freedom for the expression of a diversity of experience while it provided a basic rhythmic unity. In "Poetry and Drama" Eliot stresses that "the chief effect of style and rhythm in dramatic speech, whether in prose or verse, should be unconscious." This is especially true of verse drama today since it labors under the special handicap of suggesting artificiality to its audience. Thus verse drama should aim at a form of verse which can express everything that has to be said and a distinction should be made between "verse" and "poetry":

> "If our verse is to have so wide a range that it can say anything that has to be said, it follows that it will not be 'poetry' all the time. It will only be 'poetry' when the dramatic situation has reached such a point of intensity that poetry becomes the natural utterance, because then it is the only language in which the emotions can be expressed at all." [42]

It is important to recognize Eliot's distinction between verse and poetry because of the frequently expressed criticism of the unpoetic verse in his later plays, enforced, perhaps, by his own comment about *The Cocktail Party:* "I laid down for myself the ascetic rule to avoid poetry which could not stand the test of strict dramatic utility: with such success, indeed, that it is perhaps an open ques-

[42] Eliot, *On Poetry and Poets*, p. 78.

tion whether there is any poetry in the play at all." [43] But while the rule for *poetry* was "ascetic," *verse* was still present and was intended to do its job of unifying experience, even though the audience was not conscious of its presence.

In seeking models for his own development of this kind of dramatic verse, he returned again and again to the example of Shakespeare; Eliot's comments on his own drama from the time of *The Family Reunion* are sprinkled with references to Shakespeare's dramatic practice. In Shakespeare's plays he discovered a "musical design" which he describes in "Poetry and Drama" in his analysis of the verse of the opening scene of *Hamlet:*

> "This is great poetry, and it is dramatic; but besides being poetic and dramatic, it is something more. There emerges, when we analyse it, a kind of musical design also which reinforces and is one with the dramatic movement. It has checked and accelerated the pulse of our emotion without our knowing it. . . . The transitions in the scene obey laws of the music of dramatic poetry." [44]

This was an ideal which Eliot found worthy of modern emulation [45] and one which he himself described as the

---

[43] Raymond Williams points out that Eliot makes a joke at the expense of his "mundane verse" as well as his hidden meanings in *The Cocktail Party* when in the final act Sir Henry asks permission to "quote poetry" and Lavinia replies "I should love to hear you speaking poetry . . . if it answers my question" (*Drama from Ibsen to Eliot,* p. 243).

[44] Eliot, *On Poetry and Poets,* pp. 80–81.

[45] In "The Music of Poetry" (1942) Eliot says: "I believe that the properties in which music concerns the poet most nearly, are the sense

ultimate goal of poetic drama, "a design of human action and of words, such as to present at once the two aspects of dramatic and of musical order." It was also the ideal behind the complex plan of *The Cocktail Party*. But however productive as a dramatic ideal, its realization in Eliot's first comedy was not entirely successful. The complex system of analogies which formed the framework of his "musical" structure left his audience in a state of confusion rather than in the "condition of serenity, stillness and reconciliation" which he had hoped to induce. The chief fault lay in the intrusion of one level of meaning in another, on which the author had insisted in every drama he had thus far composed. The use of poetic allusion which Eliot had found so successful in his early nondramatic poetry was not directly transferable to the theater when it meant the destruction of a consistently believable dramatic surface. Despite the practices of Shakespeare in interrupting his dramatic surface, Eliot was forced to face the fact that he would have to choose between his dual dramatic goals of reaching a large and heterogeneous audience and including the startling entry of *deus ex machina* figures in the everyday world and cryptic references to levels of analogy which his audience did not understand. He made his choice in favor of the audience, and the dramatic result of that choice is to be seen in *The Confidential Clerk*.

---

of rhythm and the sense of structure. . . . There are possibilities for verse which bear some analogy to the development of a theme by different groups of instruments; there are possibilities of transitions in a poem comparable to the different movements of a symphony or a quartet; there are possibilities of contrapuntal arrangement of subject-matter" (*On Poetry and Poets*, p. 32).

CHAPTER VI

THE CONFIDENTIAL CLERK

WHEN *The Confidential Clerk* was presented at the 1953 Edinburgh Festival and soon after in New York, it was the "farce" or "high comedy" quality of the play which caused the most comment among audiences and critics.[1] While it was apparent to all observers that the author presented a dramatic surface with less to puzzle and more to entertain his audience, it was equally apparent that there was a serious purpose beneath Eliot's use of the age-old farce formula of the search for one's true parentage.[2] Eliot's desire to explore further the possibilities of comedy as a vehicle for his dramatic content is to

[1] That there was an intentional emphasis on farce style in the production has been made clear by E. Martin Browne: "From establishing in our minds the verse-rhythms, . . . we passed in rehearsal to the discovery of a style in which to play it. The plot, adapted from Euripides's *Ion*, produced a series of situations which seemed, on the naturalistic plane, increasingly improbable. . . . On the stage they reminded one of Gilbert or—yes—of Oscar Wilde. Here was the right indication for the players: the verse which was for us by now the foundation of the play's being must be matched in its rhythm by a rhythm of performance akin to the high comedy of the writer to whom words are weapons, and manners the garment of feeling" ("From *The Rock* to *The Confidential Clerk*," *T. S. Eliot: A Symposium for His Seventieth Birthday*, ed. Neville Braybrooke, p. 67).

[2] Walter F. Kerr, for example, commented on the purpose behind Eliot's new dramatic "tone of voice": "In order to help his perplexed characters discover their proper destinies, the author has caught them up in the machinery of old-fashioned farce: illegitimacy, mistaken identity, the long-lost child, the dishonest nurse, the astonished parent. Whether the old-fashioned farce was written by Menander, Plautus, Shakespeare or Molière, it always ended in the same way: the youngsters discovered who they were" ("T. S. Eliot Strolls the Same Garden," *New York Herald Tribune*, February 21, 1954, p. 1).

be accounted for by the same motive behind all of his
dramatic endeavors—the desire to find a dramatic form
which would be both artistically ordered and dramatically
satisfying to a popular audience. The seriousness of his
intention is indicated by his answer to an interview question asking why he had chosen to write his new play as
a comedy. Eliot replied: "If you want to say something
serious nowadays, it's easier to say it in comedy than in
tragedy. People take tragedy seriously on the surface. They
take comedy lightly on the surface but seriously underneath." [3] His comment and his director's efforts in match-
ing the play's "verse-rhythms" with the "rhythm of performance" of high comedy stress the rhythmic integration
Eliot desired to achieve between his comedy surface and
his religious meaning.

The vicissitudes of Eliot's conception of dramatic
rhythm and its function of uniting the levels of his
drama have been traced in the preceding chapters of this
study. It has been pointed out that his early efforts to
evolve a dramatic form which would be based on an elemental rhythm beneath both comedy and tragedy, together with his desire to create an ordered dramatic world,
led to his endorsement of the mythical method in order
to achieve an integration of the dramatic surface with the
spiritual depths of meaning. In his early dramatic works
the effect he sought was a kind of double-edged application of irony and analogy. Irony was achieved by stressing
the apparent contrast between the worldly and the religious interpretations of reality; at the same time, anal-

[3] Quoted by John Beaufort, " 'The Confidential Clerk' on Broadway," *Christian Science Monitor*, February 20, 1954, p. 16.

ogies with age-old religious rituals showed the hidden spiritual meanings beneath the most secular events. Thus Sweeney's state of awareness discredits the party world of Doris and Dusty and their desire for a good time, but at the same time the telling of fortunes and the party songs of island life become cryptic echoes of elemental religious impulses in the very midst of the corruption and unawareness of the party world. The use of the underlying purgation ritual of death and rebirth provided a structural formula which supported the analogy the author tried to achieve and also suggested that the origins of drama were themselves religious in nature. The final dramatic outcome was intended to be the transformation of one set of expectations and assumptions into another in order to lead the audience to a new awareness of spiritual truth.

Eliot's goal of transformation did not, however, take into consideration the practical limitations of the theater's ability to communicate and the audience's ability to understand such complexity. His efforts, therefore, to sustain an ordered dramatic surface while transforming the original dramatic situation into a new meaning did not meet with success. In particular, by choosing to dramatize the presence of supernatural forces in the natural world, he made it impossible to sustain a meaningful dramatic surface without which his works lost both their artistic unity and their audiences' involvement. Eliot's change to comedy in *The Cocktail Party* reflected his attempt to find a way around these problems by adopting a genre in which involvement was sacrificed to the supremacy of ideas and in which incongruities in the surface could be more easily tolerated. When, however, his divine agents, even though dressed in comic guise, seemed to have nothing but a distracting effect on his audiences, the playwright chose another comic form, society farce, in which the surface action was uninterrupted by spiritual intrusions and yet which demanded very little emotional involvement from the audience. Thus, in *The Confidential Clerk* divine interruptions were to be eliminated and instead the work of communicating the religious meanings was to be handled entirely by the symbolic meanings of the surface events. High comedy lent itself to this method because in the artificiality and refinement of its dramatic world the ordered flatness which Eliot had long admired but had so far failed to achieve could be used to create a fable which could be read on two levels. It could thus be "musical" [4] in the sense that the playwright's symbolic terms could communicate both the secular and the spiritual levels of meaning simultaneously, yet without disruption or contradiction of either by the other. The dual meanings of Eggerson's garden and Colby's musical nature, as well as the latter's search for his true parentage, are examples of such dramatic terminology.[5]

[4] Eliot's description of a "musical poem" as one "which has a musical pattern of sound and a musical pattern of secondary meanings of the words which compose it, and . . . [in which] these two patterns are indissoluble and one" is an example of the poet's application of this idea to other literary forms (*On Poetry and Poets*, p. 26).

[5] Denis Donoghue illustrates this process in the following comment: "In *The Cocktail Party* there were two worlds, the secular or neutral and the spiritual. Eliot named them unambiguously, the 'common routine' and the 'way of illumination.' The presentation of those worlds, it will be recalled, involved Eliot in the false tone of Celia's martyrdom and the resultant disruption of the play. In *The Confidential Clerk* there are again two worlds, but on this occasion no difficulty of tone or of doctrine arises, because instead of naming

In using the comic form to suit his own ends, Eliot took certain existing aspects of the high-comedy tradition and used them to point up his own set of spiritual meanings. He used the theme of the foundling child to express the Christian implications of the search for identity by insisting that discovering one's identity depends on discovering one's self to be a child of the heavenly Father. In addition, he used the improbability of farce to create a dramatic situation which could be resolved by magical revelations and divinely inspired insights unimpeded by the laws of probability, while at the same time using the reversals, recognitions, and reconciliations of comedy to stress the realization that the will of God often surprises the designs and desires of men. The introduction in the third act of Mrs. Guzzard in the role of the dishonest nurse who directly or indirectly holds the key to everyone's identity was intended to emphasize the operation of a divine purpose behind the scenes of our ordinary physical existence. Mrs. Guzzard is thus both the dishonest nurse and the fairy godmother, and her final questions are intentionally phrased in the language of wish-fulfillment. In the finale of the play she asks all of the characters their wishes and grants their requests by a standard

---

these worlds 'secular' and 'spiritual' Eliot presents them as 'Commerce' and 'Art.' This is a fine tactical move. Instead of tustling with his audience over thorny spiritual ground Eliot meets them in the inoffensive region which the play calls Art. Thus he ingratiates himself with his audience by introducing them into two worlds both of which they either know or can imagine; no doctrinal suspicions are aroused. The world of Art, unlike the world of Martyrdom and Beatitude, is at one and the same time 'special' enough to embody the higher reaches of aspiration and yet within the imaginative range of a secular audience" (*The Third Voice*, p. 149).

determined by higher considerations than self-interest or self-gratification.[6]

The other characters are also those of high comedy and are drawn with appropriate "flatness." Sir Claude Mulhammer, a London financier, is for the most part a stage nobleman characterized by his bafflement at the antics of his eccentric wife, Lady Elizabeth, who dabbles in occult religions. Though their marriage is childless, both have "mislaid" children whom they wish to discover or acknowledge, and much of the comedy of the play concerns their misdirected attempts to establish ties of parenthood. Sir Claude already possesses a true, but illegitimate, daughter, Lucasta Angel, whom he supports but does not publicly acknowledge. She is engaged to B. Kaghan, a brash young man of unknown origins with a great future in the City, who has been given his start by Sir Claude and who is later revealed to be Lady Elizabeth's true son, despite her dislike of him. It is Colby Simpkins, however, whom both Sir Claude and Lady Elizabeth desire to "adopt," Sir Claude believing him to be his son by a former mistress and Lady Elizabeth believing him to be her illegitimate child by a poetic guardsman. The climaxing reversal and recognition scene toward which the whole action builds is the discovery by Sir Claude and Lady Elizabeth of their true children and their relinquish-

---

[6] Mrs. Guzzard's divine origin as well as her mythical original is indicated by Eliot's reply to Alison Leggatt when she asked for help in interpreting the role for the London production. He told her that Mrs. Guzzard is "a mixture of Pallas Athene and a suburban housewife" (Alison Leggatt, "A Postscript from Mrs Chamberlayne and Mrs Guzzard," *T. S. Eliot: A Symposium for His Seventieth Birthday*, ed. Neville Braybrooke, p. 79).

ment of their claims on Colby, who finds himself to be the child of his heavenly Father.

The events of the plot are stylized in accord with the requirements of farce. The elaborate series of comic reversals begins with Sir Claude's attempt to introduce to Lady Elizabeth his plans for adopting Colby; Colby is first to take Eggerson's place as Sir Claude's confidential clerk. The trusted Eggerson is to break the news of his successor to Lady Elizabeth on her return home from a trip to her latest master of "mind control" in Switzerland. Sir Claude's reason for not revealing Colby's identity to his wife earlier in their marriage is not that he feared to admit his early indiscretions, nor that he feared her jealousy of his former mistress, but rather, by a charming comic reversal, that because of Lady Elizabeth's "strong maternal instinct" he was afraid she would be jealous of his possession of *two* children, while she had only one, who remains lost.

Despite the careful preparations for her arrival, Lady Elizabeth upsets all expectations by arriving early, then promptly decides that *she* has selected Colby as Eggerson's successor and changes his first name to his last to suit her whim. On a slim thread of evidence, she convinces herself that Colby is her son, not Sir Claude's. In different ways Lucasta and B. Kaghan also try to "adopt" Colby, Lucasta by wishing to find her own identity by becoming a part of Colby's existence, and B. by wishing to enter into a business partnership with him. Only Eggerson recognizes Colby's true direction and identity as a person of potentially religious commitment.

The meaning of the play's events is centered in these

attempts of the other characters to change Colby into an image of what they want him to be without regard for his own nature. Sir Claude, convinced that Colby is his son, wishes to have him follow in his footsteps, as Sir Claude had followed in *his* father's footsteps. He sees in Colby's acceptance of the position of private secretary and his relinquishment of his frustrated desire to become a truly great organist a repetition of his own youth; he confesses to Colby that he himself had been a frustrated potter but had given up his art and joined his father in business when he realized that he would always be a second-rate artist.

Colby, however, is not entirely satisfied with his new identity, nor with the fragmentation of his personality which he sees taking place:

I'm not at all sure that I like the other person
That I feel myself becoming—though he fascinates me.
And yet from time to time, when I least expect it,
When my mind is cleared and empty, walking in the
    street
Or waking in the night, then the former person,
The person I used to be, returns to take possession. . . .[7]

The experience of watching oneself act out a part has long been one of Eliot's representations for the loss of identity which can only be found again in relation to God. The same theme was developed in the problems of identity experienced by Celia and the Chamberlaynes in *The Cocktail Party.*

Sir Claude, however, insists that one must accept the terms and the roles which life imposes. A new life begins,

[7] T. S. Eliot, *The Confidential Clerk* (New York: Harcourt, Brace and Company, 1954), p. 45.

he explains, as a kind of make-believe and "the make-believing makes it real." Sir Claude is convinced that he made the right decision, for though he hated the business world for which his father had a passion, he came to believe that his father had been right. But his realization came too late, and the recognition that he had harbored a secret reproach against his father while he lived made him wish to atone after his death:

> And all my life
> I have been atoning. To a dead father,
> Who had always been right. I never understood him.
> I was too young. And when I was mature enough
> To understand him, he was not there.[8]

But though his professional life is an atonement to a dead father, Sir Claude has as an escape a secret room where he houses his "collection." The religious impulse behind his aesthetic terminology is clear:

> Most people think of china or porcelain
> As merely for use, or for decoration—
> .   .   .   .
> For me, they are life itself. To be among such things,
> If it is an escape, it is escape into living,
> Escape from a sordid world to a pure one.
> Sculpture and painting—I have some good things—
> But they haven't this . . . remoteness I have always
>   longed for.
> I want a world where the form is the reality,
> Of which the substantial is only a shadow.[9]

[8] *Ibid.,* p. 48.
[9] *Ibid.,* pp. 46–47.

He recognizes his experience as a substitute for religion, just as Lady Elizabeth's "investigations" are her substitute, but in his "sense of identification with the maker" of his art works he finds an "agonizing ecstasy" which makes life bearable. He is unable to achieve, however, an integration of his two lives:

I dare say truly religious people—
I've never known any—can find some unity.
Then there are also the men of genius.
There are others, it seems to me, who have at best to live
In two worlds—each a kind of make-believe.
That's you and me. . . .[10]

He seeks in his private world of form a reality which is purer and more "real" than the visible world and its experiences, and he uses the terminology of Christian neo-Platonism—identification with the maker of the forms—to describe his ecstasy in his world of pure form. He hopes that Colby as his son will follow his course and find in his private experience of music an escape into reality by going "through the private door" into "the real world." Colby, however, is unable to accept the terms of Sir Claude's solution because he does not feel, and thus cannot accept, the full burden and obligation of sonship to the man whom he knows only as a distant patron in the years of childhood.

The terminology of Sir Claude's and Colby's discussion of the relationship of earthly fathers and sons—atonement, and reconcilement after death which perfects the relationship—makes clear that it is patterned on the rela-

[10] *Ibid.*, p. 50.

tionship to the heavenly Father, just as the love of husband and wife in *The Cocktail Party* was shown to be based on the pattern of divine love. Their discussion illustrates the transparent terms used in the play both to express the dramatic events of the surface action and to suggest religious analogies below the surface. The terminology of art to suggest religious experience is made explicit in Sir Claude's statement on the forms behind reality, but it is also present in the unstated conclusion that Sir Claude as a second-rate "potter" is an inadequate substitute for the Fatherhood of God, the original Potter. Colby, in the same way, is "musical" in the literal sense in the play but also in the sense that he cannot accept the fragmentation of his spiritual life which Sir Claude's part-time ecstasy and make-believe existence would necessitate. He needs a musical order in his life which can be supplied only by God.

As the first act has developed Sir Claude's attempt to make Colby his son, the second act develops the equally persistent attempts of Lucasta and Lady Elizabeth to claim him. Colby, looking behind Lucasta's flippant coquetry, discovers her lack of security and identity. By admitting that she hardly feels that she is a person, Lucasta experiences an intimacy in the honesty of their relationship which she has not felt before. She begins to believe that Colby, because he possesses a secret garden of music, could provide her with the sense of identity she has always lacked. She envies and wishes to share his ability to retire into a world of private meaning. But Colby demands more unity of existence than a private garden can afford him. He tries to descibe to Lucasta the unreality he experiences even in his musical garden:

And yet, you know, it's not quite real to me—
Although it's as real to me as . . . this world.
But that's just the trouble. They seem so unrelated.
I turn the key, and walk through the gate,
And there I am . . . alone, in my "garden."
Alone, that's the thing. That's why it's not real.
You know, I think that Eggerson's garden
Is more real than mine.[11]

Colby perceives that of all the people in the world of the play only Eggerson has achieved the integration of ecstasy and responsibility. When he retires to his garden he does not feel alone there, for when he comes out again he brings "marrows, or beetroot, or peas" for Mrs. Eggerson. Eggerson's garden is "part of one single world," whereas Colby's music and Sir Claude's art form gardens which have nothing to do with their other lives and thus cause both lives to be "unreal." When Lucasta asks Colby what he wants instead, he replies, "Not to be alone there":

If I were religious, God would walk in my garden
And that would make the world outside it real
And acceptable, I think.[12]

Eliot used the image of the garden to represent the escape into ecstasy as early as the "hyacinth girl" passage in *The Waste Land* and later in "Ash Wednesday" and "Burnt Norton." It also appears in Harry's rose garden in *The Family Reunion* and in the magic forest where Celia seeks a lost treasure in *The Cocktail Party*. In Eliot's latest play, *The Elder Statesman,* the setting for Lord Claverton's mastery of the past through love is the sanatorium's

[11] *Ibid.,* p. 64.
[12] *Ibid.,* p. 65.

garden of memory. In Eliot's early uses of this image his emphasis was on the transitory and even illusory quality of remembered bliss, and he frequently portrayed the experience of ecstasy in sexual terms. This, the poet implied, was all that humanity had salvaged from the original Garden of Eden, where physical love and spiritual love were not separated and sexual and religious fertility were one. It is indicative of a significant change in Eliot's view of religious experience that, whereas earlier the garden of remembered bliss was opposed to the experience of everyday living, in *The Confidential Clerk* the earlier secret rose garden is rejected by Colby in favor of the totality of Eggerson's garden, where God walks among the vegetables. The rose has become "marrows, or beetroot, or peas" and, while less exotic, the products of the new garden are more useful in satisfying the needs of everyday existence.

In *The Confidential Clerk* the garden image is also used to differentiate those characters who can discover a sense of selfhood which will allow an integration of religious and secular experience from those characters who cannot. B. Kaghan and Lucasta have no private gardens and must depend on others to give them their roles in life. Sir Claude and Lady Elizabeth possess private gardens in which they can escape from the rest of their existence in order to find a temporary order and meaning. Only Eggerson has a garden which satisfies the needs of both realms simultaneously. Colby, presented in the course of the play with these three approaches to selfhood, must finally make his choice among them. The possibility of a love affair and marriage to Lucasta represents a purely secular resolution of the problem. But just as Harry's momentary desire to find purely human happiness with his cousin Mary in *The Family Reunion* is thwarted by the appearance of the Furies, so here the playwright contrives a dramatic equivalent in terms of farce techniques to thwart the developing human love affair between Colby and Lucasta. Since farce revolves around the search for identity and the discovery of paternity, Eliot has chosen to resolve this potential threat to his hero's spirituality by using a time-honored device of farce—the discovery that the lovers are really brother and sister. While this revelation is proved by the events of the third act to be false (Colby is *not* Sir Claude's son and thus not Lucasta's half-brother), Eliot wishes, I think, to use the brother-sister resolution to emphasize the hidden meaning beneath the farce surface, namely that Colby's future includes not human marriage but human brotherhood based on Colby's *divine* union with God.

The second half of the second act develops Lady Elizabeth's attempt to impose on Colby her method of coming to terms with life, as Sir Claude and Lucasta have earlier attempted to do. Her endeavors are intentionally cast in the fast-paced repartee of high comedy, and the effect is both to emphasize and caricature the pattern of "adopting" Colby established by Sir Claude and Lucasta. Lady Elizabeth has decorated Colby's flat in colors ostensibly chosen to suit his "spiritual" needs; in reality she knows nothing of his real spiritual needs and chooses his colors as she chooses his identity—to match the imaginary Colby she has created to suit her own needs. Lady Elizabeth is probably Eliot's best comic character and in an irresistibly funny parody of the earlier scenes of childhood revelations she compares her childhood with Colby's. She insists on finding similarities and thus spiritual affinities where there are only differences, and when Colby points out that there is a fundamental dissimilarity in the fact that he did not know his parents while she had many relatives, Lady Elizabeth, undaunted, answers:

These are only superficial differences:
You must have been a lonely child, having no relatives—
No brothers or sisters—and I was lonely
Because they were so numerous—and so uncongenial.

.   .   .   .

I didn't want to belong there. I refused to believe
That my father could have been an ordinary earl!
And I couldn't believe that my mother *was* my mother.[13]

Beneath the comedy of this scene lies a set of seriously proposed Christian analogues. When Lady Elizabeth confesses to Colby that as a child she had liked to think of herself as a foundling or a "changeling," she reflects the universal isolation and loneliness of man until he recognizes his spiritual Father. She explains that she first took up the "Wisdom of the East" because the doctrine of reincarnation seemed to solve the problem of identity:

That was only a phase. But it made it all so simple!
To be able to think that one's earthly parents
Are only the means that we have to employ
To become reincarnate. And that one's real ancestry
Is one's previous existences. Of course, there's something
     in us,

[13] *Ibid.*, pp. 86–87.

In all of us, which isn't just heredity,
But something unique. Something we have been
From eternity. Something . . . straight from God.
That means that we are nearer to God than to anyone.[14]

The impulse behind Lady Elizabeth's occult pursuits from the "Wisdom of the East" to "mind control" is genuinely religious, but she is looking in the wrong place for divine guidance; in the terms of the play, she is traveling abroad to study mind control rather than remaining at home to master spirit control. As the mythical stratum of the play is to make clear, Lady Elizabeth has a spiritual doctor nearer at hand than the Swiss doctors she has been visiting.

Lady Elizabeth succeeds in convincing herself, on the evidence of Mrs. Guzzard's picture, that Colby is really her misplaced son, and the second act concludes with the comic reversal produced by her insistence on her claim to Colby after Sir Claude has so carefully prepared his wife to accept Colby as his son.

Colby's reaction to the haggling over possession of him is not the state of "acute agony" which Sir Claude expects, but rather a state of numbness. Never having had parents as a child, Colby experiences a "gap that never can be filled" by human parents, and certainly not by the two potential parents who wish to claim him. He says to Lady Elizabeth:

At the time when I was born, your being my mother—
If you are my mother—was a living fact.
Now, it is a dead fact, and out of dead facts

14 *Ibid.*, p. 87.

Nothing living can spring. Now, it is too late.
I never wanted a parent till now—
I never thought about it. Now you have made me think,
And I wish that I could have had a father and a mother.[15]

For the first time Colby is seized by a desire to know who
his true parents were because he desires to replace the
"dead fact" with a living fact of his true identity. Behind
these events and the play's theme of the discovery of sonship lies the suggestion that man has a dual nature which
is part human and part divine. He is born of earthly parents but his devotion belongs primarily to his heavenly
Father, and his bond of love and obedience to his earthly
parents derives its meaning primarily from his duty to
God.

Eliot's thinking on the subject of the relationship between man's duty to his earthly father and to his heavenly
Father can be seen in his discussion of the quality of
pietas in "Virgil and the Christian World" (1951). Aeneas'
relationship to his father is characterized by filial piety,
which is more than personal affection:

"There is personal affection, without which filial piety
would be imperfect; but personal affection is not piety.
There is also devotion to his father as his father, as his
progenitor: this is piety as the acceptance of a bond
which one has not chosen. The quality of affection is
altered, and its importance deepened, when it becomes
love *due* to the object. But this filial piety is also the
recognition of a further bond, that with the gods, to
whom such an attitude is pleasing: to fail in it would be

[15] *Ibid.*, p. 98.

[200]

to be guilty of impiety also towards the gods. The gods must therefore be gods worthy of this respect; and without gods, or a god, regarded in this way, filial piety must perish. For then it becomes no longer a *duty:* your feeling towards your father will be due merely to the fortunate accident of congeniality, or will be reduced to a sentiment of gratitude for care and consideration." [16]

Eliot concludes that an essential element in the piety of Aeneas is an attitude which is "an analogue and foreshadow of Christian humility," for as a "fugitive from a ruined city and an obliterated society" his only reward is the fulfillment of his destiny. Eliot views him as "the prototype of a Christian hero" for he suffers and acts only in obedience. He is "a man with a mission; and the mission is everything." [17] Colby is also a man with a mission, although, like Aeneas, he does not know what that mission is, and he thus becomes in the play Eliot's portrayal of the Christian hero.

The third act presents, in a grand finale of revelations

---

[16] *Eliot, On Poetry and Poets,* pp. 142-43.

[17] Another of Virgil's ideas "which render him peculiarly sympathetic to the Christian mind" is his assertion of "the importance of good cultivation of the soil for the well-being of the state both materially and spiritually." This led, says Eliot, to the principle behind Christian monasticism—"the principle that action and contemplation, labour and prayer, are both essential to the life of the complete man." In *The Confidential Clerk* Eggerson's garden, which is a place for both work and prayer, represents this Virgilian ideal of the integration of the spiritual and the material. This conception of integration is also connected with Eliot's ideas on social organization as expressed in *The Idea of a Christian Society* and *Notes towards the Definition of Culture.* Eliot notes that Virgil's use of the word *pietas* "implies an attitude towards the individual, towards the family, towards the region, and towards the imperial destiny of Rome" as well as toward the gods. (*On Poetry and Poets,* pp. 141-42.)

about misplaced children, lost parents, and wishes gratified in unexpected ways, Colby's discovery of his Christian identity which is to provide him with the first step toward his future spiritual mission. Mrs. Guzzard has been summoned to reveal the true facts of Colby's parentage, and the shift from human desire to divine resolution is executed by changing the chief dramatic focus from the parents and children to Mrs. Guzzard and Eggerson. Sir Claude symbolically relinquishes his control by putting Eggerson in the role of chairman of the proceedings and seating him behind the desk where Sir Claude had sat in the first act.

The discovery of new identities extends to all of the chief characters. Before Mrs. Guzzard's arrival, Lucasta announces her decision to marry B. Kaghan, an act which represents her recognition of the limitations and potentialities of her own nature. Her revelation that she had been interested in Colby causes everyone shock, but especially Sir Claude, who is forced to admit that in his effort to adopt a new child he has neglected to get to know his own true child.

Mrs. Guzzard reveals that Lady Elizabeth's lost son is not Colby but B. Kaghan, whom she has never taken the trouble to know. Nor is Colby Sir Claude's son, but rather Mrs. Guzzard's own child whom she wished to establish in life by deceiving Sir Claude about his identity. Sir Claude and Lady Elizabeth in their disillusionment discover their mistakes and something about their own natures. Sir Claude, so certain earlier of the rightness of his course as a model for Colby to follow, comes to realize that perhaps he had not truly followed his father's ideal by taking up finance. He says to Lady Elizabeth:

> What he wanted to transmit to me
> Was that idea, that inspiration
> Which to him was life. To me, it was a burden.
> You can't communicate an inspiration,
> Like that, by force of will. He was a great financier—
> And I am merely a successful one.
> I might have been truer to my father's inspiration
> If I had done what I wanted to do.[18]

Sir Claude and Lady Elizabeth come to a new understanding of each other as well. Each realizes that he has assumed things about the other which he wished to believe. Sir Claude believed his wife to be a "Lady" who wanted a husband of importance and would despise an artist. He finds out that her real desire in life was "to inspire an artist." Lady Elizabeth, on the other hand, had believed that her husband was interested in nothing but financial affairs when in reality he longed to be the artist that she might have inspired. Actually, their needs are complementary, but because each acted on false assumptions about the other, they frustrated rather than satisfied each other's desires. Their joint conclusion, pointed up in the aphoristic and mannered style of comedy is that "It's a great mistake . . . For married people to take anything for granted."

The resolution of Colby's problem of identity comes when Mrs. Guzzard grants Colby's wish to have a father

---

[18] Eliot, *The Confidential Clerk*, p. 105.

whose image he could create for himself. She tells him that his father was a disappointed musician, a man who died "obscure and silent." Colby thus feels himself free to pursue his music, and he accepts Eggerson's offer, as the "Vicar's Warden," of the position of church organist at Joshua Park. Colby thereby becomes the spiritual son of Eggerson, who predicts that he will not spend a lifetime as an organist but will find that he has "another vocation" which will lead to his "reading for orders." Thus while the wishes granted by Mrs. Guzzard are different from the previous desires of the wishers, they lead to a resolution fitted to Christian comedy. The members of the older generation realize their mistakes and the members of the younger generation choose more wisely and with more self-understanding than their chastened elders. A new conception of the meaning of Christian marriage has been realized by the couples of both generations, and Sir Claude and Lady Elizabeth can expect to establish the familial ties with their "new" children which they hoped to establish with Colby. Colby himself must follow the higher mission of pursuing sonship of another Father in whose image all human bonds have their meaning. The play thus ends with an endorsement of both the order of the Christian family and the more "musical" pursuit of the "orders" of the church as valid paths to salvation.

The Christian implications of the events and characters of *The Confidential Clerk* become clearer when their prototypes in Eliot's Greek source, Euripides' *Ion,* are examined. The *Ion* is also a story of a misplaced child and the conflicting parental claims upon him. In the prologue to the Greek play it is revealed that Apollo had once ravished Creusa, princess of Athens, and the child Ion was born of the union. Creusa abandoned the child to the elements, expecting him to die of exposure but Apollo, unwilling to see his own son destroyed, sent Hermes to rescue Ion and take him to the shrine at Delphi to be reared by the priestess and to become a servant of Apollo at the temple. Creusa, meanwhile, had married Xuthus, never revealing the birth of her child by the god. The action of the play takes place years later when Creusa and Xuthus, their marriage childless, journey to the oracle to ask for aid. Apollo, wishing Ion to claim his birthright of the kingdom of Athens, reveals to the king through the oracle that the first person he meets after leaving the temple will be his natural son. Apollo plans to reveal Ion's identity secretly to his mother later. Xuthus meets Ion outside the temple and, embracing him as his son, plans to take him home and establish him as his heir. Ion, however, is not eager to leave his sacred life for the wealth and power of life at court. He points out to Xuthus that Creusa may be displeased by being forced to accept her husband's child, but the king tells him that he must learn to be happy with his lot. Xuthus plans to keep Ion's identity secret until he can gain the approval of Creusa, but before this can be accomplished, the chorus interferes and tells the queen of Xuthus' new son. In her jealousy and anger at Apollo for favoring her husband, she plans the murder of Ion, but when her plan miscarries she is forced to seek refuge at the altar of the god. She is met there by Ion seeking vengeance, but before he can take action the altar priestess intervenes and, showing the cradle, wrappings, and birth trinkets, reveals to mother and son their true relationship. In disbelief, Ion asks Apollo directly for the truth and the god sends Pallas Athene to confirm Ion's parentage and his inheritance.

In Eliot's version of this story Colby is, of course, Ion and Lady Elizabeth and Sir Claude the childless Creusa and Xuthus. Colby, born of the union of humanity and divinity,[19] has an obligation to both worlds, but whereas in Euripides' play Ion must accept his human heritage and leave the altar of Apollo, Eliot focuses the interest of his plot on the divine parentage of his hero which takes precedence over every human relationship. Both plays, however, emphasize the point that human desires are not always fulfilled as men would wish but instead as the gods determine. Just as Apollo does not wish his son to go without his birthright, so the Christian God finds a birthright for Colby superior to that of wealth or power, and at the play's end Eggerson becomes Colby's substitute father.[20]

[19] Eliot's use of the *Ion* suggests that he wished to merge the child-of-divinity theme present in Euripides' play with the ritual hero's search for his parentage which he discovers to be partly divine. (See Lord Raglan's *The Hero*, pp. 178–221.) The statement of the young Jesus that he must be about his Father's business, a phrase which echoes unspoken behind many of the speeches in *The Confidential Clerk*, is a Christian instance of this idea.

[20] Grover Smith in *T. S. Eliot's Poetry and Plays*, pp. 237–43, argues that Eliot based his changes in his source on A. W. Verrall's controversial interpretation of Euripides' *Ion:* "Verrall's rationalistic interpretation of the play affected the plot of *The Confidential Clerk*. His main points may be summarized as follows: First, that Hermes and Athena cannot be trusted, because Euripides always depicted the gods as frauds. Second, that for the same reason Ion is not the son of Apollo. Third, that the tokens identified by Creusa do not constitute trustworthy evidence and that the recognition scene is stage-managed by the priestess to avert the impiety of a crime on the altar. Fourth,

Lady Elizabeth and Sir Claude, like Creusa and Xuthus, have a childless marriage, but both have lost children earlier whom they desire to discover. In *The Confidential Clerk* Lucasta and B. Kaghan, the "true" children of the Mulhammers, replace Colby, who as the child of Apollo follows *his* true father. Thus Colby inherits his "musical" nature naturally, or, more accurately, supernaturally, as the child of the god of music. As Ion was reared by the temple priestess of Apollo, Colby has been raised by Mrs.

---

that although Creusa accepts the solution because it is what she wants, Ion is not her son. Fifth, that Ion is the son of Xuthus. Sixth, that the priestess knows this fact to be true because one of the temple women, perhaps herself, is Ion's mother. Euripides . . . expected the wisest of his audience to see through the duplicities of the oracle and to be scornful of fanaticism." Smith, finding Verrall's view "plausible," asserts that Eliot, following Verrall, "let his resolution depend on imperfect evidence and even on possible trickery by certain of the characters. When scrutinized, the questions of doubtful parentage permit answers far different from those believed by the leading personages and by the average audience." Smith concludes that Colby is Sir Claude's son, not Mrs. Guzzard's, but that Mrs. Guzzard lies in order to allow Colby to adopt the profession he desires. Smith's conclusions seem to me to be based on unconvincing conjectures and questions foreign to the world of farce, such as whether Mrs. Guzzard could produce the proper documents as proof of her statements and "whether her [Mrs. Guzzard's sister's] child could have been carried to term." In addition, it seems very unlikely that Eliot would wish to appropriate the approach of the rationalist Verrall, when the more conventional interpretation of the *Ion* suited his purposes more exactly. Smith's hypothesis may reflect William Arrowsmith's discussion of the process of "transfiguration" of one level of meaning into another in the plays of Euripides and Eliot ("Transfiguration in Eliot and Euripides," *Sewanee Review*, LXIII, No. 3 [1955], 421–42). While Arrowsmith describes Verrall's theories, he carefully avoids asserting that Eliot used Verrall's interpretations. In conversation, Arrowsmith has indicated to me that he asked Eliot if he had read or had used Verrall's arguments in his plays. Eliot replied that he was familiar with Verrall's ideas but that he had never consciously used them in his plays.

Guzzard, and her role as granter of divinely approved wishes comes from Eliot's merging of Apollo's priestess and Pallas Athene into one character.[21]

Although Eliot has avoided supernatural disruptions of the play's surface, important elements of the ritual scheme still remain in *The Confidential Clerk*. Renewal by divine agency is still the fundamental dramatic theme, although the author has now expanded his conception of the meaning of renewal beyond the ascetic confines expressed in his first plays. The secular renewal portrayed in *The Confidential Clerk* is achieved by the rejection of the false substitutes tried by the older generation—Sir Claude's attempt to atone to his dead father in the wrong way and Lady Elizabeth's inadequate efforts to find religious inspiration —and the replacement of these false aspirations by the understanding of one's own nature and of one's own family. The domestic circle is fuller in *The Confidential Clerk* than in *The Cocktail Party* because the dramatist has added the relationship of parents and children to his earlier treatment of Christian marriage as a means of following the Affirmative Path to salvation. Thus the marriage relationships of both the older and the younger couple will be complemented by their mutual roles as parents and children; Colby's renewal will be of a different kind—the consecration of a life of service to the musical principle of the spirit.

But more remains of Eliot's early enthusiasm for the

[21] To those members of the audience familiar with the source there is an excellent comic effect in some of Eliot's "revisions" of the *Ion*. Two examples are the conversion of the priestess of Apollo and Pallas Athene into a suburban housewife and Creusa, princess of Athens, into an English dowager.

Greek ritual drama than a generalized re-use of its theme. In my opinion, the only satisfactory explanation of the role played in *The Confidential Clerk* by Eggerson is one which recognizes his ritual origins.[22] The importance of Eggerson's function is indicated both by the title of the play and by the fact that the action and the theme of the play are stated in the events surrounding Sir Claude's outgoing and incoming confidential clerks. Moreover, Eggerson, whose name itself suggests his ritual source, invariably appears, almost miraculously, at the most crucial moments of the play. He is indispensable to Sir Claude and is called up from "retirement" in the country to assist in the delicate matters of paternity and identity. Sir Claude desires his help in making Colby his legal son and heir. Eggerson, however, though deferential, continually reminds Sir Claude of Colby's spiritual predisposition and his musical

[22] There has been much critical puzzlement over the role of Eggerson in *The Confidential Clerk*. C. L. Barber, for example, frankly admits his bafflement: "Eggerson, whose nod is final, is the one character I have difficulty with. He is . . . a Christian adaptation of the Admirable Crichton. That is to say, he is a better man than his boss but never shows it because of the admirable class system. . . . It may be only my American middle class prejudice against the whole English lower middle class, but these lines [in which Eggerson offers the post of church organist and predicts Colby's clerical future] seem to me to be silly. It would perhaps be sillier still to say the same thing with deep ecclesiastical pedal-point; no matter what local habitation and name Eliot might decide to give religion, there will be the difficulty that troubling social concomitants come into play. The aim with Eggerson is to show how the church transcends class lines, for this is the first moment where Eggerson has stepped out of the role of perfectly disciplined, self-effacing helpfulness. . . . Perhaps in Eggerson Eliot *has* salvaged for his own purposes the stock role of perfect servant. But even if one can forgive the simper, it is troubling to have Christian selflessness so nearly indistinguishable from servile selflessness" ("The Power of Development . . . in a Different World," in

nature. Throughout the play only Eggerson sees that Col-by's future lies in the acceptance of the orders of the church. Eggerson's gift of foresight also extends to knowl-edge of the futures of other characters, for he predicts the marriage of Lucasta to B. Kaghan. It is also significant that in the abortive "love scene" between Colby and Lu-casta it is Eggerson's unity of existence that Colby cites as an ideal that he would like to emulate. At the end of the play when Colby accepts Eggerson's offer of a position as church organist and a place in Eggerson's home at Joshua Park, he exchanges the sonship of Sir Claude for the sonship of Eggerson.

These and other evidences point to Eggerson's identity as a spiritual agent whose function is to assist the neophyte on his way toward God; his role parallels that of Agatha, Mary, and the doctor in *The Family Reunion* and Sir Henry and the other guardians in *The Cocktail Party*. Assisted by Mrs. Guzzard, another spiritual agent in dis-guise, he enacts the role, present in nearly all of Eliot's plays, of the cook-doctor who assists in the process of re-birth or conducts the spiritual cure. The action of the play takes place, appropriately, in the spring of the year and the imagery of planting the new seed, made quite explicit

---

The Achievement of T. S. Eliot, by F. O. Matthiessen, pp. 224–25). The point which is overlooked by this criticism is that Eliot is at-tempting to present his religious content in the accepted modes of farce and the wise or witty servant is a well-known formulation in that genre. Eliot is not, I think, trying "to show how the church transcends class lines," nor is he presenting in Eggerson "Christian selflessness." Rather, he is trying to cast in comic form the divine agent who, though eternally present, intervenes in the spiritual cure only when the time is ripe for decision. He is a "confidential clerk" in the sense that he is a secret representative of divinity.

in the many references to gardening, suggests the spring fertility ceremonies.

In *The Confidential Clerk* the ritual battle between the old and the new is enacted between Colby and the characters who try to gain possession of him to satisfy their own human needs. The members of the human family lose their struggle for possession of the child of divinity, and he is thus reborn through the ministry of Eggerson and Mrs. Guzzard, his spiritual doctor and his guardian angel. A further evidence of the playwright's use of the ritual struggle is his treatment of Sir Claude at the end of the play. Sir Claude, as the central representative of the principle which must be rejected, is portrayed as suffering a shock so great at Colby's renunciation of his fatherhood that he virtually loses his grip on reality. He speaks very little at the end of the third act and in the last lines of the play he cries out to Lucasta, his new-found daughter, beseeching her not to leave him. The play ends with Sir Claude's request for confirmation of Mrs. Guzzard's story from Eggerson and Eggerson's nod confirming the death of the old and the birth of the new. The ending of *The Confidential Clerk* is therefore strikingly similar to the ending of *The Family Reunion,* where Amy's death symbolized her son's divestment of the corruption of the earth mother. Amy, like Sir Claude, called out for the final support of Agatha and Mary in her demise, just as Sir Claude calls out for Lucasta and Eggerson. In both cases, a son has been lost by the material world and gained by the world of the spirit. And in both cases, by the circling around the birthday cake in the earlier play and by Eggerson's final confirming nod in the later one, there is a visible assertion by the playwright that his hero has followed the path leading to spiritual renewal and salvation.

In *The Confidential Clerk* Eliot moved farther away from overtly poetic verbal effects than in any of his previous plays.[23] It seems evident that he at last achieved his goal of creating a conversational verse form which can be employed for everyday conversation without self-consciousness. The measure of his success is the fact that the same verse form moves without the audience's awareness from the comedy repartee of the first act to the discussion of identity in the "love scene" of the second act. The poetic qualities that are present are introduced in the gradual development of the multi-level theme of fatherhood and sonship and in the use of recurrent images, such as the garden image, which exist on both a literal and a symbolic level in the play.

Despite the objections to the direction Eliot's poetic drama has taken, he has succeeded in satisfying the two objectives which he himself has seen as his major dramatic goals; he has succeeded in presenting a dramatic surface which could be understood by his audience, while at the same time including deeper levels of symbolic meaning implicit in that surface but developed by mythical anal-

[23] While the judgments of the verse used in *The Confidential Clerk* have been mixed, its "unpoetic" quality has been frequently noted. D. E. Jones comments: "*The Confidential Clerk* does belong to the realm of poetic drama, if only by the fineness with which it delineates feeling, but perhaps it is only just across the border from prose" (*The Plays of T. S. Eliot*, p. 178). Grover Smith states the point even more strongly: "The characters in *The Confidential Clerk*, where Eliot sacrificed poetry even more ruthlessly than in *The Cocktail Party*, speak lines which are verse in typography but prose in cadence" (*T. S. Eliot's Poetry and Plays*, p. 228).

ogies beneath. In *The Confidential Clerk* the devices of farce enabled him to develop resolutions and reversals which might be improbable in real life but which served to carry out the theme of spiritual quest for identity. They presented, in other words, a means of introducing his religious content without interference with the most immediately apparent level of meaning. In response to an audience insulated against both religious meaning and poetic method, Eliot has gradually evolved a new kind of religious drama which could introduce both religion and poetry without either being immediately obvious. To objections on the one hand that his content was unpoetic and on the other that it was undramatic, it can only be said that in trying to solve the problem of creating a satisfying dramatic product applicable to modern experience he turned to a dramatic genre which precluded much that was poetic in his earlier plays. What was necessarily left out was religious emotion, the quality of the religious experience. It was this missing range of emotional experience, especially the complexity of human and divine love, which Eliot attempted to emphasize in his next play, *The Elder Statesman*.

CHAPTER VII

THE ELDER STATESMAN

꿏 *The Elder Statesman* is a fitting play with which to close a study of Eliot's drama for it stresses the quality of divine resolution and reconciliation to God's will through human love which are the keynotes of Eliot's thought in his most recent writings.[1] Both the relationship between Lord Claverton and his daughter and the playwright's use of *Oedipus at Colonus* as his Greek source are important elements in establishing the play's tone.

The poet's attitude of conciliation and resolution of differences is also evident in the fact that he has removed the last interference between himself and his audience by changing his dramatic tone of voice from that of farce to that of romantic comedy in order to make the mood of the surface compatible with the play's religious theme of the relationship between human and divine love. Indeed, so well has the author matched his surface action to his deeper meanings that *The Elder Statesman,* at first, seems to conceal no further undercurrents of meaning than those present in the relationship between Lord

[1] Of Eliot's many recent comments on the importance of human love for salvation, the following, in Henry Hewes, "T. S. Eliot at Seventy," *The Saturday Review of Literature,* September 13, 1958, p. 32, is typical: "For the Christian, . . . there is that perpetual living in paradox. You must lose your life in order to save it. One has to be otherworldly and yet deeply responsible for the affairs of this world. One must preserve a capacity for enjoying the things of this world such as love and affection."

[214]

Claverton and his children and their mutual search for personal happiness.

But while the dramatic mood has been changed to soften the discrepancies between the surface action and the underlying meanings, the fundamental dramatic conception behind the play is the same one that has operated in each play which has been examined. The plot of *The Elder Statesman* is just as much a transparent mask for religious meanings as the plots of Eliot's earlier plays, and the author's theory of dramatic levels is still in effect. In fact, when the whole body of Eliot's drama is surveyed it can be seen that the genre he has attempted to evolve has as its predominant characteristic a surface action which is a dramatic fable for the expression of Christian meanings which the author feels to be universal in human experience.[2]

In *The Elder Statesman* Eliot has expanded his conception of the play as a transparent mask meant to be looked through for the religious meanings which lie behind the dramatic events. The mask itself becomes a

---

[2] Hugh Kenner, in *The Invisible Poet: T. S. Eliot,* pp. 331, 337, notes the transparent quality of Eliot's plays: "These plays of masked actors in Savile Row costumes, each work turning on the establishment of someone's moral identity, Eliot has reduced in the twenty years since *The Family Reunion* to a nearly ritual simplicity of means. The Eliot play, in fact, seems on the way to becoming a distinct dramatic genre, like the Shaw play or the Wilde play, in which a special language, a corresponding moral climate, and a whimsically melodramatic kind of plot irradiate one another's possibilities." Kenner cites particularly Eliot's "unemphatic use of a structure of incidents in which one is not really expected to believe, thus throwing attention onto the invisible drama of volition and vocation. The plot provides, almost playfully, external and stageable points of reference for this essentially interior drama. . . ."

major symbol in the play for the social identities which must be seen through before spiritual selfhood can be achieved. It has already been noted that Eliot has in his earlier plays frequently used the imagery of plays and players to convey the idea of false roles and conceptions of identity. In *The Family Reunion,* for example, the chorus characters feel themselves to be unwilling actors given their parts by Amy and released only when Amy's play is replaced by Harry's salvation drama. In *The Cocktail Party* both Edward and Lavinia feel that they are forced to play the parts given them by their mates without the recognition of their true identities. The same imagery is again used in *The Confidential Clerk* when Lucasta tells Sir Claude and Lady Elizabeth that they had given their true children false roles which they faithfully tried to play until Colby released them by denying his human heritage in order to become the son of his heavenly Father. In *The Elder Statesman* Eliot further explores the idea of the role or dramatic mask given us by others, or assumed to protect ourselves from others, which must fall off before love can be freely offered or received. Lord Claverton must strip himself of his false roles as distinguished statesman, retired executive of "public companies," and irreproachable father and husband, and accept the truth about his real nature and his shabby past. Only by confession to his daughter Monica can he fully experience self-acceptance in the peace of her forgiveness and love. The stripping off of false masks before death makes up the chief dramatic action of the play.

Both the tone and the structure of *The Elder Statesman* are carefully arranged to stress the importance of love in the process of self-knowledge. Although the most important part of the play's content deals with the events leading to Lord Claverton's death, the author opens the play with a love scene between Monica and her suitor, Charles. The developing relationship between the young lovers is used throughout the play to exert an emotional control over the other events and to reflect the effect of these events upon their love. The first view of the lovers shows them in a graceful drawing-room scene engaged in a playful courtship argument. Having accompanied Monica home after luncheon and a shopping expedition, Charles vainly tries to be alone with her in order to propose, while she teasingly keeps him at a distance. Their conversation serves to introduce the play's more serious dilemma of love: the relationship between Monica and her father, which is chiefly responsible for keeping Charles and Monica apart.

Lord Claverton, after a highly successful political career followed by a term in "public companies," is about to begin an enforced retirement on doctor's orders at Badgley Court, an expensive convalescent home. Charles is jealous of Lord Claverton's dependence on Monica and remonstrates against her father's insistence that she accompany him. The lightness of the opening love scene suddenly changes at the moment when Monica first recognizes and admits her love for Charles:

> How did this come, Charles? It crept so softly
> On silent feet, and stood behind my back

Quietly, a long time, a long long time
Before I felt its presence.[3]

While Monica expresses love newly discovered, Charles describes the negative side of the same emotion—the torment of unexpressed and unaccepted love and the lover's desperate need for reassurance. Their conversation states the theme which is developed throughout the stages of Lord Claverton's spiritual re-education. They recognize the transforming power of love which he is finally brought to recognize when, after a life spent in selfish exploitation of others because of his inability to face the responsibilities of loving and being loved, he is visited by the ghosts of his guilty past. It is only at the end of the play that Lord Claverton discovers that his ghosts can be exorcised by his hard-won recognition of what loving costs and its curative effects on the soul.

The love duet between Charles and Monica gives ample evidence that Eliot has learned to integrate his poetic and his dramatic goals. His first dramatic use of the love duet was in the "beyond character" scene between Harry and his cousin in *The Family Reunion;* the fact that the playwright purged such poetic "intrusions" from his later plays is an indication that he judged such devices to interfere with the dramatic expression of his theme. In *The Elder Statesman* he has reintroduced the poetic interlude, but it now serves to forward the main love theme of the play. The lovers' discovery of a private world in the midst of the public world is conveyed by Charles' question:

[3] T. S. Eliot, *The Elder Statesman* (London: Faber and Faber Limited, 1959), p. 13.

I'm not the same person as a moment ago.
What do the words mean now—*I* and *you*? [4]

and Monica's astonished reply:

In our private world—now we have our private world—
The meanings are different. Look! We're back in the
    room
That we entered only a few minutes ago.[5]

In these lines and in Lord Claverton's final spiritual cure,
the poet expresses the necessity of a private world of personal love before either selfhood or salvation can be
achieved. Neither the pretense of a public personality nor
the isolation of a private life filled with unconfessed secrets can give a sense of identity. Lord Claverton has
sacrificed his private world of personal relationships for
his public roles and has lost hold of both worlds. The love
of Monica and Charles is meant to exemplify the positive
and beneficial power of love, while Lord Claverton's unawakened state before his act of contrition exemplifies the
destructive and malignant power of love perverted and
betrayed.

The anatomy of Lord Claverton's spiritual disease is
precisely described by Monica when Charles insists on
knowing why she must accompany her father to Badgley

---

[4] *Ibid.*

[5] *Ibid.* According to Henry Hewes' review of the Edinburgh Festival
production, some additional lines were part of this speech in the first
production which make even clearer the thematic meaning of this
speech. Monica says, according to Hewes, "We must keep our private
world private to ourselves, learn the path of transition out into the
public world and back again to ours" ("T. S. Eliot at Seventy," *The
Saturday Review of Literature,* September 13, 1958, p. 30).

Court. Lord Claverton has a "terror of being alone" and, at the same time, a "fear of being exposed to strangers." Finally, and most imperative, his doctor has disclosed that he is "much iller than he is aware of." Monica's diagnosis is, of course, a description of man's universal dilemma: man, because he continually faces the possibility of imminent death, lives in terror of being alone, yet at the same time he fears "encountering" other people without his customary roles and masks, thereby cutting himself off from the Affirmative Way, one valid path to eternal life. It is indicative of Eliot's most recent analysis of man's spiritual disease that he presents in *The Elder Statesman* only the Affirmative Way to salvation, with no alternative representation of the Negative Way. Even in *The Confidential Clerk*, Colby, although choosing Eggerson's garden of integration between the natural and the spiritual worlds, gave up human love for his divine mission. In *The Elder Statesman* the only complete means of salvation presented is through the recognition of human love as an earthly image of the divine love of God.

Lord Claverton's cure begins with his recognition of the meaninglessness of his public triumphs. He is faced, at his retirement, with the insincerity of the speeches at his farewell banquet, the parting gift bought with begrudged contributions, and the newspaper articles with "the established liturgy of the Press." He has nothing to look forward to but the usual obituary with "a portrait taken twenty years ago," representing the outworn mask of his public personality. He expresses his spiritual state before death in the imagery of a passenger who waits vainly for a train that never comes in:

It's just like sitting in an empty waiting room
In a railway station on a branch line,
After the last train, after all the other passengers
Have left, and the booking office is closed
And the porters have gone. What am I waiting for
In a cold and empty room before an empty grate?
For no one. For nothing.[6]

Made ready for the painful exploration of his spiritual malady by his enforced rest and his new recognition of the hollowness of his public honors, Lord Claverton is visited by the ghosts of his past in the persons of Fred Culverwell and Maisie Montjoy. Fred Culverwell (Coverwell), alias Frederico Gomez, has been engaged in profitable duplicities in a Central American state since he left England years before after an imprisonment for forgery. He holds Lord Claverton responsible for his youthful crime and his subsequent loss of country and identity because his misplaced adoration and imitation of his college friend had made him accustomed to expensive tastes and unscrupulous in his methods of satisfying them. Maisie Montjoy, former revue star, is Lord Claverton's second ghost, and her claim upon him is that as her first lover he had allowed his father to pay her off in order to avoid a breach of promise suit. Both hold him responsible for corrupting their natures and violating their love, and both attempt a kind of moral blackmail whereby in exchange for his company they agree to conceal the facts

[6] Eliot, *The Elder Statesman*, p. 20. Other examples of Eliot's use of the imagery of trains and train stations to represent spiritual states and debased spiritual journeys are to be found in the unpublished fragment of *Sweeney Agonistes,* "East Coker," and "The Dry Salvages."

of Lord Claverton's true nature from the world and from his children.

Lord Claverton's first painful lesson in love begins with his recognition not only of the wrong he has done Culverwell through the misuse of the bond of friendship, but also of the analogies between his friend's life and his own. Culverwell's role as Lord Claverton's alter ego is subtly developed in their first conversation in which the elder statesman is forced, step by step, to lose his feelings of superiority. His contempt for his visitor's worldly success, because it is based on the kind of "systematic corruption" which would be illegal in England, is countered by Culverwell's ironic retort that like Lord Claverton, at whose secret political "mistakes" he hints, he has merely matched his morality to the society in which he found himself.

Moreover, they both suffer from the same spiritual disease, the loss of self and the isolation which ensues; Culverwell's return to England for a "rest cure" intended to restore his sense of identity is matched by Lord Claverton's spiritual rest cure at Badgley Court. Just as Culverwell has lived in exile from his country and his past for thirty-five years with a wife and children who did not share his language or his thinking, so Lord Claverton has lived as a spiritual exile from himself in the same kind of isolation. Culverwell, in order to "fabricate for [himself] another personality," took on his wife's name, just as Lord Claverton, who had been "plain Dick Ferry" at Oxford, took on his wealthy wife's name to become first Richard Claverton-Ferry and finally Lord Claverton. Both have left behind their former selves and, as Culverwell points out to him, the only difference between them is that Lord

Claverton has not yet fully recognized the cause of his spiritual illness:

I parted from myself by a sudden effort,
You, so slowly and sweetly, that you've never woken up
To the fact that Dick Ferry died long ago.

.   .   .   .

It's only when you come to see that you have lost *yourself*
That you are quite alone.[7]

Culverwell explains that he now needs a friend he can "trust" who will "accept both Culverwell and Gomez" and thus give him reality once more. He knows he can force his college friend to accept him because he remembers an event in Lord Claverton's past when he had run over a man on the road and had not stopped. Culverwell thus proposes to use as his means of becoming whole again the same person whom he holds responsible for his loss of wholeness. He means to haunt Lord Claverton by a perversion of the trait of human friendship earlier used to pervert him.

With the appearance of his second ghost, Lord Claverton is forced to probe even more deeply into his spiritual wound, this time into the *cause* of his loss of self and his destruction of others. At Badgley Court he meets Mrs. Carghill, formerly Maisie Montjoy, and before that Maisie Batterson. Her changes of identity, indicated by her changes of name, (as the changed names of Lord Claverton and Fred Culverwell reflect their changed identities) have been caused by Lord Claverton's abandonment. She reminds him of their past love affair and of his love let-

[7] Eliot, *The Elder Statesman*, pp. 29–30.

ters which she hopes to use in order to keep him from abandoning her again. She too has followed his career and accuses him of posing in the role of elder statesman as he has always posed in one role or another, as a lover or as a friend, without true regard for others. Because he has "touched [her] soul—pawed it, perhaps," her love has turned to hate, and she intends to make sure that she is revenged. In the most grotesque sense, she insists that they "belong together":

It's frightening to think that we're still together
And more frightening to think that we may *always* be
    together.
There's a phrase I seem to remember reading somewhere:
Where their fires are not quenched. . . .[8]

Both of Lord Claverton's ghosts have perverted the saving power of love into the destructiveness of hate. Together they choose to enact their revenge upon him through his son Michael, who is not only "the image" of his father at his age but onto whom all of his father's youthful follies are projected. Lord Claverton's unconscious recognition of this fact is indicated by his continual concern lest his son run over someone or become involved with the wrong women and the wrong friends. Michael, who has been forced to live in the false world of his father's public roles, wants only to escape his name and heritage by going abroad and taking another name and identity. His rebellion has led him, not to a discovery of himself through mastery of the past, but, ironically, to the same form of escape taken years before by his father, a

[8] *Ibid.,* p. 57.

course which will lead not to release but to the duplication of his father's failures. In watching the re-enactment of his own false course in the actions of his son, Lord Claverton is finally brought to the awareness of his own responsibility for his son's nature and his need to face the past himself; with a new humility he vows to learn the lessons of the past if time will allow him:

> Do I understand the meaning
> Of the lesson I would teach? Come, I'll start to learn
> again.
> Michael and I shall go to school together.
> We'll sit side by side, at little desks
> And suffer the same humiliations
> At the hands of the same master. But have I still time?
> There is time for Michael. Is it too late for me, Monica? [9]

Lord Claverton realizes that his only cure lies in confession to someone he truly loves:

> If a man has one person, just one in his life,
> To whom he is willing to confess everything—
> . . . .
> Then he loves that person, and his love will save him.[10]

His greatest impediment is the fear that his daughter will not love the actor "off the stage, without his costume and make-up," but with her encouraging love and her assurance that Fred Culverwell and Mrs. Carghill are "only ghosts, who can be exorcised," Lord Claverton confesses to Charles and Monica the failures of his past. He determines that he will no longer flee from his specters but

[9] *Ibid.*, p. 79.
[10] *Ibid.*, p. 83.

will turn and confront them, for although his confession is the first step toward his freedom it is necessary for expiation to occur before he is cleansed. He must endure the humiliation and suffering inherent in his past sins as a sign of his recognition of personal guilt and responsibility.[11]

The ordeal which Lord Claverton must endure is to witness the inevitable outcome of his sacrifice of his son to his enemies, with the full recognition that he has forced Michael into the path he takes. Mrs. Carghill and Culverwell contrive to lure Michael to San Marco with an offer of a new job and a new life as an escape from his father's world. Thus Culverwell, by consciously duplicating the role of tempter which Michael's father had earlier played in his youth, plans to become the custodian and corrupter of the son's morals. Although Monica implores her brother not to commit the kind of suicide which abandonment of his family and his "very self" will involve, he cannot be persuaded to change his decision. Lord Claverton, however, practicing the new lesson in Christian freedom which he has so recently learned himself, realizes that every man must assume the responsibility for his own moral choices:

---

[11] In *The Elder Statesman* the author draws the same distinction between moral and social guilt as that described as early as "Eeldrop and Appleplex" and made explicit in *The Family Reunion* with Agatha's reference to Dostoevski's *Crime and Punishment*. Lord Claverton says:

> It's harder to confess the sin that no one believes in
> Than the crime that everyone can appreciate.
> For the crime is in relation to the law
> And the sin is in relation to the sinner.
> (Eliot, *The Elder Statesman*, pp. 89–90.)

Michael's a free agent. So if he chooses
To place himself in your power, Fred Culverwell,
Of his own volition to contract his enslavement,
I cannot prevent him. . . .[12]

Though Michael is temporarily lost, Monica realizes what
the future holds for him and accepts the responsibility of
being his link in future years with his former self. She
tells him that whoever he is when they meet again she
will "always pretend that it is the same Michael."

Lord Claverton, with a presentiment that the time of
his death is near, at last feels at peace in a new understanding of his past and a new unity of existence:

It is the peace that ensues upon contrition
When contrition ensues upon knowledge of the truth.
Why did I always want to dominate my children?
Why did I mark out a narrow path for Michael?
Because I wanted to perpetuate myself in him.
Why did I want to keep you to myself, Monica?
Because I wanted you to give your life to adoring
The man that I pretended to myself that I was,
So that I could believe in my own pretences.
I've only just now had the illumination
Of knowing what love is. . . .[13]

He blesses the lovers as he leaves them, and the action of
the play concludes, as it began, with a love scene between
Monica and Charles in which they face together the
knowledge and meaning of Lord Claverton's death. They
realize that the love they feel for each other will be their

[12] *Ibid.*, p. 99.
[13] *Ibid.*, pp. 104–05.

salvation, for it will insure the preservation of their Christian identities; they will find in human love the reflection of divine love. In Lord Claverton's suffering and death they find rebirth as "a new person Who is you and me together." The play ends as Charles says, "The dead has poured out a blessing on the living," and Monica answers:

Age and decrepitude can have no terrors for me,
Loss and vicissitude cannot appal me,
Not even death can dismay or amaze me
Fixed in the certainty of love unchanging.
    I feel utterly secure
In you; I am a part of you. Now take me to my father.[14]

Eliot's choice of Sophocles' *Oedipus at Colonus* [15] as his Greek source for *The Elder Statesman* suggests that he wished the play to express the final resolution of his theme of spiritual quest. At the time of the first production of *The Family Reunion*, Eliot had written to his director, E. Martin Browne, that "Harry's career needs

---

[14] *Ibid.*, p. 108.

[15] When asked in a recent interview about the Greek "model" behind *The Elder Statesman*, Eliot replied:

"The play in the background is the *Oedipus at Colonus*. But I wouldn't like to refer to my Greek originals as models. I have always regarded them more as points of departure. That was one of the weaknesses of *The Family Reunion;* it was rather too close to the *Eumenides*. I tried to follow my original too literally and in that way led to confusion by mixing pre-Christian and post-Christian attitudes about matters of conscience and sin and guilt.

"So in the subsequent three I have tried to take the Greek myth as a sort of springboard, you see. After all, what one gets essential and permanent, I think, in the old plays, is a situation." ("The Art of Poetry I: T. S. Eliot," an interview by Donald Hall, *The Paris Review,* No. 21 [Spring-Summer 1959], p. 61.)

to be completed by an *Orestes* or an *Oedipus at Colonnos.*" [16] *The Elder Statesman* is the fulfillment of that promise. It is indicative, however, of Eliot's changed conception of the qualifications necessary for salvation that between *The Family Reunion* (1939) and *The Elder Statesman* (1958) Harry had been replaced as the archetype for the penitent by a hero less spiritually gifted, less ascetically oriented, and more corrupted by personal sin. Eliot's choice of the old king Oedipus as his prototype for Lord Claverton stresses expiation by prolonged suffering and devotion to the will of the gods.

In Sophocles' *Oedipus at Colonus* the exiled king has grown old expiating his youthful crimes of patricide and incest; having arrived at a state of reconciliation and acceptance, he nears the sacred grove of the Eumenides, where it is ordained that he is to die. Because of his blindness, he is led by his faithful daughter, Antigone, and later joined by his other daughter, Ismene, who assists him in conducting his prayers to the gods. Oedipus begs Theseus, king of Athens, for asylum and protection, and Theseus grants his request since his death place has been ordained by Apollo and since his burial at Colonus will bring a blessing on the city.

However, the oracle has also prophesied that if Thebes is to prosper, Oedipus must be buried there, and his peaceful and sacred death is threatened by the appearance of Creon, who desires to take him back to Thebes by force if necessary. Creon's motives are those of personal ambition, for by insuring his city's salvation he hopes to

---

[16] Eliot's letter is quoted in F. O. Matthiessen, *The Achievement of T. S. Eliot*, pp. 167–68.

regain the crown which has been wrested from him by Polynices and Eteocles, Oedipus' two sons. Finally, with the help of Theseus, Oedipus is able to resist all efforts to take him away from the sacred grove of the Eumenides.

Oedipus is then visited by his son Polynices, who, having been exiled by his brother, is planning to attack Thebes by force. Polynices comes to ask his father's blessing on his endeavor, but Oedipus, instead, curses both his sons for thinking only of the throne instead of recalling him when they received word of the oracle. Thunder is heard and, after a loving farewell to his daughters, Oedipus obeys the divine summons which urges him toward his fated place of death.

In Eliot's version of Sophocles' play, Lord Claverton re-enacts the final purgation of the aged Oedipus, laden with sins but purified and blessed by the gods before death. Lord Claverton, like Oedipus, has been blind to his guilt and has lived in a state of spiritual darkness. The sins of his past parallel those of Oedipus. He has run over an old man, lived with his wife without recognizing her identity, and reared a son who, like Polynices, is an outcast from the world of spirit. Michael's desire for worldly power and wealth can be equated with Polynices' planned attack on Thebes, which represents a city of destruction, pestilence, and conflict. The irony of Lord Claverton's public role as elder statesman in the face of his private guilt is made painfully clear when his correspondence to the aged Oedipus is seen, for Oedipus is an elder statesman in the most grotesque sense.

As Oedipus is supported in his purgation ordeal by his faithful daughter Antigone, so Lord Claverton is both supported and finally cured by the love of Monica. And as Antigone vowed to carry out the burial rites for her brother Polynices if his assault on Thebes failed, Monica assumes the obligation of being her brother Michael's link with his lost self, thus insuring his ultimate means of salvation.

Finally, as Oedipus is drawn to the sacred grove of the Eumenides, Lord Claverton is drawn to the great beech at Badgley Court where he will find salvation. The emphasis in both plays is on obedience to the will of God and faithful observance of the bonds of love as a means of redemption.[17]

By using *Oedipus at Colonus* as his source, Eliot is able to emphasize a more positive side of the ritual symbolism than that used in his other plays. In his earlier portrayal of the ritual battle, the struggle between the old and the new involved the violent rejection and annihilation of the corrupt old god and the complete endorsement of the new and the young. In *The Elder Statesman,* however, while the representative of corruption dies, it is not as the result of a struggle with the new principle in the person of the young hero. Rather, the struggle is now enacted within the hero himself, who represents both the sin-laden old god and the reborn new god.

Medical imagery and the presence of a doctor figure, which have recurred in virtually all of Eliot's plays, are

[17] D. E. Jones, in *The Plays of T. S. Eliot,* p. 181, comments that the final words of Oedipus to his daughters "might serve as an epigraph to Eliot's play:

> one word
> Makes all those difficulties disappear:
> That word is love."

present in a more overt form in *The Elder Statesman*. Lord Claverton is ill, both literally and figuratively, with the disease of self, and his cure is wrought by the spiritual agency of his daughter's saving love which enables him to acknowledge the ghosts of his past iniquity. Badgley Court is another instance of a sanatorium where the human condition is cured by saving grace, and Lord Claverton has been ordered there by his doctor, who knows that he is near death. Mrs. Piggott, the "matron," serves a symbolic purpose similar to that of Mrs. Guzzard in *The Confidential Clerk* and Julia and Alex in *The Cocktail Party;* she represents a comic version of the spiritual doctor's assistant. Her ritual function is indicated by the fact that she is a "Trained Nurse," that she has always lived in a "medical milieu," and that her father was "a specialist in pharmacology" and her husband "a distinguished surgeon." As Oedipus entered the sacred grove at Colonus for his ultimate cure, so Lord Claverton comes to Badgley Court on his spiritual doctor's orders, accompanied by his daughter, who will perform the sacred rite of Christian confession. It should not be overlooked that the time of his arrival is the early spring, the season used so frequently by Eliot to suggest the annual fertility ceremonies.

At the end of the play the pattern of double marriage which Eliot has used in *The Cocktail Party* and *The Confidential Clerk* is repeated. As Lord Claverton is about to become married to God in his new purification and rebirth, he bestows his marriage blessing on the love of Charles and Monica. Through Christian death he gains eternal life and in his blessing bestows fertility in the form of Christian love on the young lovers. The imagery of death and rebirth is emphatic in the close of *The Elder Statesman* when Lord Claverton says:

I've been freed from the self that pretends to be someone;
And in becoming no one, I begin to live.
It is worth while dying, to find out what life is.[18]

Finally, the structure of the play is again based on the pattern of the ritual cure. In the first act Lord Claverton, as a representative of the old god, is ill with the corruption of earth and self. In the second act, through his struggle with the ghosts of his past and the images of his former selves which they project, he is brought to recognize the source of his illness. In the third act, through his daughter's saving love and his admission of guilt, he is purged through death of his mortality and made ready for his rebirth as spirit.

Since Eliot's present theological position includes a greater unity between human and divine love, he sought to achieve a greater unification between the elements of his dramatic methods. Most obviously, though his theory of dramatic levels is still in effect, there is a closer fusion between the events presented on the surface of the play and their symbolic level of meaning. The poet's treatment of the ritual scheme is a case in point; the ritual plot is quite literally translated into the surface action and the play now deals with a sinful old man near death who is advised by his doctor to visit a "convalescent home" and whose cure takes place before our eyes. The ritualistic and naturalistic meanings of the play are thus more closely

<hr>

[18] Eliot, *The Elder Statesman*, p. 106.

integrated and the dramatic mood of both levels is consistent.

In the same way, the poet has integrated his poetic form with his dramatic theme by reintroducing a more lyric tone than he has used since *The Family Reunion.* The renewed use of the love duet in the opening scene between Charles and Monica has already been noted. In Eliot's plays the love lyric is associated with moments of human love and because his early plays are characterized by the rejection of purely human love in favor of a more ascetic means of union with God, the lyric tone, if introduced at all, is presented in order to be disavowed. Thus in *Sweeney Agonistes,* where the poet wishes to discredit physical love, he caricatures the love song by presenting it as a debased jazz chant. In *The Family Reunion,* the love duet between Harry and his cousin Mary is interrupted by the grim reminder of the Furies that human love must be rejected. The same kind of treatment occurs in *The Confidential Clerk* when the love scene between Colby and Lucasta ends in a misunderstanding meant to suggest that another path, one which does not include human marriage, is meant for Colby. Only in *The Elder Statesman,* when the poet at last wishes to endorse the possibility of finding divine love in human love and marriage, does he find the lyric note appropriate to his dramatic theme, thereby providing a closeness between the verse form and the religious meaning which has been lacking in his drama since *Murder in the Cathedral.*

It will be remembered that Eliot had said in "Poetry and Drama" (1951):

"I . . . believe that while the self-education of a poet trying to write for the theatre seems to require a long period of disciplining his poetry, and putting it, so to speak, on a very thin diet in order to adapt it to the needs of the stage, he may find that later, when (and if) the understanding of theatrical technique has become second nature, he can dare to make more liberal use of poetry and take greater liberties with ordinary colloquial speech. I base this belief on the evolution of Shakespeare, and on some study of the language in his late plays." [19]

In the light of the play's atmosphere of resolution and harmony which suggests *The Tempest,* it might be concluded that Eliot felt both the necessities of his theme and the stage of his dramatic development at last made it possible for him to "make more liberal use of poetry." [20] In any case, he has broken his ascetic rule of putting his poetry on a thin diet and in *The Elder Statesman* has used a verse which includes, along with patterned speech for everyday dramatic moments, more lyric interludes for extraordinary dramatic moments.

One further element in Eliot's movement toward dramatic unity should be noted because of its relevance to

[19] Eliot, *On Poetry and Poets,* p. 92.

[20] Eliot has recently commented, after noting that he had concentrated on mastering the techniques of dramatic structure in *The Confidential Clerk:* "I hope that *The Elder Statesman* goes further in getting more poetry in, at any rate, than *The Confidential Clerk* did. I don't feel that I've got to the point I aim at and I don't think I ever will, but I would like to feel I was getting a little nearer to it each time" ("The Art of Poetry I: T. S. Eliot," an interview by Donald Hall, *The Paris Review,* No. 21 [Spring-Summer 1959], p. 61).

his early views on the "problem of personality" in poetic composition. Eliot had endorsed the mythical method and had evolved his "impersonal theory of poetry" as an antidote to the dangers of personality in art; spiritual and artistic pride could operate together, he felt, to destroy the artistic validity of the art work by allowing excessive emotion to overcome the standards of disciplined artistic perfection. In *The Elder Statesman,* however, the playwright gives evidence of a view more tolerant of personal statement and one which includes a more comprehensive conception of the elements involved in dramatic creation.

Eliot's fullest exposition of his revised view is to be found in "The Three Voices of Poetry" (1953). In the poetry of the first voice, "the voice of the poet talking to himself—or nobody," the poet has "something germinating in him for which he must find words," but he does not know what those words are or what their arrangement will be until he has written the poem. The second voice is "the voice of the poet addressing an audience, whether large or small." It is best illustrated by the dramatic monologue in which the author puts on "fancy dress and a mask" in order to conceal his identity. The third voice is that of "the poet when he attempts to create a dramatic character speaking in verse." Here the author must create characters who are more than his mouthpieces and, while he may put something of his own personality into them, they must also have an identity of their own.

The point which Eliot draws from this analysis is that not the third voice alone but all three voices are found together in dramatic poetry—the poet's most personal expressions when he talks to himself, the poet's remarks with his mask and costume on, and the speeches of characters given a separate identity by the author. Eliot concludes with the statement that "the world of a great poetic dramatist is a world in which the creator is everywhere present, and everywhere hidden."

As if to draw particular attention to the merger of personal and universal meanings in *The Elder Statesman*, Eliot has included in the printed version of the play a dedication to his wife Valerie which expresses the same idea in more personal terms:

The words [of the play] mean what they say, but some
    have a further meaning
For you and me only.[21]

The unity which the poet hopes to achieve between private and public experience is thus both appropriate to the play's theme of the necessity to integrate one's private and public worlds and representative of the poet's personal satisfaction with his achievement of the major goal of his dramatic career—the development of a dramatic unity which can express his religious perspective without compromise while satisfying the demands of art and the demands of a lay audience. The private experience of the poet as expatriate, as elder statesman, and as lover is

---

[21] Eliot, *The Elder Statesman*, p. [5]. Hugh Kenner comments on this dedication and the relevance of the dual love story of father and daughter and young lovers to Eliot's dedication. He also states that "this simplest of Eliot's plays is the most personal of his works. . . . The Invisible Poet, we sense after the curtain, has occupied the stage at length, and in more than one guise. . . ." (*The Invisible Poet: T. S. Eliot*, p. 340.)

merged in his latest play with his most recent methods of expressing artistic and religious integration to form a literary product which, of all his plays, most nearly satisfies his own standards and thus provides a fitting end point for this survey of Eliot's dramatic development.

It is an irony of Eliot's dramatic career, however, that after a long and complex development, the playwright has evolved a dramatic form which, in attempting to communicate to a wide audience the profundities of religious meaning, has excluded the quality of allusive fascination so characteristic of his early plays. Eliot has not, as it has often been claimed, embraced naturalism in an effort to meet his audience more than half way; rather, he has continued to compose theatrical fables meant to disclose religious meanings. Therefore, he cannot expect nor does he desire to achieve the compelling effects of naturalism to be gained from the audiences' identification with characters like themselves. But, by the same token, as the fable becomes more luminous, the alternative appeal of the dramatic charade is also sacrificed to a theatrical work which is doomed to the no man's land between two kinds of theater. In giving up the intellectual appeal of the early plays, and by substituting none of the compelling effects of naturalism, Eliot has lost the best of both theaters. His goal of developing a new theater, and training an audience to respond to it, had thus been frustrated by the inability of his current dramatic methods to reach the emotions of his audience, on the one hand, or to fascinate and stimulate their intellect, on the other.

The one hopeful possibility lies in Eliot's move back to a more lyric surface, for his poetry is the one dramatic tool he has yet to exploit fully. If he could create a poetry which could infuse the fable with dramatic excitement and verbal beauty, he might recoup his losses and yet not lose his gains. Nevertheless, Eliot's endeavor to create a new genre which would be both dramatically compelling and spiritually profound in terms meaningful to the modern age is a goal which must be endorsed, especially when it has been espoused by one of the major poetic talents of the twentieth century.

BIBLIOGRAPHY

Note: The following is a bibliography of works cited in the present study. For the most complete listing of T. S. Eliot's own works Donald Gallup's *T. S. Eliot: A Bibliography* (New York: Harcourt, Brace and Company, 1953) should be consulted. D. E. Jones, in *The Plays of T. S. Eliot* (London: Routledge & Kegan Paul, 1960), provides an up-to-date listing of the most important critical studies dealing with Eliot's plays.

BOOKS AND ARTICLES BY T. S. ELIOT

Eliot, T. S. *After Strange Gods: A Primer of Modern Heresy* New York: Harcourt, Brace and Company, 1934.

——. "The Beating of a Drum," *The Nation and the Athenaeum,* xxxiv (October 6, 1923), 11–12.

——. *The Complete Poems and Plays: 1909–1950.* New York: Harcourt, Brace and Company, 1952.

——. *The Confidential Clerk.* New York: Harcourt, Brace and Company, 1954.

——. "Eeldrop and Appleplex. I," *Little Review,* iv (May 1917), 9.

——. *The Elder Statesman.* London: Faber and Faber Limited, 1959.

——. *Essays Ancient and Modern.* London: Faber and Faber Limited, 1936.

——. *For Lancelot Andrewes: Essays on Style and Order.* London: Faber and Gwyer, 1928.

——. *The Idea of a Christian Society.* London: Faber and Faber Limited, 1939.

——. Introduction to *Savonarola: A Dramatic Poem,* by Charlotte Eliot. London: R. Cobden-Sanderson, [1926], pp. viii–xii.

——. "Last Words," *The Criterion,* xviii (January 1939), 269–75.

Eliot, T. S. "Notes on the Way" [I], *Time and Tide,* XVI (January 5, 1935), 6–7.

——. *Notes towards the Definition of Culture.* London: Faber and Faber Limited, 1948.

——. *On Poetry and Poets.* New York: Farrar, Straus and Cudahy, 1957.

——. *The Rock.* New York: Harcourt, Brace and Company, 1934.

——. *The Sacred Wood: Essays on Poetry and Criticism.* London: Methuen & Co. Ltd., 1928.

——. *Selected Essays.* New York: Harcourt, Brace and Company, 1950.

——. "Shakespearian Criticism: I. From Dryden to Coleridge," *A Companion to Shakespeare Studies.* Edited by Harley Granville-Barker and G. B. Harrison. Cambridge: Cambridge University Press, 1934, pp. [287]–99.

——. "Ulysses, Order, and Myth," *Dial,* LXXV (November 1923), 480–83.

——. *The Use of Poetry and the Use of Criticism: Studies in the Relation of Criticism to Poetry in England.* Cambridge, Massachusetts: Harvard University Press, 1933.

—— and Hoellering, George. *The Film of Murder in the Cathedral.* New York: Harcourt, Brace and Company, 1952.

BOOKS BY OTHER AUTHORS

Bethell, S. L. *Shakespeare & the Popular Dramatic Tradition.* London: P. S. King and Staples Limited, 1944.

Bodkin, Maud. *The Quest for Salvation in an Ancient and a Modern Play.* Oxford: Oxford University Press, 1941.

Cornford, Francis M. *The Origin of Attic Comedy.* London: Edward Arnold, 1914.

Dawson, Christopher. *The Making of Europe.* London: Sheed & Ward, 1932.

Donoghue, Denis. *The Third Voice: Modern British and American Verse Drama.* Princeton, New Jersey: Princeton University Press, 1959.

Fenollosa, Ernest, and Pound, Ezra. *Certain Noble Plays of Japan*. Churchtown, Dundrum, Ireland: The Cuala Press, 1916.

Fergusson, Francis. *The Idea of a Theater*. Princeton, New Jersey: Princeton University Press, 1949.

Flanagan, Hallie. *Dynamo*. New York: Duell, Sloan and Pearce, 1943.

Gallup, Donald. *T. S. Eliot: A Bibliography*. New York: Harcourt, Brace and Company, 1953.

Gardner, Helen. *The Art of T. S. Eliot*. London: The Cresset Press, 1949.

Harrison, Jane Ellen. *Themis: A Study of the Social Origins of Greek Religion*. Cambridge: Cambridge University Press, 1912.

Heath-Stubbs, John. *Charles Williams*. London: Published for the British Council by Longmans, Green, 1955.

Henn, T. R. *The Harvest of Tragedy*. London: Methuen & Co. Ltd., 1956.

Isaacs, J. *An Assessment of Twentieth-Century Literature*. London: Secker & Warburg, 1951.

Jones, David E. *The Plays of T. S. Eliot*. London: Routledge & Kegan Paul, 1960.

The Journals of Arnold Bennett. III, 1921–1928. Edited by Newman Flower. London: Cassell and Company, 1933.

Kenner, Hugh. *The Invisible Poet: T. S. Eliot*. New York: McDowell, Obolensky, 1959.

Matthiessen, F. O. *The Achievement of T. S. Eliot: An Essay on the Nature of Poetry*. 3rd ed. revised. New York: Oxford University Press, 1958.

Murray, Gilbert. *The Classical Tradition in Poetry*. Cambridge, Massachusetts: Harvard University Press, 1927.

Peers, E. Allison (ed.). *The Complete Works of Saint John of the Cross*. Vol. 1. Westminster, Maryland: The Newman Bookshop, 1945.

Raglan, Lord. *The Hero: A Study in Tradition, Myth, and Drama*. New York: Oxford University Press, 1937.

Smith, Grover, Jr. *T. S. Eliot's Poetry and Plays: A Study in Sources and Meaning.* Chicago, Illinois: The University of Chicago Press, 1956.

Underhill, Evelyn. *Mysticism.* 17th ed. London: Methuen & Co. Ltd., 1949.

Weisinger, Herbert. *Tragedy and the Paradox of the Fortunate Fall.* London: Routledge and Kegan Paul, 1953.

Wells, Henry W. *New Poets from Old.* New York: Columbia University Press, 1940.

Weston, Jessie L. *From Ritual to Romance.* Cambridge: The University Press, 1920.

Williams, Charles. *Descent into Hell.* New York: Pellegrini & Cudahy, 1949.

——. *The Descent of the Dove: A Short History of the Holy Spirit in the Church.* Reprinted ed. New York: Meridian Books, 1956.

——. *The Figure of Beatrice: A Study in Dante.* London: Faber and Faber Limited, 1943.

Williams, Raymond. *Drama from Ibsen to Eliot.* London: Chatto & Windus, 1954.

Wilson, Edmund. *Axel's Castle: A Study in the Imaginative Literature of 1870–1930.* New York: Charles Scribner's Sons, 1931.

ARTICLES BY OTHER AUTHORS

Arrowsmith, William. "The Comedy of T. S. Eliot," *English Stage Comedy.* Edited by W. K. Wimsatt, Jr. New York: Columbia University Press, 1955, pp. 148–72.

——. "Transfiguration in Eliot and Euripides," *Sewanee Review,* LXIII, No. 3 (1955), pp. 421–42.

"The Art of Poetry I: T. S. Eliot," an interview by Donald Hall, *The Paris Review,* No. 21 (Spring–Summer 1959), pp. 47–70.

Barber, C. L. "The Power of Development . . . in a Different World," appearing as the final chapter in *The Achievement of T. S. Eliot: An Essay on the Nature of Poetry,* by F. O.

Matthiessen. 3rd ed. revised. New York: Oxford University Press, 1958, pp. 198–243.

——. "T. S. Eliot After Strange Gods," *T. S. Eliot: A Selected Critique.* Edited by Leonard Unger. New York: Rinehart & Company, Inc., 1948, pp. 415–43.

Battenhouse, Roy. "Eliot's 'The Family Reunion' as Christian Prophecy," *Christendom,* x (Summer 1945), 307–21.

Beaufort, John. " 'The Confidential Clerk' on Broadway," *Christian Science Monitor,* February 20, 1954, p. 16.

Blackmur, R. P. "T. S. Eliot: From *Ash Wednesday* to *Murder in the Cathedral,*" *T. S. Eliot: A Selected Critique.* Edited by Leonard Unger. New York: Rinehart & Company, Inc., 1948, pp. 236–62.

Browne, E. Martin. "The Dramatic Verse of T. S. Eliot," *T. S. Eliot: A Symposium.* Compiled by Richard March and Tambimuttu. London: Editions Poetry London, 1948, pp. 196–207.

——. "From *The Rock* to *The Confidential Clerk,*" *T. S. Eliot: A Symposium for His Seventieth Birthday.* Edited by Neville Braybrooke. New York: Farrar, Straus & Cudahy, 1958, pp. 57–69.

Heilman, Robert B. "*Alcestis* and *The Cocktail Party,*" *Comparative Literature,* v (Spring 1955), 105–16.

Hewes, Henry. "T. S. Eliot at Seventy," *The Saturday Review of Literature,* September 13, 1958, pp. 30–32.

Kerr, Walter F. "T. S. Eliot Strolls the Same Garden," *New York Herald Tribune,* February 21, 1954, p. 1.

Leggatt, Alison. "A Postscript from Mrs Chamberlayne and Mrs Guzzard," *T. S. Eliot: A Symposium for His Seventieth Birthday.* Edited by Neville Braybrooke. New York: Farrar, Straus & Cudahy, 1958, pp. 79–80.

Martz, Louis L. "The Wheel and the Point: Aspects of Imagery and Theme in Eliot's Later Poetry," *T. S. Eliot: A Selected Critique.* Edited by Leonard Unger. New York: Rinehart & Company, Inc., 1948, pp. 444–62.

Murray, Gilbert. "Excursus on the Ritual Forms Preserved

in Greek Tragedy," appearing as a special chapter in *Themis: A Study of the Social Origins of Greek Religion,* by Jane Ellen Harrison. Cambridge: Cambridge University Press, 1912, pp. 341–63.

Ransom, John Crowe. "T. S. Eliot as Dramatist," *Poetry: A Magazine of Verse,* LIV, No. 5 (1939), 264–71.

Smith, Grover, Jr. "T. S. Eliot and Sherlock Holmes," *Notes and Queries,* CXCIII (October 2, 1948), 431–32.

Stamm, Rudolf. "The Orestes Theme in Three Plays by Eugene O'Neill, T. S. Eliot and Jean-Paul Sartre," *English Studies* (Amsterdam), XXX, No. 5 (1949), 244–55.

Ward, Anne. "Speculations on Eliot's Time-World: An Analysis of *The Family Reunion* in Relation to Hulme and Bergson," *American Literature,* XXI (March 1949), 18–34.

Wimsatt, W. K., Jr. "Eliot's Comedy," *Sewanee Review,* LVIII (Autumn 1950), 666–78.

INDEX

Aeschylus, 11, 72; *Choephoroi,* 32, 59, 113; *Eumenides,* 228n; *Oresteia,* 128n, 132, 133, 134, 229
Affirmative Way, 157–62, 167–70, 172, 178, 180, 208, 220. *See also* Negative Way
Andrewes, Lancelot, 15
Anglo-Catholicism, 14, 15, 24–25, 78, 159. *See also* Church of England
anthropology, 41–42. *See also* Cambridge School of Classical Anthropology
Aristophanes, 44, 58, 72
Aristotle, 44, 47–49, 53; *De Anima,* 110n; *De Generatione et Corruptione,* 110n
Arrowsmith, William, 176n, 207n
Athenian drama, 35. *See also* Greek drama
Auden, W. H., *Dance of Death,* 90n

Babbitt, Irving, 5, 17–18
Barber, C. L., 27–28, 77n, 113n, 147n, 152n, 155n, 209n
Battenhouse, Roy, 136n
Baudelaire, 16, 17
Beaufort, John, 185n
Bennett, Arnold, 51n
Bergson, Henri, 5, 136n; *durée,* 6n
Bethell, S. L., *Shakespeare & the Popular Dramatic Tradition,* 150–56
Blackmur, R. P., 77n, 96n
Bodkin, Maud, 133n
Bradley, F. H., 5, 6n
Bramhall, John, 15
Brecht, Berthold, 90n

Browne, E. Martin, 52n, 76, 84, 101, 102, 115n, 128n, 147n, 149n, 163n, 184n, 228
Buddha, 123, 173

Cambridge School of Classical Anthropology, 43, 62. *See also* Cornford, Francis M.; Harrison, Jane Ellen; Murray, Gilbert; ritual drama
Chaplin, Charlie, 48
Chesterton, G. K., 22n
chorus, 13, 24, 72, 84, 85, 86–88, 89, 92, 100, 101, 103, 106, 109, 110–11, 116, 119, 125, 145–46, 152n, 216
Christian neo-Platonism, 193
Christie, Agatha, 148
Church of England, 14, 78. *See also* Anglo-Catholicism
classicism, 6n, 8, 14, 15
Cornford, Francis M., 43, 44–46, 47, 58, 62–72, 104, 106, 109n, 138–39, 145. *See also* Cambridge School of Classical Anthropology; ritual drama
Criterion, The, 32, 51, 78, 81

Dante, 14, 30, 156, 160–61; *Inferno,* 109
Dawson, Christopher, 83; *The Making of Europe,* 22n, 82
Dionysius the Areopagite, 157
Donoghue, Denis, 112n, 148n, 155n, 187n
Dostoevski, *Crime and Punishment,* 132, 226n

Eliot, Charlotte, *Savonarola,* 51
ELIOT, T. S., *After Strange Gods,* 22–24; "Andrew Marvell," 56;

Eliot, T. S. (*continued*)
"Ash Wednesday," 195; "Baudelaire in Our Time," 16; "The Beating of a Drum," 47, 65n; "Catholicism and International Order," 79; *The Cocktail Party,* 26, 27, 64n, 66, 131n, 139, 146, 147–83, 186, 187n, 191, 194, 195, 208, 210, 212n, 216, 232; *The Confidential Clerk,* 26, 27, 64n, 139, 183, 184–213, 216, 220, 232, 234, 235n; "Dans le Restaurant," 124; "Eeldrop and Appleplex," 123, 226n; *The Elder Statesman,* 26, 27, 66, 128n, 139, 195, 213, 214–39; *The Family Reunion,* 17, 26, 27, 66, 111, 112–46, 147, 148–50, 152n, 158n, 182, 195, 197, 210, 211, 215n, 216, 218, 226n, 228, 229, 234; "Five Points on Dramatic Writing," 53n; *For Lancelot Andrewes,* 13, 15–18; "Four Elizabethan Dramatists," 10; *Four Quartets,* 158n ("Burnt Norton," 136, 195; "The Dry Salvages," 129n, 221n; "East Coker," 66, 221n; "Little Gidding," 158n); "The Function of Criticism," 7–10; "Gerontion," 180; "The Humanism of Irving Babbitt," 17; *The Idea of a Christian Society,* 22, 27n, 201n; "John Bramhall," 15; "Lancelot Andrewes," 15; "The Love Song of J. Alfred Prufrock," 124; "Modern Education and the Classics," 78; *Murder in the Cathedral,* 17, 24–25, 26, 33, 46n, 76, 77, 80–81, 83, 85, 87, 89, 91–111, 112, 113, 115, 116, 117, 119, 147, 149n, 151n, 158n, 234; "The Music of Poetry," 182n–183n; "Niccolo Machiavelli," 15; "Notes on the Way," 91; *Notes towards the Definition of Culture,* 28, 201n; *On Poetry and Poets,* 27, 28; "The 'Pensées' of Pascal," 19; "Poetry and Drama," 29, 103, 133n, 176, 181–83, 234–35; "The Possibility of a Poetic Drama," 35, 46; "Religion and Literature," 20; *The Rock,* 24, 76, 77, 78, 83, 84–91, 103, 110, 111, 115; *The Sacred Wood,* 5, 14; "Second Thoughts about Humanism," 79; "The Social Function of Poetry," 28; *Sweeney Agonistes,* 12–13, 24, 26, 32–75, 76, 79, 83, 86, 100, 101, 104, 110, 111, 112, 113, 114, 115, 118, 119, 139, 142, 149, 221n, 234; "Sweeney Erect," 60n; "The Three Voices of Poetry," 236; "Tradition and the Individual Talent," 6, 8, 22; *The Use of Poetry and the Use of Criticism,* 20, 24, 33n; "Virgil and the Christian World," 200; *The Waste Land,* 33n, 41, 51n, 60, 66, 67n, 72, 106, 124, 195; "Wilkie Collins and Dickens," 58

Elizabethan drama, 3, 35, 37, 38
Elizabethan theater, 55, 151
Erinys, 113. *See also* Eumenides; Furies
ethnology, 40–42
Eumenides, 117, 127–29, 229–31. *See also* Erinys; Furies
Euripides, *Alcestis,* 176–79; *Ion,* 184n, 204–08
Everyman, 10, 103
Existentialism, 130n

Fergusson, Francis, 33, 105n
Fitzgerald, F. Scott, *The Great Gatsby,* 61n
Flanagan, Hallie, 52, 62n–63n, 68

Foerster, Norman, 79
Frazer, J. G., 43, 72; *The Golden Bough,* 40, 41–42
Freud, 42
Furies, 59, 72, 112, 114, 118, 125–29, 138, 149n, 154, 197, 234. *See also* Erinys; Eumenides

Galsworthy, John, 10
Gardner, Helen, 33n
Gilbert, W. S., 184n
Gilbert and Sullivan, *Iolanthe,* 72n
Goethe, 27; *Faust,* 36
Grail legends, 41. *See also* Weston, Jessie
Greek drama, 13, 43, 46, 53n, 56, 57, 86, 103, 133. *See also* Aeschylus; Aristophanes; Euripides; Sophocles

Hall, Donald, 24n
Hamlet, 134n, 140n
Harrison, Jane Ellen, 43. *See also* Cambridge School of Classical Anthropology; ritual drama
Heath-Stubbs, John, 159–61
Heilman, Robert B., 176n
Henn, T. R., 133n
Hewes, Henry, 214n, 219n
Hobbes, 15
Homer, *Odyssey,* 39
Hulme, T. E., 136n

Ibsen, 36, 150; *A Doll's House,* 48–49
I'll Take My Stand, 22n
Isaacs, J., 53n

Jacobean drama, 3, 35
jazz, 12, 51–53, 60–61, 76, 86, 100, 110, 234
John the Apostle, St., 98

John of the Cross, St., 32, 70–71, 79, 118, 123, 130, 157; *The Ascent of Mount Carmel,* 59–60, 73–74. *See also* mysticism; Negative Way
Jones, David E., 33–34, 90n, 96n, 105n, 119n, 142n, 162n, 212n, 231n
Jonson, Ben, 50, 52, 59, 120
Joyce, James, *Ulysses,* 39
Jung, Carl, 42

Kenner, Hugh, 34n, 215n, 237n
Kerr, Walter F., 184n
Kipling, 27
Kyd, Thomas, 10, 11

Laforgue, Jules, 38
Leggatt, Alison, 189n
Lindsay, Vachel, "Daniel Jazz," 100
Lloyd, Marie, 53–54
Lotinga, Ernie, 53n
Luke, St., 106

Machiavelli, 15–16
Maeterlinck, 36, 39
Marlowe, Christopher, 50
Martz, Louis L., 94n
Massine, 48
Matthew, St., 106–08
Matthiessen, F. O., *The Achievement of T. S. Eliot,* 4, 90n, 128n, 131n, 140n, 145n
melodrama, 58–59
metaphysical poets, 38, 56
Milton, 27; *Samson Agonistes,* 57
Molière, 184n
Mummers' Play of St. George and the Dragon, 65n
Murray, Gilbert, 43, 44, 46n, 47, 67, 106, 109n, 123n, 134n, 140n. *See also* Cambridge School of

Murray, Gilbert (*continued*)
Classical Anthropology; ritual drama
Murry, J. Middleton, 8
music-hall, 37, 53–54, 55, 58, 76, 151n
mysticism, 60, 70–74, 130, 157, 162, 176
myth, 39, 40–41, 42, 46, 113, 114, 132–33, 134n, 178, 185–86, 189n, 199, 228n, 236

Negative Way, 157–62, 170–74, 178, 180, 220. *See also* Affirmative Way
Newman, John Henry, 19
Noh drama, 35, 62n

O'Neill, Eugene, *The Emperor Jones,* 49n
Orestes, 134n, 140n; myth of, 111, 113, 117

Pascal, 25, 33
Paul, St., 17
Peter, St., 85
Plato, *Symposium,* 161
Pound, Ezra, 35, 62n
psychology, 40–42, 104
Punch, 65n

Racine, 48
Raglan, Lord, *The Hero,* 104n, 206n
Ransom, John Crowe, 113n
Rastelli, 48–49
Richards, I. A., 15, 20
ritual drama, 13, 41, 43, 44–46, 48, 56, 58, 61, 62–72, 104–09, 114, 116, 117, 123–24, 132, 134–46, 179–81, 186, 206n, 208–12, 231–34. *See also* Cambridge

School of Classical Anthropology
Russell, Bertrand, 15

Samson, 88n, 95
Sartre, Jean-Paul, *The Flies,* 130n
Shakespeare, 14, 48, 50, 54–55, 103, 150–56, 182–83, 184n, 235; *Hamlet,* 182; *Lear,* 65n; *The Tempest,* 152n, 235
Shaw, G. B., 17, 36, 39, 215n
Shelley, *Prometheus Unbound,* 174
Smith, Grover, Jr., 32, 60n, 61n, 88n, 100n, 105n, 109n–110n, 117n, 129n, 130n, 132n, 138n, 148n, 174n, 179n, 206n, 212n
Sophocles, 58, 88n; *Oedipus at Colonus,* 128n, 214, 228–32
Stephen, St., 98, 105
Spender, Stephen, *The Trial of a Judge,* 90n
Stamm, Rudolf, 133n
Symbolist poetry, 5, 38

Tate, Allen, 22n
Tchehov, 36
Tiresias, 88n

Verrall, A. W., 206n–207n
vers libre, 89
Virgil, 30, 201n

Ward, Anne, 6n, 136n
Weisinger, Herbert, 104n
Wells, H. G., 17
Wells, Henry W., 72n
Weston, Jessie, 72, 135; *From Ritual to Romance,* 41
Wilde, Oscar, 184n, 215n
Williams, Charles, 159–62; *Descent into Hell,* 160, 174n; *The Descent of the Dove,* 161–62; *The Figure of Beatrice,* 160

Williams, Raymond, 112n, 147n, 156n, 182n

Williams, Tennessee, *A Streetcar Named Desire*, 136n

Wilson, Edmund, *Axel's Castle*, 3

Wimsatt, W. K., Jr., 155n

wit, 56–57, 60, 114, 149, 162n

Yeats, W. B., 35, 37, 40; *The Hawk's Well*, 62n